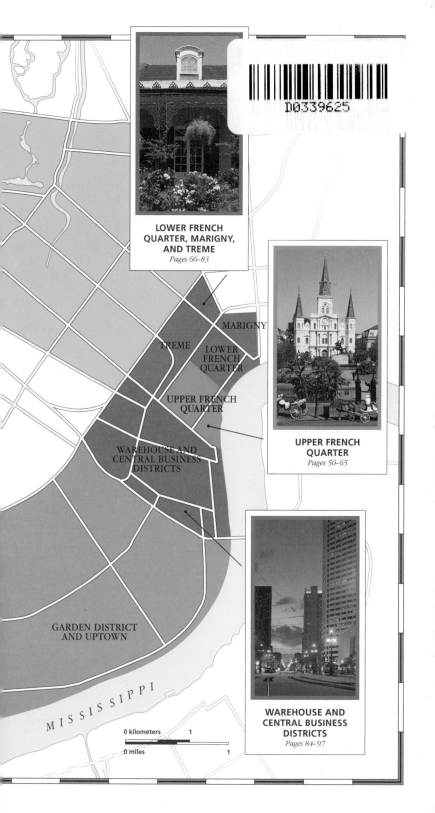

LOWER FRENCH QUARTER, MARIGNY, AND TREME
Pages 66–83

UPPER FRENCH QUARTER
Pages 50–65

WAREHOUSE AND CENTRAL BUSINESS DISTRICTS
Pages 84–97

MARIGNY

TREME

LOWER FRENCH QUARTER

UPPER FRENCH QUARTER

WAREHOUSE AND CENTRAL BUSINESS DISTRICTS

GARDEN DISTRICT AND UPTOWN

MISSISSIPPI

0 kilometers 1

0 miles 1

NEW
ORLEANS

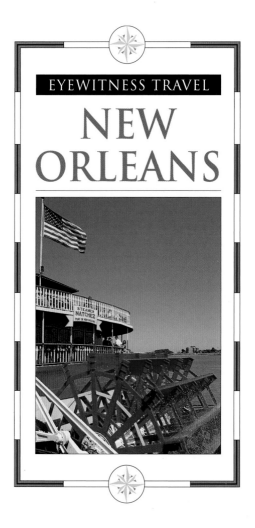

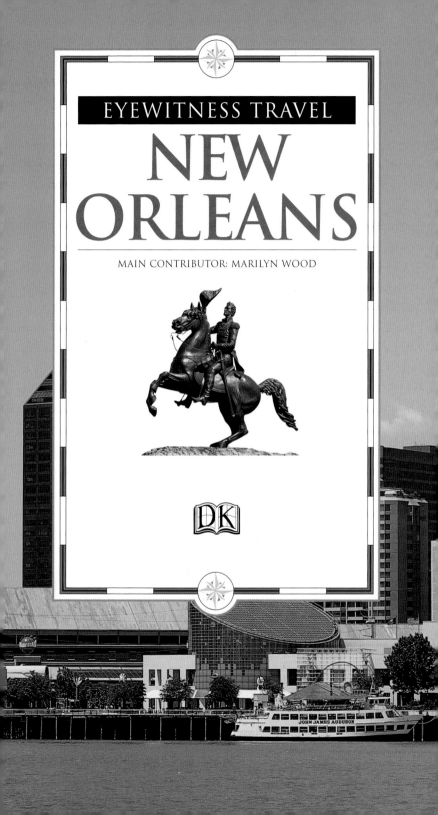

EYEWITNESS TRAVEL

NEW ORLEANS

MAIN CONTRIBUTOR: MARILYN WOOD

DK

LONDON, NEW YORK,
MELBOURNE, MUNICH AND DELHI
www.dk.com

PROJECT EDITOR Alejandro Lajud
ART EDITOR Victor Hugo Garnica
EDITOR Karla Sánchez
DESIGNERS Carlos Muñoz, Alejandro Lajud, Victor Hugo Garnica

Dorling Kindersley Limited
SENIOR PUBLISHING MANAGER Louise Bostock Lang
PUBLISHING MANAGER Kate Poole
DIRECTOR OF PUBLISHING Gillian Allan
EDITORS Stephanie Driver, Mary Sutherland, Andrew Szudek
MAP CO-ORDINATORS David Pugh, Casper Morris
DTP CO-ORDINATORS Jason Little, Conrad van Dyk
PRODUCTION CONTROLLER Joanna Bull

MAIN CONTRIBUTOR
Marilyn Wood

MAPS
Ben Bowles, Rob Clynes and James Macdonald at Mapping Ideas Ltd.

PHOTOGRAPHERS
Julio Rochon, Jaime Baldovinos

ILLUSTRATORS
Ricardo Almazan, Ricardo Almazan Jr.

Printed and bound by South China Printing Co. Ltd., China

First American Edition, 2002
12 13 14 15 10 9 8 7 6 5 4 3 2 1

Published in the United States by DK Publishing,
375 Hudson Street, New York, New York 10014

Reprinted with revisions 2004, 2005, 2008, 2010, 2012

Copyright 2002, 2012 © Dorling Kindersley Limited, London

PUBLISHED IN GREAT BRITAIN BY DORLING KINDERSLEY LIMITED.

A CATALOG RECORD FOR THIS BOOK IS AVAILABLE
FROM THE LIBRARY OF CONGRESS.

ISSN 1542-1554
ISBN 978-0-7566-8582-9

Front cover main image:
Wrought-iron balcony in the French Quarter

MIX
Paper from
responsible sources
FSC™ C018179
www.fsc.org

**The information in this
DK Eyewitness Travel Guide is checked regularly.**
Every effort has been made to ensure that this book is as up-to-date
as possible at the time of going to press. Some details, however,
such as telephone numbers, opening hours, prices, gallery hanging
arrangements, and travel information are liable to change. The
publishers cannot accept responsibility for any consequences arising
from the use of this book. We value the views and suggestions of
our readers very highly. Please write to: Publisher, DK Eyewitness
Travel Guides, Dorling Kindersley, 80 Strand, London WC2R 0RL,
Great Britain, or email: travelguides@dk.com.

CONTENTS

New Orleans ironwork,
Lower French Quarter

INTRODUCING
NEW ORLEANS

The bustling Central
Business District

◁ View of the Central Business District from the Mississippi River

Mansion on St. Charles Avenue

Vegetables and fruit for sale in the French Market

Preservation Hall, one of New Orleans' best jazz venues

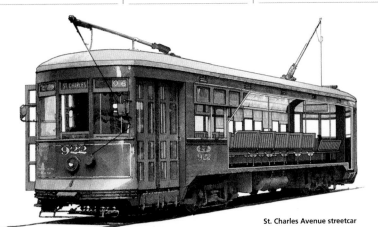

St. Charles Avenue streetcar

HOW TO USE THIS GUIDE

This DK Eyewitness Travel Guide helps you to get the most from your visit to New Orleans. It provides detailed information and expert recommendations.

The chapter titled *Introducing New Orleans* maps the city and the region, and sets it in its historical and cultural context; it also describes the most salient events of the year. *New Orleans at a Glance* is an overview of the city's main attractions. *New Orleans Area by Area* starts on page 44. This is the main

sightseeing section, and it covers all of the important sights, with photographs, maps and illustrations. *Beyond New Orleans* covers nearby Cajun Country, as well as the historic plantations.

Information about hotels, restaurants, shops and markets, entertainment, and sports is found in *Travelers' Needs*. The *Survival Guide* section has advice on everything from using New Orleans' medical services, telephones, banking, and post offices to the public transportation system.

FINDING YOUR WAY AROUND NEW ORLEANS

The city has been divided into five sightseeing areas, each with its own section in the guide. Each section opens with a portrait of the area, summing up its character and history, and listing all the sights to be covered. The sights

are numbered and clearly located on an *Area Map*. After this comes a *Street-by-Street Map* focusing on the most interesting part of the area. Finding your way about the area section is made easy by a numbering system.

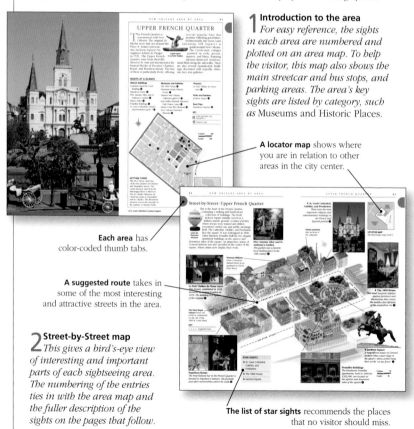

1 Introduction to the area
For easy reference, the sights in each area are numbered and plotted on an area map. To help the visitor, this map also shows the main streetcar and bus stops, and parking areas. The area's key sights are listed by category, such as Museums and Historic Places.

A locator map shows where you are in relation to other areas in the city center.

Each area has color-coded thumb tabs.

A suggested route takes in some of the most interesting and attractive streets in the area.

2 Street-by-Street map
This gives a bird's-eye view of interesting and important parts of each sightseeing area. The numbering of the entries ties in with the area map and the fuller description of the sights on the pages that follow.

The list of star sights recommends the places that no visitor should miss.

NEW ORLEANS AREA MAP

The colored areas shown on this map *(see inside front cover)* are the five main sightseeing areas used in this guide. Each is covered in a full chapter in *New Orleans Area by Area (see pp44–135)*. They are highlighted on other maps throughout the book. In *New Orleans at a Glance*, for example, they help you locate the top sights *(see pp30–31)*.

Numbers refer to each sight's position on the area map and its place in the chapter.

Practical information provides everything you need to know to visit each sight. Map references pinpoint the sight's location on the *Street Finder* map *(see pp222–9)*.

3 Detailed information
All the important sights in New Orleans are described individually. They are listed in order, following the numbering on the area map at the start of the section. Practical information includes a map reference, opening hours, and telephone numbers. The key to the symbols is on the back flap.

The visitors' checklist gives all the practical information needed to plan your visit.

Façades of important buildings are often shown to help you recognize them quickly.

4 New Orleans' major sights
Historic buildings are dissected to reveal their interiors; museums and galleries have color-coded floor plans to help you find the most important exhibits.

Stars indicate the features that no visitor should miss.

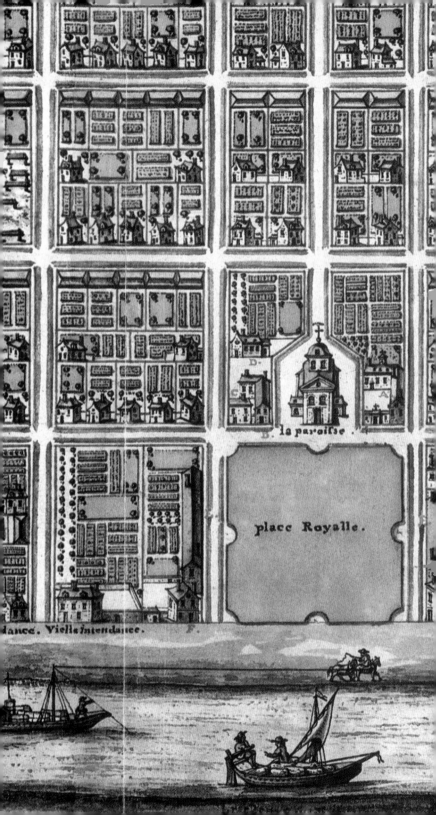

B. la paroisse.

place Royalle.

...dance. Vielle intendance.

INTRODUCING
NEW ORLEANS

fleuve S. loüis

a 400 pieds de profundeur

FOUR GREAT DAYS IN NEW ORLEANS

New Orleans has always been a city where many cultures mingle. Today, that heritage is reflected in a great diversity of things to do and see. Here are four great days out, each showing different slices of life in this exuberant city. One reveals the French Quarter with its Gallic ambience; another explores

Music, New Orleans-style

elegant Uptown by streetcar; a third taps into the exciting visual and performing arts scene, and the fourth is aimed at entertaining families with children. Important sights have page references so you can check for more details. The price guides include cost of travel, food, and admission charges.

FRENCH QUARTER AND MISSISSIPPI CRUISE

- *Beignets* for breakfast
- **Mardi Gras exhibit**
- **Lunch at Napoleon House**
- **Cruise on the *Natchez* and go for a Bourbon stroll**

TWO ADULTS allow at least $125

Morning
Start the day with a classic coffee and *beignets* (donuts) breakfast at the **Café du Monde** (*see p76 and p176*). Cross Decatur Street to **Jackson Square** (*see p54*), where street performers entertain. Visit the Mardi Gras exhibit at the **Presbytère** (*see pp56–7*), a landmark state museum. Then, amble down Chartres Street to **Napoleon House** (*see p59 and p178*) for lunch. This mansion, built for the French

Oysters, at the Acme Oyster House

emperor, is now a charming café and bar that oozes French Quarter ambience.

Afternoon
Head to the riverfront and the **Steamboat *Natchez*** (*see pp64–5*) for a 2-hour cruise (departs at 2:30pm), with calliope music, fascinating narratives on the city, and views of the busy waterway. Back on land, a short walk from the dock, the **French Market** (*see p70*) is ideal for a spot of browsing in the shops, crafts booths, and flea market stalls. Return to Jackson Square and hire a carriage for a ride through the Quarter; you will be intrigued by the local architecture. Finally, stroll along **Bourbon Street** (*see pp46–7*), and relish its neon-lit, bawdy glory before heading to the **Acme Oyster House** (*see p176*) for oysters or gumbo (stew).

Stunning architecture at the Contemporary Arts Center

STYLE, ART, AND CREOLE CULTURE

- **Explore the Arts District**
- **Creole history, art and antiques on Royal Street**
- **An evening at the theater**

TWO ADULTS allow at least $120

Morning
Breakfast at the world-famous **Brennan's** restaurant (*see p176*) starts the day in laidback but elegant style. Catch the **St. Charles Avenue streetcar** (*see pp104–5*) or take a cab to **Lee Circle** (*see p96*) where, within a three-block radius, you can happily overdose on art at the **Ogden Museum of Southern Art** (*see p96*), the **Contemporary Arts Center** (*see p97*), and Julia Street galleries, which are clustered together in the district.

A few blocks away, built into an old river warehouse on S. Peters and Fulton

Garlic, and plenty of it, at the French market

◁ *Plan de la Ville/La Nouvelle Orléans/Capitale de la Province de la Louisiane, by Thierry, 1755*

streets, you'll find restaurants offering a variety of lunch options, including tapas, sushi, and Mexican food.

Afternoon

Head back to the French Quarter and visit the **Historic New Orleans Collection** *(see pp60–61)*, where exhibits illustrate Creole life in the 19th century. Take a stroll along **Royal Street** *(see pp48–9)*, with its galleries and antiques stores, where for six blocks performers and musicians are found on nearly every corner. If you want to experience Creole fine dining, stop at **Galatoire's** *(see p177)*, an upscale bistro on Bourbon Street. Culture fans will love a modern play at the Southern Repertory Theatre in **Canal Place** *(see p94)*, or a classic at **Le Petit Théâtre** *(see p55)*.

A group of jazz players on Jackson Square

A streetcar named St. Charles

THE HISTORIC CHARM OF THE STREETCAR

- **Go up and down town on stately streetcars**
- **Admire mansions and tombs in the Garden District**
- **Lunch in the Riverbend**
- **Cocktails at sunset**

TWO ADULTS allow at least $75

Morning

Get your $1.25 fares ready and head to the first stop of the historic **St. Charles Avenue streetcar** *(see pp104–5)* at the corner of Canal and Carondelet streets. Passengers travel at a steady pace past the mansions and towering oaks. Disembark at Washington Avenue and head into the **Garden District** *(see pp100–1)*, where you'll see opulent homes and splendid gardens that bear witness to the wealth of the antebellum South. Drop into the lobby of the renowned **Commander's Palace** *(see p182)* restaurant to pick up a free guide to historic homes.

Explore the maze of tombs at **Lafayette Cemetery** *(see p100)*. Return to the streetcar route and board the next Uptown-bound car. At **Audubon Park** *(see p111)*, walk through lush grounds, or cross the street to visit the campuses of **Tulane and Loyola universities** *(see p110)*. Walk, or jump onto another Uptown-bound streetcar, to the **Riverbend** *(see p111)*, an outdoor recreation area. If hungry, grab a counter seat at **Camellia Grill** *(see p180)*, a charmingly retro diner.

Afternoon

After crossing Carrollton Avenue, window shop along bustling Maple Street, with its fine book stores and upscale boutiques. Return to St. Charles Avenue to board a downtown-bound streetcar to the **Columns Hotel** *(see p166)*, and reward yourself with a cocktail at the Victorian Bar, either on its regal porch or inside at the ornate bar.

A predatory jaguar in the lush jungle at Audubon Zoo

A FUN DAY OUT FOR THE FAMILY

- **Clowns and caricatures**
- **A streetcar ride to the zoo**
- **Swamps and rare alligators**
- **History and horror in wax**

FAMILY OF 4 allow at least $150

Morning

Start in the French Quarter, at **Jackson Square** *(see p54)*, where clowns, artists, and street performers put on a show for all. A caricature drawn here makes for a unique souvenir. Then, head across Decatur Street to check out the dance troupes and other acts in the performance area next to the Jax Brewery. Pick up the St. Charles Avenue streetcar on Canal Street and take a leisurely 30-minute ride to the acclaimed **Audubon Zoo** *(see pp112–13)*. If you get hungry, grab a bite at one of the zoo's cafés (you'll find the swamp section's popular eatery is heaving). While there, check out the Louisiana swamp exhibit of local wildlife, especially the rare white alligator.

Afternoon

Jump aboard the streetcar for the return trip. Back in the French Quarter, enjoy scary dungeon settings, scenes from New Orleans' history, and famous figures in wax at the **Musée Conti Wax Museum** *(see p58)*. End the afternoon by grabbing a *muffuletta* at the popular **Central Grocery** *(see p177)* – you've earned it.

Putting New Orleans on the Map

New Orleans is located in southeast Louisiana, between Lake Pontchartrain and the Mississippi River. The airport handles international and domestic flights, and there are good road and rail links to the rest of the country. Prior to Hurricane Katrina, in August 2005, the population of central New Orleans was approximately 485,000. Many New Orleanians lost their homes as a result of the terrible floods and had to move away. By 2010 the population had rebounded to around 340,000.

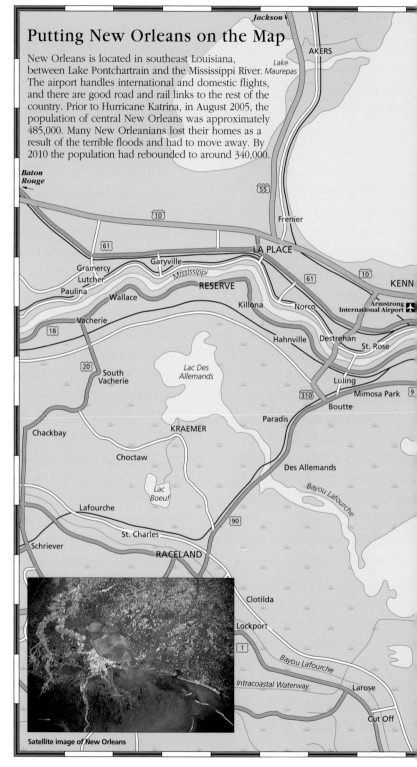

Satellite image of New Orleans

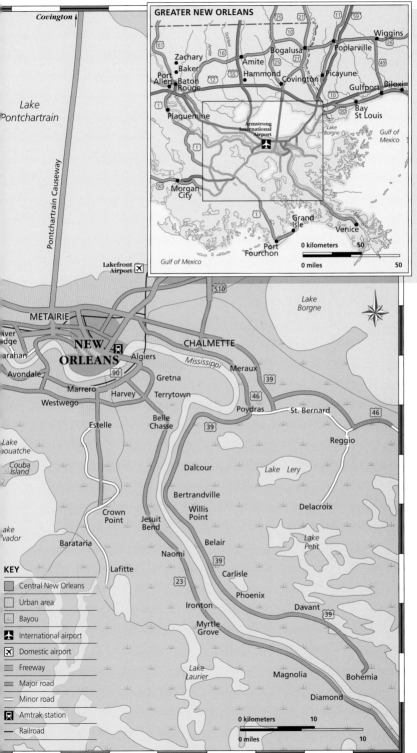

GREATER NEW ORLEANS

Covington

Wiggins

Zachary
Baker
Port
Allen
Baton
Rouge
Amite
Hammond
Bogalusa
Poplarville
Covington
Picayune
Gulfport
Biloxi

Plaquemine
Bay
St Louis
Gulf of
Mexico

Armstrong
International
Airport
Lake
Borgne

Morgan
City

Grand
Isle
Venice

Port
Fourchon

Gulf of Mexico

0 kilometers   50

0 miles   50

Lake
Pontchartrain

Pontchartrain Causeway

Lakefront
Airport

510

Lake
Borgne

METAIRIE

iver
idge
arahan

NEW
ORLEANS

Algiers
CHALMETTE

Mississippi
Meraux

Avondale
90

Gretna
39

Marrero
Harvey
Terrytown
46
Poydras
St. Bernard
46

Westwego

Belle
Chasse
39

Reggio

Estelle

Dalcour
Lake   Lery

Lake
ouatche

Bertrandville
Willis
Point
Delacroix

Couba
Island

Crown
Point
Jesuit
Bend

Belair
Lake
Petit

ake
vador
Barataria
Naomi
39

KEY

Lafitte
Carlisle

Central New Orleans

Phoenix

Urban area

23
Ironton
Davant
39

Bayou

Myrtle
Grove

International airport

Domestic airport

Freeway

Lake
Laurier
Magnolia
Bohemia

Major road

Diamond

Minor road

Amtrak station

Railroad

0 kilometers   10

0 miles   10

THE HISTORY OF NEW ORLEANS

I n 1541, Spanish explorer Hernando de Soto discovered the Mississippi River, but it was the Frenchman Robert de La Salle who sailed down the river for the first time in 1682 and erected a cross somewhere near the location of modern New Orleans, claiming it and the whole of Louisiana for his king, Louis XIV.

FRENCH COLONY

The first French settlements were established on the Gulf Coast at Biloxi. It took another 19 years before Jean Baptiste Le Moyne, Sieur de Bienville, established a settlement on the Lower Mississippi at New Orleans in 1718. In 1721, the engineer Adrien de Pauger laid out the French Quarter behind the levees that had been constructed. Two years later the capital of the colony was moved from Biloxi to New Orleans.

Jean Baptiste Le Moyne, founder of New Orleans

However, the colony did not prosper, and the French Regent, Philippe d'Orléans, turned over control to a private financier and speculator, Scotsman John Law, who floated stock in his Company of the West and promoted Louisiana as a utopia, which it was not. The natives were hostile, the land was a swamp, and the climate pestilential, but, lured by Law's advertisements, thousands of Germans and Swiss left for Louisiana and, if they survived the perilous ocean crossing, settled along the Mississippi. Whenever immigration to the new colony diminished, criminals and prostitutes were deported from France to New Orleans, the first 88 women arriving from La Salpêtrière, a Paris house of correction, in 1721. The first slaves had arrived a year earlier, and in 1727 the Ursuline Sisters arrived and founded their convent. The Company of the West speculative bubble eventually burst and Law's company collapsed. In 1731 the king resumed control and sent Bienville back to govern and to deal with the troublesome Chickasaw and Natchez Indians. Commerce began to grow, despite the restrictions that the French had imposed on trade with England, Spain, Mexico, Florida, and the West Indies. Much of it was illegal. By 1763 river traffic had grown so prodigiously that exports (indigo, sugar, rum, skins, and fur) totaled $304,000.

By that time, the contest for the control of North America had begun in earnest; in 1755 the Seven Years' War had broken out between Britain and France, Spain, and other European powers.

TIMELINE

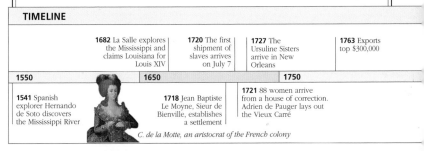

1550	1650	1750
1682 La Salle explores the Mississippi and claims Louisiana for Louis XIV	**1720** The first shipment of slaves arrives on July 7	**1727** The Ursuline Sisters arrive in New Orleans
		1763 Exports top $300,000

1541 Spanish explorer Hernando de Soto discovers the Mississippi River

1718 Jean Baptiste Le Moyne, Sieur de Bienville, establishes a settlement

1721 88 women arrive from a house of correction. Adrien de Pauger lays out the Vieux Carré

C. de la Motte, an aristocrat of the French colony

◁ **Americans take control of the city after the Louisiana Purchase**

St. Louis Cathedral, flanked by the Cabildo (left) and Presbytère, built during Spanish rule

SPANISH CITY

The Seven Years' War ended in 1763, and Louis XV signed the Treaty of Paris, which ended French ambitions in North America. Before signing, however, he had secretly ceded Louisiana to his cousin, the Spanish king, Charles III. The French settlers in Louisiana were outraged at the news, and when the Spanish governor Don Antonio de Ulloa arrived in 1766 to take control, they rebelled, driving him back to Havana. Alexander O'Reilly, an Irish-born Spanish general, arrived with 24 warships, 2,000 soldiers, and 50 artillery pieces. He executed six ringleaders of the rebellion at the site of the Old US Mint, on October 25, 1769, and firmly established Spanish power.

During the American Revolution (1775–83), Governor Bernardo de Galvez supported the American colonists and skillfully defended Baton Rouge, Natchez, Mobile, and Pensacola. He also relaxed trade restrictions, allowing citizens to trade

Spanish Governor Bernardo de Galvez (1776–85)

with countries other than Spain. In 1788, a fire on Good Friday, March 21, destroyed 856 buildings. The destruction was so extensive that most of the French-style buildings were lost. After the fire, the Spanish decreed that all buildings of two stories or more were to be constructed of brick, thus giving the rebuilt city a definite Mediterranean look.

In the 1790s, under Baron Carondelet (1792–7), New Orleans thrived. He granted free trade to the Americans on the Mississippi and made New Orleans the port of deposit for three years. The city's first theater and first newspaper were soon established, gas lamps lit the streets, and a basic police force were recruited. Drainage ditches were dug too, to protect the city against flooding by the Mississippi. Prosperity increased, and the sugar industry was created in 1796, when Jean Etienne de Boré first granulated sugar on a commercial scale. The city was home

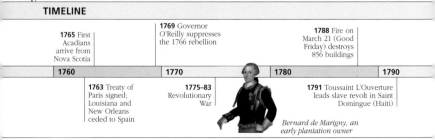

TIMELINE

1765 First Acadians arrive from Nova Scotia

1769 Governor O'Reilly suppresses the 1766 rebellion

1788 Fire on March 21 (Good Friday) destroys 856 buildings

| 1760 | 1770 | 1780 | 1790 |

1763 Treaty of Paris signed; Louisiana and New Orleans ceded to Spain

1775–83 Revolutionary War

1791 Toussaint L'Ouverture leads slave revolt in Saint Domingue (Haiti)

Bernard de Marigny, an early plantation owner

to important plantations like the one owned by Bernard de Marigny in the Lower French Quarter. New Orleans also received an infusion of talented men from the French colony of Saint Domingue (now Haiti), who had fled the slave uprising there in 1791. By 1804, refugee planters and slaves were pouring into New Orleans. They added a distinct Caribbean cast to the colony, erecting West Indian-style houses. The planters' slaves

Andrew Jackson leading the Battle of New Orleans

and free people of color expanded the practice of voodoo in the colony.

THE LOUISIANA PURCHASE AND THE BATTLE OF NEW ORLEANS

Although Spain ceded Louisiana to France in 1800, Napoleon, who was preoccupied in Europe, soon sold it to the United States for $15 million to help pay for his wars. General James

Representation of the Battle of New Orleans at Chalmette

Wilkinson and William C.C. Claiborne officially ratified the transfer on December 20, 1803, at the Cabildo. On April 30, 1812, Louisiana was admitted to the Union, six weeks before the United States declared war on Great Britain because of restraint of trade and the impressment of Americans into the British navy. In January 1815, despite the Treaty of Ghent, which had theoretically ended the war the month before, British forces launched a fresh attack on New Orleans. Under General Andrew Jackson, a ragtag army of pirates, American frontiersmen, French gentlemen, and free men of color beat back the British, validating the peace treaty and finally ending hostilities.

In 1812 the first steamboat had arrived in New Orleans, and soon after the victory at the Battle of New Orleans waves of newcomers, attracted by rapid commercial growth, drove the population to more than 40,000. Nevertheless, friction between the French Creoles and the Americans gave rise to the creation of two separate districts; the French Quarter and an uptown American section. Canal Street separated the two, and the space between was known as the neutral ground.

			Spanish treaty of 1794	**1812** The steamer *New Orleans* arrives in the city in January	
	1796 Sugar industry established		**1803** Louisiana Purchase ratified on December 20		**1815** Andrew Jackson triumphs at the Battle of New Orleans on January 8
		1800		**1810**	**1820**
1795 United States and Spain sign a treaty opening the Mississippi to American trade		**1800** Louisiana ceded from Spain to France	**1812** Louisiana admitted to the Union on April 30		
				1814 Treaty of Ghent, signed on December 24, ends the War of 1812	

STEAMBOATS, COTTON, AND SUGAR

The arrival of the first steamboat, in 1812, opened the city's trade to the interior and the upcountry plantations. Before the steamboat, cargo was carried on flatboats, which floated down the Ohio and Mississippi from Louisville, Kentucky, on a journey that took several weeks.

The *Robert E. Lee* steamboat on the Mississippi

The new steamboats cut the journey to a fraction of that time. Between 1803 and 1833, about 1,000 boats a year docked at the port of New Orleans. By the mid-1830s, the port was shipping half a million bales of cotton, becoming the cotton capital of the world. By 1840 it was the second most important port in the nation, after New York, and the population had passed 80,000. Other commodities that enriched the city were sugar, indigo, coffee, and bananas. As many as 35,000 steamboats docked at the wharves in 1860, clearing $324 million worth of trade.

By this time, New Orleans was the largest city in the South, and, with a population of 168,000, it was the sixth largest city in the nation. The immense wealth that was being generated led to the city's further expansion and cultural development. The city of Lafayette (now the Garden District) was annexed in 1852; the French Opera House was built in 1858; the Mardi Gras festival became more widely celebrated when the first parading krewe, Comus, was found-ed in 1857; it also developed a reputation for its courtly life, riverboat gambling, and easy living. The only blights were the frequent epidemics of cholera and yellow fever. Between 1817 and 1860 there were 23 yellow fever epidemics, killing more than 28,000 people. The worst, in 1853, killed 10,300 people.

1845 portrait of a family

CIVIL WAR AND RECONSTRUCTION

The Civil War brought pros-perity to an end. In 1861 Louisiana seceded from the Union. In 1862, Union Navy Captain Farragut captured New Orleans, and General Benjamin "Beast" Butler occupied the city on May 1, 1862. Butler hanged William Mumford for tearing the United States flag down from the Mint, confiscated the prop-erty of those who refused to sign an oath of allegiance, and passed an ordinance declaring that any woman who insulted a Union soldier would be regarded as a pros-titute and locked up. The citizens chafed under his rule and that of his successor, General Nathaniel Banks. After the war, the city struggled to

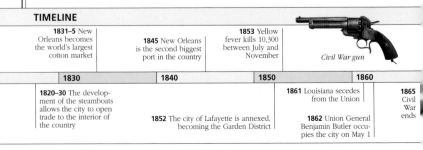

TIMELINE

1831–5 New Orleans becomes the world's largest cotton market	**1845** New Orleans is the second biggest port in the country	**1853** Yellow fever kills 10,300 between July and November	*Civil War gun*
1830	**1840**	**1850**	**1860**
1820–30 The development of the steamboats allows the city to open trade to the interior of the country	**1852** The city of Lafayette is annexed, becoming the Garden District	**1861** Louisiana secedes from the Union **1862** Union General Benjamin Butler occupies the city on May 1	**1865** Civil War ends

recover, but the source of so much of the city's wealth – the upriver plantations – had been destroyed. The "Old South" never recovered; the steamboat era was over, and the economic shift toward the northeast left New Orleans languishing.

Poor race relations troubled the city after the Civil War. In 1865, at the end of the Civil War, slaves were freed but lived in legal limbo. In 1866, a race riot broke out near Mechanics Hall in downtown New Orleans, where a group of white and black men were

Slave cabin in a cotton plantation, circa 1860

drafting a new state constitution to extend full rights to black men (women would not vote until the 20th century). During the attack, 37 delegates were killed and 136 wounded; the violence of the Mechanics Hall riot was a key element in Congress's decision to organize Reconstruction as a military occupation of the old Confederacy by federal troops.

In 1877 federal troops withdrew, but the legal and social gains made by African Americans during Reconstruction soon began to erode as old Confederates resumed full political, civil, and economic power. Segregation became entrenched in 1896 when in Plessy v. Ferguson the US Supreme Court established the so-called "separate but equal" mandates. Segregation was not successfully challenged again for more than 50 years. Racial tensions only worsened as waves of Italians and Irish immigrants arrived in the late 19th century.

Although the 1884 Cotton Centennial Exposition boosted the city's profile as a major commercial center, crime, prostitution, and corruption remained rampant. In 1897, in an attempt to control the lawlessness that was troubling the city, Alderman Sidney Story sponsored a bill that legalized prostitution in a 38-block area bounded by Iberville, Basin, Robertson, and St. Louis streets. This area, which became known as "Storyville", fostered the beginnings of a new style of improvisational music, called jazz *(see pp20–21)*. It was later demolished to make way for low-income housing.

Painting of a fleet of Civil War frigates

1866 Mechanics Hall Riot

1877 Reconstruction ends; federal troops leave

1890 Racial tensions reach their peak in New Orleans

1897 Sidney Story proposes official red light district

1870   1880   1890   1900

1884 Cotton Centennial Exposition

1896 Supreme Court decision in Plessy v. Ferguson permits racial segregation

General Robert E. Lee

History of New Orleans Jazz

Blue Lu Barker

Jazz is America's original contribution to world culture. It evolved slowly and almost imperceptibly from a number of sources – from the music played at balls, parades, dances, and funerals, and New Orleans' unique blend of cultures. Its musical inspirations included classical music (the original jazz musicians were classically trained), spirituals, marches, and American folk influences – the entire mélange of music that was played in 19th-century New Orleans.

Trumpeter Oscar "Papa" Celestin
The founder of the Tuxedo Brass Band in 1911 also composed "Down by the Riverside."

Congo Square
On Sundays, slaves gathered here to celebrate their one day off, playing music and dancing.

Papa Jack's Dixieland Jazz Band
This all-white band, led by Nick LaRocca, made the first jazz recording in 1917.

Louis Armstrong
This world-famous jazz trumpeter began singing on the streets of New Orleans. He played with Kid Ory before leaving the city in 1923 to join King Oliver's band in Chicago.

Bordellos, or "sporting houses," were where jazz gained its popularity.

TIMELINE

Buddy Bolden (1877–1931), a barber born in New Orleans, played cornet and formed one of the first jazz bands in the 1890s

Joe "King" Oliver (1885–1938) started playing cornet in New Orleans in 1904, but moved to Chicago with his Creole Jazz Band

"King" Oliver

1880	1900	1920

Jelly Roll Morton (1890–1941) began his piano career in the brothels of Storyville. He was the first great jazz composer and pianist

Sidney Bechet (1897–1959) played clarinet and soprano saxophone with early leaders like Freddie Keppard

Riverboat Jazz Bands
After Storyville was closed down in 1917, New Orleans' best musicians moved onto the boats or migrated to northern cities. Pianist Fate Marable's band included Louis Armstrong, who played the cornet.

Kid Ory's Trombone
Edward "Kid" Ory played with King Oliver and Louis Armstrong's famous Hot Five band.

The Boswell Sisters
Connie, Martha, and Vet Boswell sang and recorded in the early 1930s. This was the most popular female jazz group of its time.

Musicians were screened off so that they could not see the patrons.

STORYVILLE JAZZ SALON
Many early jazz artists entertained in Storyville at the bordellos, playing behind screens – Buddy Bolden, King Oliver, Jelly Roll Morton, Sidney Bechet, Kid Ory, Freddy Keppard, and Manuel Perez among them.

Jelly Roll Morton
Ferdinand "Jelly Roll" Morton, who formed the band The Red Hot Peppers, claimed to have invented jazz in 1902.

Louis Armstrong (1901–1971) was the greatest of all jazz musicians. From 1940 to 1960 he played with his All Star Band

Louis Armstrong

Terence Blanchard (1962–), a trumpeter, played with Lionel Hampton and Art Blakey before forming his own quintet. He is famous for composing and playing the music for Spike Lee's films

1940	1960	1980	2000

Danny Barker (1909–1994) played guitar and banjo with the big bands in the 1930s and 1940s before returning to New Orleans

Pete Fountain (1930–) is considered one of the best clarinetists in the world

Harry Connick, Jr. (1967–) played in New Orleans clubs as a teenager, later becoming a major jazz-pop music star and arranging the score for *When Harry Met Sally*

A World War II Higgins boat

20TH-CENTURY NEW ORLEANS – FROM STORYVILLE TO 2000

Until it was abolished on October 2, 1917, Storyville was the most extraordinary spectacle of legalized vice in the United States. Patrons could pick up a copy of the "Blue Book" in a bar or hotel and find the names and addresses of 700 prostitutes listed with their prices and their color. Storyville also gave jazz a boost, because many early jazz artists began their musical lives in the brothels *(see pp20–21)*.

The Department of the Navy closed Storyville down in 1917, because it feared that it was too tempting to sailors shipping out from New Orleans to World War I battlefronts. Although the war briefly boosted business in the shipyards, the economy languished in the early 1930s. The effects of the Depression were evident by 1933, when five New Orleans banks failed and 11 percent of the citizenry was on welfare. Under the New Deal, Mayor Robert Maestri used federal dollars to build roads, bridges, parks, and public buildings. During World War II, business

picked up again in the shipyards, and New Orleans produced thousands of the famous Higgins boats that were used in Allied amphibious landings on all war fronts.

In 1946 Mayor de Lesseps Story "Chep" Morrison was elected as a reformer and served until 1961. During his administration the city began to take on its current appearance. He constructed the Pontchartrain Expressway, a new airport, and, in 1958, the $65-million Mississippi River Bridge (later renamed the Crescent City Connection), which opened the West Bank area to suburban development. In 1954, the Supreme Court ruling Brown v. the Board of Education ordered the desegregation of public education. Schools were integrated by federal marshals in 1960.

During the 1960s there was some economic regeneration when NASA took over an old aviation plant to build the Saturn rocket booster, and a ship channel was opened, enabling very large ships to enter the port. In 1969 the port was still the second in the nation. During the boom, new

The Crescent City Connection Bridge, reconstructed in the 1990s

TIMELINE

1910	1920	1930	1940	1950	1960

1933 Five New Orleans banks fail; 11 percent of the citizens are on relief

1936–46 Mayor Robert Maestri uses federal funds to repair the city's infrastructure

1961 NASA acquires the old Michoud aviation plant to assemble Saturn booster rockets

1917 Storyville abolished on October 2

1936 Vieux Carré Commission established

Storyville brothel sign

1954 Brown v. Board of Education orders desegregation

1941–45 Higgins boats produced at the shipyards

1960 N. O. schools are desegregated by federal marshals

LULU WHITE

buildings like the World Trade Center, Rivergate, and One Shell Square were erected, and several hotels rose up along Canal Street. In 1967 the city was granted an NFL (National Football League) franchise.

The 1965 Voting Rights Act changed the political picture in the city. In 1969, Mayor Moon Landrieu was elected primarily thanks to the support of black voters, and he appointed the first black to a senior position in his administration, paving the way for the election of Ernest N. "Dutch" Morial, the first black mayor, in 1978.

NASA Saturn rocket, built in the 1960s at the Michoud plant

The early years of the Morial administration benefited greatly from the oil boom, but by 1986 the bubble had burst, due to the drop in international oil prices; as a result, the city's economy was devastated. Meanwhile, the white and middle class flight to the suburbs, which began in the 1950s, continued, leaving parts of the inner city to the poor. Morial sought to salvage city fortunes by advancing construction on the Convention Center, farther developing the waterfront, and encouraging tourism investment, but racial tensions increased, finally spilling over into Mardi Gras. In 1991 the City Council passed a stringent anti-discrimination law, refusing to grant parade permits to all; the Comus, Proteus, and Momus krewes refused to comply, and canceled their parades. The ordinance

Millennium celebrations on the Mississippi River

was later toned down, and Proteus resumed its parade in 2000. In 1994, Dutch's son, Marc Morial, was elected mayor. He served two terms, building a powerful political machine. Some economic diversification and the boom in the late 1990s helped restore prosperity, but the city still suffers from a dependence on tourism and oil, and from the persistent problems of corruption. C. Ray Nagin was elected mayor in 2002 on a reform platform. In August 2005, a disastrous flood caused by Hurricane Katrina *(see pp24–7)* hit the city, killing more than 1,400 people, but sparing most historic neighborhoods. In 2010, Moon Landrieu's son Mitch was elected mayor. Several years after Katrina, much remains to be done, but the city is steadily recovering, doing what it does best; delivering the pleasures of food, drink, music, and art to the many visitors that flock here.

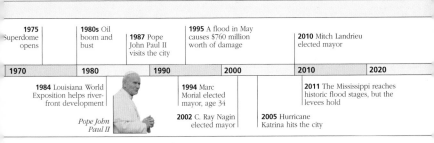

Hurricane Katrina

A satellite image of Hurricane Katrina

Hurricane Katrina – and the subsequent levee failures – which hit New Orleans in August 2005 have been called the most expensive disaster in US history. More than 850,000 homes were damaged and entire communities along the Gulf Coast of Louisiana, Mississippi, and Alabama were destroyed overnight. The official death toll in Louisiana alone exceeded 1,400 people, and many more were forced to relocate across the country. Much of the destruction in the city was caused by floodwaters. The recovery effort has been a monumental undertaking: billions of dollars in insurance proceeds and government funds have been committed so far.

17th Street Canal and London Avenue Canal
Katrina's storm surge overwhelmed these canals and flooded much of the city.

Tulane and Loyola Universities
These institutions had to contend with damage to the facilities and the displacement of most employees and students. They managed to reopen in 2006.

The St. Charles Avenue streetcar was severely damaged by the winds, which tore down the overhead power lines. The rolling stock, however, survived the storm, and service was resumed in 2007.

The massive Mississippi River levees that help contain the river weathered Katrina without a problem, ensuring that the French Quarter, Central Business District, Uptown, and parts of the Garden District remained dry.

TIMELINE

Aug 28 Mayor Ray Nagin orders the mandatory evacuation of New Orleans

Aug 26, 2005 State of emergency declared in Louisiana

Aug 31 Attempts to plug levee breaches fail; flooding continues until waters reach the level of Lake Pontchartrain

Sep 24 Hurricane Rita makes landfall; parts of New Orleans are flooded again

Mayor Nagin

Feb 28, 2006 First post-Katrina Mardi Gras

2005

2006

Aug 29 Katrina makes landfall; storm surge inundates some communities; levees fail around New Orleans and massive flooding reported

Sep 6 Evacuation of Superdome is completed

Sep 15 President Bush pledges to rebuild the city

Sep 12 Federal Emergency Management Agency (FEMA) director Michael Brown resigns

Nov 28 City's first public school reopens

Oct 6 Drinking water declared safe in most of the city

THE CITY UNDERWATER

The historic neighborhoods built on higher ground did not flood, while the newer communities, built on reclaimed swamp land, were devastated as lake water surged through the levee breaches.

The New Orleans Fair Grounds race-track flooded, but the venue was still able to host the New Orleans Jazz & Heritage Festival in 2006. Horse racing resumed in November 2007.

St. Louis Cathedral and other landmarks in the historic French Quarter were built on high ground and therefore avoided flooding.

WHY THE LEVEES FAILED

New Orleans relies on a network of man-made canals supported by concrete walls and earthen levees to drain water from the low-lying city into Lake Pontchartrain. The storm surge from Hurricane Katrina forced a massive amount of water from the lake back into the canals, and eventually this water overflowed the walls meant to contain it.

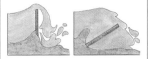

Water cascaded *over the canal walls with such force that it eroded the supporting earthen banks. This eventually weakened the levees so much that the walls collapsed and flood-water poured into the city.*

The Mississippi River-Gulf Outlet, a man-made shipping channel outside of New Orleans, helped funnel the storm surge into the city via the Industrial Canal.

Roof Damage at the Superdome

Storm winds tore off the roof of the city's largest sports arena, a refuge for several thousand residents. It took days for the people trapped there to be evacuated.

Lower Ninth Ward

In this area, water blasted through the failed levees with such force that homes were ripped from the ground, leaving little to salvage in the flood's wake.

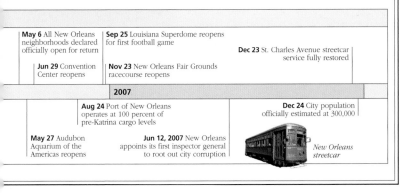

New Orleans streetcar

The Impact of Hurricane Katrina

Scrawled messages on a house in New Orleans

Hurricane Katrina was a disaster of unprecedented magnitude for New Orleans, combining the destructive force of a powerful hurricane with levee failures that left much of the city inundated by floodwaters for weeks. It was clear from the start that the city's recovery would take years, and early results materialized very slowly as bureaucratic issues mounted. However, the spirit and improvisation that have long made New Orleans such a captivating place for visitors have also fueled the city's recovery. As the rebuilding work continues, New Orleans has emerged as a showcase and proving ground for new ideas, while the warm atmosphere and unique charms of the historic city have survived to greet visitors once again.

Destruction in the wake of Hurricane Camille (1969)

A HISTORY OF HURRICANES

Like many other communities on the Gulf of Mexico, New Orleans has had to contend with powerful, devastating hurricanes throughout its history. In particular, Hurricane Betsy in September 1965, and Hurricane Camille in August 1969, caused much destruction in the metro area.

Each hurricane season, local residents would follow the storm forecasts, but while there had been several close calls, the city had managed to escape major damage for many years. However, rapidly accelerating coastal erosion was stripping away the massive wetlands that stand between New Orleans and the open waters of the Gulf. These wetlands would prove crucial as they provide a natural buffer against tropical storms.

LEVEE FAILURES AND A FITFUL RESPONSE

Hurricane Katrina formed over the Atlantic in late August 2005. As storm-track forecasts zeroed in on the New Orleans area, government officials and residents began making preparations. On August 26, the Louisiana governor declared a state of emergency, and on August 28, Mayor Ray Nagin ordered a mandatory evacuation of New Orleans. Several thousand residents took to the highways, but many others stayed put; the Louisiana Superdome was opened as a refuge to shelter them.

Katrina made landfall on August 29: winds knocked down trees, shattered windows, and tore roofs across the area. But much worse damage came from the wall of seawater the hurricane had driven towards the Gulf Coast. This storm surge

inundated entire communities outside of the region's protection levees. In New Orleans itself, the levee walls collapsed, allowing water from Lake Pontchartrain to pour into the city.

The paralyzed city descended into chaos, with thousands of desperate citizens pleading for help from their rooftops. The Federal Emergency Management Agency (FEMA) was criticized for its disorganized, slow response, but eventually the military arrived in force to oversee a massive evacuation.

A MODERN DIASPORA

Amid the turmoil were moments of great courage and generosity. The US Coast Guard rescued an estimated 33,500 people from the area, and countless individuals stepped up to help those displaced and in dire need. When the evacuation was complete, the flooded city and its suburbs sat virtually empty as residents spread out across the US in search of temporary shelter.

On September 15, President George W. Bush delivered a televised speech from Jackson Square to pledge that the nation would do "whatever it takes" to rebuild New Orleans. Recovery efforts began by plugging levee breaks and draining the flooded neighborhoods, leaving behind endless vistas of washed-out destruction and a body count that would exceed 1,400 in Louisiana alone.

Aerial image of the city revealing the extent of the devastation

THE NEW ORLEANS SAINTS

With their hometown devastated and their stadium, the Superdome, in ruins, the New Orleans Saints football team ended the 2005 season with one of the National Football League's worst records. However, the team came roaring back the following year. The restored Superdome reopened in September 2006, just in time for the Saints' first home game since Katrina. The team won that game and went on to end the season with a trip to the conference championship. Along the way, the Saints' success provided an uplifting cause for New Orleanians, who embraced the team as a symbol of their city's recovery.

The grand reopening of the Louisiana Superdome

PICKING UP THE PIECES

Neighborhoods built on high ground, such as the French Quarter and the Garden District, did not flood and were open for re-entry just weeks after Katrina. For other areas, a slow planning process for rebuilding began as the government debated how to fund the immense recovery effort. Residents slowly trickled back and were provided with thousands of trailers for temporary lodging.

Debris amassed in front of a house in the aftermath of Katrina

OPEN FOR BUSINESS

Despite the devastation and lack of urban infrastructure, the recovery of New Orleans began to spread from the relatively intact historic core to the surrounding neighborhoods. Restaurants and businesses slowly reopened, sometimes in makeshift conditions, and the first schools resumed lessons before the end of 2005. The New Orleans port, the city's long-standing economic powerhouse, also

got back to business, and volunteers from around the world flocked to the area to help with the recovery effort. Though the tourism and convention industries were severely reduced, and staffing shortages were rampant, New Orleans managed to host its traditional Mardi Gras celebration in February 2006.

REBUILDING BETTER

As residents continued to return to the city, the Army Corps of Engineers began building a stronger, more advanced flood-control system. This project will take years to complete, but it has already increased the city's level of protection, as the river's levees held in 2011. The federal government eventually approved billions of dollars in aid to repair local infrastructure and help residents rebuild their homes and businesses. After several central planning processes fell apart, frustrated neighborhood groups began

crafting their own redevelopment plans. Private programs have also grown to encourage environmentally sensitive designs in rebuilding the city.

A NEW NEW ORLEANS

Today it is possible to visit New Orleans without seeing a trace of the disaster, though outside the historic areas signs of the devastation still linger. Recovery continues on a block-by-block basis, even as large-scale reconstruction projects begin to take shape.

The city's population is still significantly smaller than before Katrina. However, many of the residents who have returned, and newcomers drawn to New Orleans since the disaster, have embraced the city's cultural heritage and are reinvigorating its many unique traditions. The population has also taken a renewed interest in politics and wide-ranging political reforms have been created to hold officials more accountable, and improve civic institutions.

Homes being built in the New Orleans Musicians' Village

History of Mardi Gras

Mardi Gras costume

Culminating on Mardi Gras – the day before Ash Wednesday – the Carnival celebrations in New Orleans attract visitors from across the United States and around the world. Since the 1700s the period between Twelfth Night (January 6) and Ash Wednesday, the start of Lent, has been celebrated with lavish balls, presented by private citizen groups known as "krewes." Although most balls are private, many krewes also put on parades, with ornate costumes and floats. These take place for 10 days before Mardi Gras, with the oldest and most famous parades on Tuesday itself.

Bacchus Kings
The Krewe of Bacchus has invited Bob Hope, Kirk Douglas, and Charlton Heston to be their king.

Rex
This krewe was founded in 1872 to organize a spectacle for Grand Duke Alexis, a younger son of Czar Alexander II.

King Cake
The traditional food of Carnival, each king cake contains a small plastic figure of a baby, representing the baby Jesus.

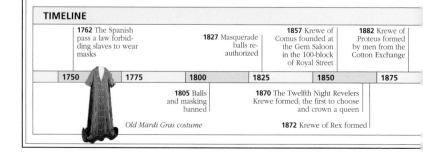

Parade Floats
Each krewe has 14 or more colorful floats, some still made of traditional papier-mâché, that are pulled through the city in the parades.

TIMELINE

1762 The Spanish pass a law forbidding slaves to wear masks		**1827** Masquerade balls re-authorized	**1857** Krewe of Comus founded at the Gem Saloon in the 100-block of Royal Street		**1882** Krewe of Proteus formed by men from the Cotton Exchange
1750	1775	1800	1825	1850	1875
	1805 Balls and masking banned		**1870** The Twelfth Night Revelers Krewe formed; the first to choose and crown a queen		
	Old Mardi Gras costume		**1872** Krewe of Rex formed		

French Quarter Celebrations
Crowds jam the French Quarter to watch the costumed crowds and impromptu parades.

WHERE TO SEE MARDI GRAS

The history of Mardi Gras is displayed at a permanent exhibition in the Presbytère *(see pp56–7)*. Many floats are constructed at Blaine Kern's Mardi Gras World *(see p106)* and can be seen there all year long.

Throws
Souvenir doubloons (coins), beads, and dolls are thrown from the floats to the crowds. This tradition began with Rex in 1881.

The Presbytère *presents a colorful display of Mardi Gras history.*

Blaine Kern's Mardi Gras World *is the place where many of the floats are made.*

MARDI GRAS COLORS

The purple, green, and gold masks, banners, and other decorations that adorn buildings everywhere during the Carnival season are derived from the original costume worn by Rex in the 1872 parade. He used a theatrical costume made for *Richard III*, consisting of a purple velvet cloak with green rhinestones and a golden scepter and crown. Today, these colors are still used: purple symbolizing justice, green for faith, and gold for power.

Rex's Scepter
The King of Mardi Gras, a prominent New Orleans citizen, is chosen by the Rex organization every year.

Rex knight

1968 Krewe of Bacchus breaks traditions. It opens its ranks to all and invites celebrities to become its king

1909 Zulu, the first black krewe, organized as a parody

1991 A city ordinance requires parading Krewes to open their membership to all. Comus, Momus, and Proteus cancel their parades

1900	1925	1950	1975	2000	2025

1889 The first marching krewe, Jefferson City Buzzards, founded

1935 The Elks organize the first truck krewe

2000 Proteus resumes parading after a nine-year absence

2008 The city returns to its pre-Katrina Mardi Gras parade schedule, with 11 days of festivities

NEW ORLEANS AT A GLANCE

There are more than 100 places of interest described in this book. They range from the legendary Bourbon Street to the quiet and beautiful live oaks in City Park, and from Jackson Square, with its spontaneous jazz street-musicians, to the scientific exhibits in the Audubon Aquarium of the Americas. The following eight pages are a time-saving guide to the best New Orleans has to offer. Architecture, wrought and cast iron, and culture have their own sections. There is also a guide to the diverse cultures that have given this city its unique character and feeling. Below is a selection of sights that no visitor should miss.

NEW ORLEANS TOP TEN SIGHTS

Old US Mint
See pp74–5

Garden District and Uptown
See pp98–113

Royal Street
See pp48–9

Bourbon Street
See pp46–7

St. Charles Avenue Streetcar *See pp104–5*

Audubon Aquarium of the Americas *See pp90–91*

Audubon Zoo
See pp112–13

Jackson Square
See p54

City Park
See pp116–17

Steamboat *Natchez*
See pp64–5

◁ **Chartres Street, near Jackson Square**

Exploring New Orleans' Many Cultures

New Orleans' unique flavor derives from the incredible mix of peoples and cultures assembled on the banks of the Mississippi River; Native American, French, Spanish, African, Anglo-American, Jewish, Italian, German, and Irish. They have all contributed to the "gumbo" that is New Orleans.

African mask

French colonists signing a treaty with Native Americans

THE NATIVE AMERICANS

Numerous Native American tribes lived in the Delta: Attakpas, Bayougoula, Okelousa, Choctaw, Houma, Tunica, and Chitimacha. They were either wiped out like the Natchez, who were destroyed in the war of 1730, or removed, like the Choctaw, to Oklahoma. Only scattered traces of these tribes remain, mostly outside the city.

THE FRENCH

The French came down the Mississippi from Canada and explored and settled the region in the late 17th and

The French Market, where the city's diverse cultures mix

early 18th centuries. Refugees from the French colony of Saint Domingue added a distinct West Indian flavor to the culture at the beginning of the 19th century. There was a continuous flow of immigration from France throughout the rest of the century. Their influence is most clearly seen in the cuisine as well as in architecture and decorative arts, such as the furniture created by Prudence Mallard.

THE AFRICAN CULTURES

The first slaves arrived in 1720, and by 1724 there were enough to justify the *Code Noir* for their control. New Orleans became known for its large number of free people of color, many of whom came from Haiti during the 1791–1808 Haitian Revolution. On the eve of the Civil War, the city of 168,000 people had 13,000 slaves and free people of color. From Africa and the West Indies came music that influenced the birth of jazz (*see pp20–21*). During Mardi Gras and on St. Joseph's Day (March 19), the Mardi Gras Indians pay homage to native Americans who hid runaway slaves.

THE SPANISH

The Spanish took over from the French as administrators of Louisiana from 1763 to 1800 (*see pp16–17*), but few immigrants from Spain actually settled in New Orleans. Spanish is still spoken by descendants of the "Isleños" – people who came at the request of the Spanish from the Canary Islands in the 1770s. In the 1950s, Latin American refugees from Cuba, Nicaragua, and Honduras flooded into the city. The most obvious Hispanic influence can be seen throughout the French Quarter in the design of the buildings.

THE GERMANS

The first Germans arrived in 1722, lured by John Law's promotion of the colony as an earthly paradise (*see p15*). About 10,000 had left their homes in the Rhineland between 1719 and 1720 after the Thirty Years' War. Nearly 2,000 arrived in the region, settling as small farmers about 25 miles (40 km) upstream from New Orleans, in an area known as the "German Coast." A second wave followed between 1820 and 1850, bringing thousands more, who were fleeing political turmoil in Europe. Another wave followed just before the

Mardi Gras Indian, unique to New Orleans

Civil War, and then another from 1865 to the 1890s. By 1870 there were more than 15,000 living in New Orleans itself. For a time they were the largest immigrant group in Louisiana.

THE CAJUNS

When the British gained control of French Canada, they insisted that the Acadians swear an oath to the British crown. When they refused, they were exiled. Many returned to France, but others traveled south to Catholic Spanish Louisiana. The first 650 people arrived in the region in 1765 and settled as farmers along the bayous west of New Orleans. Today, Cajun culture is undergoing a renaissance, assisted by Cajun and zydeco artists and chefs such as Paul Prudhomme, of K-Paul's Louisiana Kitchen *(see p177)*. While Cajun culture is separate from New Orleans' Creole-influenced culture, Cajun food, and music can be sampled here.

Cajun craftsman sitting at a traditional workbench

THE ANGLO-AMERICANS

The rough-and-ready men who piloted the riverboats down the Mississippi were the first Americans to arrive in New Orleans and give it its reputation as a City of Sin. They came in search of "dixies," or 10-dollar bills, and their carousing became notorious. After the Louisiana Purchase in 1803 *(see p17)*, government workers and land speculators migrated from the east coast, all seeking fortunes in the new territory.

A jazz band marching in the French Quarter

Many of them were of Scots-Irish or English descent. They settled in what became the American Sector on the upriver side of Canal Street, and brought another new architectural style to the city.

THE JEWS

The Jewish community made a big impact on New Orleans from the 19th century, when many Jews emigrated from Germany and Eastern Europe, and in 1828 the first synagogue was organized. In the 19th century, Samuel Zemurray, for one, started a fruit-importing company, which eventually became the United Fruit Company. He was a great philanthropist, and donated enormous sums of money to Tulane University *(see p110)*.

THE IRISH

The Irish arrived in the mid-19th century, fleeing the 1840 potato famine in Ireland. By 1860 there were 24,000 Irish in New Orleans, crowded into a narrow area dubbed the "Irish Channel" between the river and Magazine Street, east of Louisiana Avenue. The majority of them worked as laborers (building the New Basin Canal), and as stevedores. The later generations became very successful in politics.

THE ITALIANS

Although some Italians arrived before the Civil War, many more arrived later and replaced slaves as agricultural laborers. By 1890 there were more than 25,000 living in New Orleans, and more arrived at the turn of the century. Most came from Sicily and settled in the poor French Quarter, where they started out as laborers, peddlers, and market vendors, bringing interesting new flavors to the French Market. Their influence can be seen mainly in the cuisine, including the popular *muffaletta* sandwich *(see p172)*.

A New Orleans canal, built by Irish laborers

The Architecture of New Orleans

French dormer

New Orleans is one of the few American cities that has managed to retain much of its historic architecture. The French Quarter has many buildings dating back 150 years or more, while the Garden District has splendid mansions designed in a variety of styles. Beautiful houses line Esplanade Avenue, historically the residential nucleus of the Creole elite, and the city also possesses a good stock of 19th-century public buildings built in Greek Revival style. It is not always easy to categorize buildings by style, for many of them are hybrids, like the Gallier House, which incorporated both Creole and American features.

Eastlake-style townhouse on Esplanade Avenue

FRENCH COLONIAL

Only a few buildings, such as the Old Ursuline Convent *(see p68)* and Lafitte's Blacksmith Shop *(see p78)*, remain from this period, which combines various French styles of the 18th century. Most were destroyed by a series of fires: in 1788, 856 wooden buildings were destroyed; in 1794, 212 buildings. However, the city's many Creole cottages are reflective of this era.

Brick, stucco, and timber walls

The roof was made of wood tiles.

The brick chimney rose through the center of the house.

Lafitte's Blacksmith Shop *is a fine example of brick between posts, in which soft local bricks are supported by cypress timbers and protected by plaster.*

Water channels protected the wood from water damage.

Gas lamps were added in the 19th century.

SPANISH COLONIAL

After the 1788 and 1794 fires, the Spanish decreed that any building of more than one story must be constructed of brick. The houses that were subsequently built can still be seen in the French Quarter. They often combine residence and store, and feature arcaded walls, heavy doors and windows, and a flagstone alleyway leading to a loggia and fountain-graced courtyard.

The second floor was the family home.

The attic was used as a warehouse.

Walls were built of brick instead of wood.

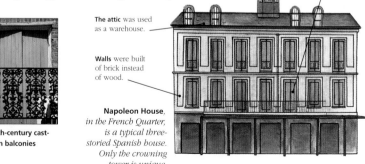

19th-century cast-iron balconies

Napoleon House, *in the French Quarter, is a typical three-storied Spanish house. Only the crowning tower is unique.*

FEDERAL TOWNHOUSE

Americans from the Atlantic states brought their own architectural preferences with them, and the successful among them erected Federal-style homes that stand out from the French or Spanish cottages surrounding them in the Quarter.

Greek Revival elements, like the columns, were used in these houses.

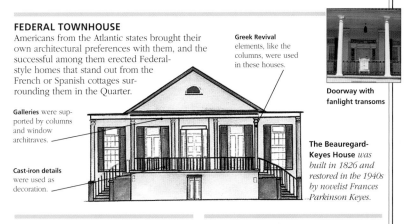

Doorway with fanlight transoms

Galleries were supported by columns and window architraves.

Cast-iron details were used as decoration.

The Beauregard-Keyes House *was built in 1826 and restored in the 1940s by novelist Frances Parkinson Keyes.*

RAISED AMERICAN COTTAGE

Most of these raised cottages feature extensive eaves and an alleyway leading to a rear garden or courtyard. The interior usually contains four rooms arranged symmetrically and separated by a center hall. The kitchen and servants' quarters are away from the house at the rear.

Gabled roofs were popular and were often high enough for an attic.

Main bedrooms were usually at the front of the house.

A wide balcony faced the street.

Esplanade Avenue *is lined with several kinds of these raised cottages.*

The ground floor was used as a storage area.

SHOTGUN HOUSE

These cottages were so called because a bullet fired from a shotgun through the front door would go straight through the house and out the back as all the doors were aligned. They come in single and double versions, and usually have a set of box steps in front.

The main doorway leads directly into the first room.

Simple balconies overlook the porch.

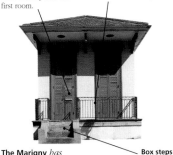

The Marigny *has several examples of traditional shotgun houses.*

Box steps

THE CREOLE PLANTATION HOUSE

The refugees from Saint Domingue (Haiti) brought this Caribbean-style dwelling to New Orleans. This one-story residence is usually raised on brick pillars (to catch the breezes and to cope with flooding) and incorporates a wraparound veranda. The space below the house and the flagstone piazza below the veranda are used as service or storage areas.

French doors gave access to the veranda.

Wide verandas were built at the front entrance.

Brick pillars raised the house.

Plantation houses *were the most popular style of residences built along the Bayou St. John.*

Famous New Orleanians

Because of its cultural roots, geographic importance, and easy-going ways, New Orleans has been a magnet for creative people since the 18th century. A great many writers and artists came here to live, and, like Tennessee Williams, called New Orleans their spiritual home. Others, like Louis Armstrong, were born here. Nurtured by its culture, they carried their musical, literary, and artistic creations to the rest of the world.

Marie Laveau
The most famous voodoo queen in New Orleans (see pp82–3), Laveau celebrated her rituals on the banks of Bayou St. John.

Louis Armstrong
Born in a shack at 723 Jane Alley, Louis Armstrong strongly influenced the development of solo jazz performances (see pp20–21). Armstrong Park (see p79), near the French Quarter, and the city's airport are named after him.

GARDEN DISTRICT
AND UPTOWN

Mahalia Jackson
This gospel singer (see p80) was born on Water Street and grew up at an aunt's house at 7467 Esther (now Pitt) Street.

Truman Capote
This famous author was born in Touro Infirmary in the Garden District. He wrote his first work, Other Voices, Other Rooms, *in a rented room at 711 Royal St.*

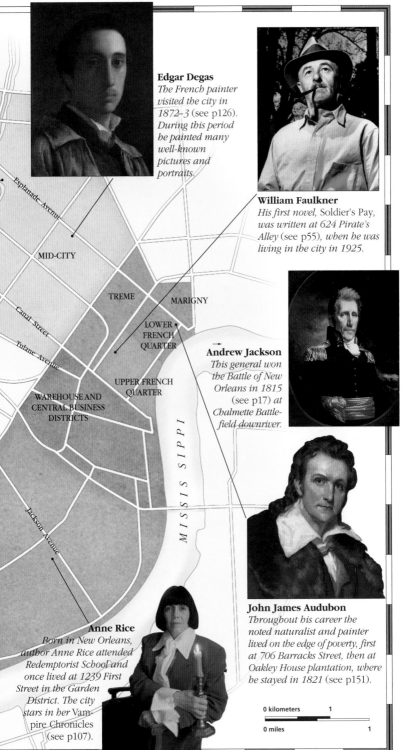

Edgar Degas
The French painter visited the city in 1872–3 (see p126). During this period he painted many well-known pictures and portraits.

William Faulkner
His first novel, Soldier's Pay, *was written at 624 Pirate's Alley (see p55), when he was living in the city in 1925.*

MID-CITY

TREME

MARIGNY

LOWER
FRENCH
QUARTER

UPPER FRENCH
QUARTER

WAREHOUSE AND
CENTRAL BUSINESS
DISTRICTS

Esplanade Avenue

Canal Street

Tulane Avenue

Jackson Avenue

MISSISSIPPI

Andrew Jackson
This general won the Battle of New Orleans in 1815 (see p17) at Chalmette Battlefield downriver.

John James Audubon
Throughout his career the noted naturalist and painter lived on the edge of poverty, first at 706 Barracks Street, then at Oakley House plantation, where he stayed in 1821 (see p151).

Anne Rice
Born in New Orleans, author Anne Rice attended Redemptorist School and once lived at 1239 First Street in the Garden District. The city stars in her Vampire Chronicles (see p107).

0 kilometers   1

0 miles   1

New Orleans Ironwork

Cast-iron detail

The shadows cast by New Orleans ironwork add a romantic touch to the city. Wrought iron, which came first, was fashioned by hand into beautiful shapes by German, Irish, and black artisans. Cast iron, on the other hand, was poured into wooden molds and allowed to set. As a result, the latter has a somewhat solid, fixed appearance, unlike wrought iron, which is handmade and has a more fluid aspect. Examples of both kinds of work can be seen throughout the city, particularly in the French Quarter and the Garden District.

Colonial-style house, Royal Street

Decorative iron balconies *with unique designs and patterns are seen on many galleries. They are admired as much today as they were in antebellum times.*

Royal Street's famous corn-stalk fence

The Pontalba Buildings, *commissioned by Baroness Pontalba (see p55), spurred on the craze for ironwork. Completed in 1850, they transformed the profile of Jackson Square (see p54). Some of the patterns were designed by the Baroness's son.*

The signature of New Orleans *is Creole ironwork, which appears in many forms, including fences, gates, window grilles, balconies, hinges, doorknobs, and lanterns.*

Wrought ironing *contains a purer iron. Handmade and stronger than cast iron, it is very common in the French Quarter.*

Ironwork details *were added to many buildings in the 1850s. Lacy balconies depicting oak leaf and acorn can be seen on the LaBranche House at 700 Royal Street.*

Cast iron *shaped in elaborate designs was often used in homes in the Garden District. It was superior to wood because it withstood humidity.*

CORNSTALK FENCES

There are three "cornstalk" fences in New Orleans, so-called because of their decorative motifs. One is at 915 Royal Street *(see p77)*, another at Colonel Short's Villa in the Garden District *(see p107)*, and a third is at the Dufour-Plassan house on the corner of White and Bell streets in Faubourg St. John.

IRONWORK MOTIFS

Cast-iron railing detail

In the 1850s, Philadelphia iron-mongers Wood & Perot opened a branch office in New Orleans. Offering hundreds of patterns specially designed for the city, the company quickly grew, its motifs including abstracts, acorns, fruits, cherubs, bacchants, vines, and animals. These were soon seen in railings throughout the city.

Popular balcony motifs

NEW ORLEANS
THROUGH THE YEAR

The spring and fall, enjoying the most temperate weather, are the best times to visit. Although the pace slows with the heat of the summer, the city is still alive with indoor and outdoor events. Some festivities celebrate themes specific to New Orleans, such as the French Quarter Festival in April. The city also throws parties for the major holidays,

Jazz Fest musician

especially 4th of July, Bastille Day, and New Year's Eve. At Christmas time, local restaurants celebrate with traditional French "Reveillon" dinners. The high points of the year, however, are Mardi Gras, with all the Carnival festivities stretching from January to as late as early March, and the New Orleans Jazz and Heritage Festival (Jazz Fest) in late April and early May.

SPRING

During the spring the weather is at its best in New Orleans, neither too hot nor too humid. There are two main events in the city, both of which are internationally renowned: Mardi Gras, with its parades, street celebrations, and masked balls all over the city, and the Jazz Fest, which is held over two long weekends. It is very important to have confirmed reservations for transportation and lodging during this peak season.

MARCH

Mardi Gras *(Feb, dates vary).* The lively Carnival festivities *(see pp28–9)* begin two or three weeks before Mardi Gras and end with the last

A family dressed in colorful Mardi Gras costumes

parade on Mardi Gras ("Fat Tuesday," or the Tuesday before Lent). There are day and night parades, and masked balls (few of which are open to the public). The whole city is in party mode, so it's advisable to book hotels well in advance (for parade dates and times see www.mardigras.com).

St. Patrick's Day Parade *(weekend before and on Mar 17).* The city commemorates Ireland's famous patron saint with parades through the French Quarter, Irish Channel, and Old Metairie Road, where cabbages are thrown to the public. An all-day street party around Parasol's Bar in the Irish Channel takes place on St. Patrick's Day itself.

St. Joseph's Day *(on and around Mar 19).* The city's Italian population honors the patron saint of Sicily with elaborate altars of food. Angelo Brocato's ice-cream parlor *(see p183)* is one of the best places to see an altar.

Crescent City Classic *(Saturday before Easter).* Since 1979, world-class runners have gathered in New Orleans for this 10,000-meter race from the French Quarter to City Park. Thousands of amateur runners join in (www.ccc10k.com).

Tennessee Williams New Orleans Literary Festival and Writers' Conference *(late Mar).* This five-day cultural festival takes place in various

locations to honor the celebrated writer, with theatrical productions, lectures, readings, literary walking tours, and panel discussions on New Orleans-based authors and books. Don't miss the "Stella and Stanley" screamfest held in Jackson Square (www. tennesseewilliams.net).

A huge jazz brunch at the French Quarter Festival

APRIL

French Quarter Festival *(second weekend).* To celebrate the food and music of New Orleans, this festival is held in the French Quarter, with free musical entertainment, "the world's largest jazz brunch," fireworks over the Mississippi River, and children's activities (www. frenchquarterfestivals.org).

Spring Fiesta *(begins Fri night after Easter, lasting five days).* With the French Quarter's historic homes as the main attraction, this celebration also has a parade

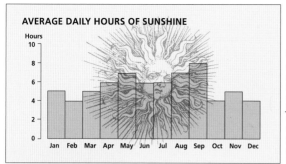

AVERAGE DAILY HOURS OF SUNSHINE

Hours

Jan Feb Mar Apr May Jun Jul Aug Sep Oct Nov Dec

Sunshine Chart
From May through September the weather is hot and humid, and the sun shines for 6 to 8 hours a day. From October through March the temperature is colder, and there are often heavy fogs.

Crowds enjoying the music at the Jazz Fest

that ends with the coronation of a local queen.

New Orleans Jazz and Heritage Festival (Jazz Fest) *(last weekend in Apr and first weekend in May)*. In this seven-day festival, held at the Fair Grounds, more than 4,000 jazz musicians entertain, with a large selection of traditional food, crafts, and evening concerts (www.nojazzfest.com).

MAY

Zoo-to-Do *(first Fri in May)*. The largest one-night fund-raising event in the country takes place at Audubon Zoo *(see pp112–13)*, with unforgettable dances among the animals, under the stars.
Greek Festival *(Memorial Day weekend)*. The Hellenic Cultural Center, near Lake Pontchartrain, hosts two days of cuisine, music, and arts and crafts.
New Orleans Wine & Food Experience *(Memorial Day weekend)*. US and European wineries come to town for parties, talks, and tastings (www.nowfe.com).

SUMMER

Hot and extremely humid weather along with daily thunderstorms make summertime in New Orleans the off-season period. Since the late summer is also the time when hurricanes and tropical storms are frequent, it is wise to be prepared for weather alerts. The biggest celebration in the city is 4th of July (Independence Day).

JUNE

Great French Market Creole Tomato Festival *(first weekend)*. Held in and around the French Market, this unique festival offers cooking demonstrations and local cuisine (www.frenchmarket.org).

JULY

Go 4th on the River *(Jul 4)*. The riverfront hosts the Independence Day celebrations. There is music, food, and entertainment for the whole family, plus a spectacular fireworks display (www.go4thontheriver.com). This coincides with Essence, which draws top acts in black entertainment (www. essencemusicfestival.com).

AUGUST

White Linen Night *(first Sat)*. An open-air event in which a number of art galleries take their exhibits outdoors to the Warehouse Art District.
Satchmo SummerFest *(first weekend)*. This annual festival is usually scheduled to coincide with the great jazz icon's birthday. Held in the French Quarter, with jazz, food, kids' events, and special programs (www. satchmosummerfest.com).
Southern Decadence *(last week of Aug to Labor Day)*. Southern Decadence is a gay street party that has over-the-top costumes, parades, and rowdy behavior, and is a great time for adults. Centered in the French Quarter, it culminates on Labor Day, the first Monday of September (www. southerndecadence.com).

Go 4th on the River celebration at Woldenberg Park

AVERAGE MONTHLY RAINFALL

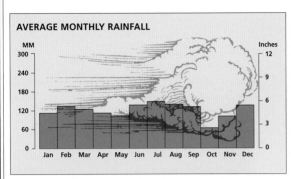

MM: 300, 240, 180, 120, 60, 0

Inches: 12, 9, 6, 3, 0

Jan Feb Mar Apr May Jun Jul Aug Sep Oct Nov Dec

Rainfall Chart
New Orleans is one of the rainiest cities in the United States, and July and August are its rainiest months, with daily showers. Tropical storms can cause widespread power failures. The hurricane season lasts from June to November, peaking in August and September.

Alligator close-up at the Louisiana Swamp Festival

FALL

Although there may still be rainy days in September, the driest months of the year are October and November, when both humidity and heat decrease. Halloween is the most important celebration of this season, and it launches the biggest selling period of the year. The New Orleans' Saints football team starts the NFL season which lasts through December.

SEPTEMBER

Madisonville Wooden Boat Festival *(last weekend of Sep).* The largest gathering of wooden water craft in the the New Orleans area, at picturesque Madisonville on the Tchefuncte River. A Kids Dingy Workshop, Quick and Dirty Boat Building Contest, and live entertainment (www. woodenboatfest.org).
Saints Football *(Sep–Dec, Louisiana Superdome).* The NFL football season starts in September with games at the Louisiana Superdome *(see p95)* through December or January *(see pp196–7).*

Louisiana Swamp Festival *(late Sep, early Oct).* For two weekends, at the Audubon Zoo *(see pp112–13)*, live Louisiana swamp animals are the center of attention. Those brave enough to touch them are allowed to do so, under close supervision. There is also Cajun food, music, and crafts.

OCTOBER

Oktoberfest *(every weekend).* The German community celebrates its cultural roots at the Deutsches Haus (200 Galvez St, (504) 522-8014) with music, food, and beer.
New Orleans Film Festival *(early to mid-Oct).* This week-long event takes place at various venues around the city and presents the works of filmmakers from all over the world. Visiting celebrities, authors, and film stars always attend the event.
Jazz Awareness Month *(all month).* Celebrating jazz at its birthplace, daily concerts are held throughout the city.

Halloween in New Orleans *(on and around 31 Oct).* A mini-Mardi Gras with masking, costumes, and impromptu street parties on Decatur Street. Kids get a big party at Audubon Zoo – the Boo-at-the-Zoo.

NOVEMBER

Turkey Day Race *(fourth Thu in Nov).* This 5-mile (8-km) run has celebrated Thanksgiving for a century.
New Orleans Fair Grounds Horse Racing Season *(opens Thanksgiving Day).* The thoroughbred racing season lasts from late November through March, at the country's third-oldest racetrack *(see p126).*
Celebration in the Oaks *(late Nov through early Jan).* City Park *(see pp116–17)* is transformed by countless sparkling Christmas lights.
Bayou Classic *(late Nov).* Football fans swarm downtown for the annual showdown between Louisiana's historically black colleges.

The Fair Grounds, home to thoroughbred racing in the Deep South

AVERAGE MONTHLY TEMPERATURE

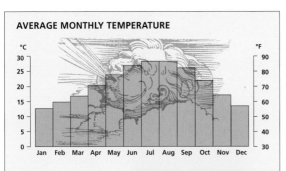

°C **°F**
30 — 90
25 — 80
20 — 70
15 — 60
10 — 50
5 — 40
0 — 30

Jan Feb Mar Apr May Jun Jul Aug Sep Oct Nov Dec

Temperature Chart
New Orleans is a semi-tropical city, and during the summer the temperature may rise above 90°F (33°C). Winters are relatively mild, as are spring and fall, which are the most comfortable times of year to visit.

WINTER

The winter months are enlivened by the holiday spirit of Christmas and New Year. As soon as Christmas festivities end on Twelfth Night (Jan 6), the excitement of Mardi Gras begins to build with events and preparations for the main celebrations before Lent.

DECEMBER

Christmas *(all month)*. Candlelight caroling in Jackson Square *(see p54)*, Reveillon dinners, and historic homes decorated for Christmas in the French Quarter and Garden District.
Festival of Bonfires *(early to mid-Dec and on Christmas Eve)*. Both riverboats *(see pp64–5)* and paddlewheelers ply the Mississippi River in this blazing festival in which local people build bonfires to guide Santa Claus to their hometown for Christmas.
Countdown *(Dec 31)*. On New Year's Eve, people gather at Jackson Square *(see p54)* to await and celebrate the arrival of the New Year with live music, food, and fireworks.

JANUARY

Sugar Bowl *(first week)*. Thousands of college football fans gather in the Louisiana Superdome *(see p95)* for this important postseason game.
Battle of New Orleans Anniversary *(weekend closest to Jan 8)*.

Mardi Gras Parade at Lafayette Square

A live reenactment of this 1815 battle *(see p17)* is performed at Chalmette Battlefield in St. Bernard Parish, featuring colorful period costumes and artillery demonstrations.

FEBRUARY

New Orleans Boat & Sportfishing Show *(second week)*. A display at the Louisiana Superdome *(see p95)*, with all the latest fishing accessories.

Mardi Gras *(early Feb to early Mar)*. Carnival begins on Jan 6 with masked balls and other celebrations. However, the majority of the parades do not begin until the second weekend before Mardi Gras itself (the Tuesday before Lent).

PUBLIC HOLIDAYS

New Year's Day (Jan 1)
Martin Luther King Day (3rd Mon, Jan)
Mardi Gras Day (varies, Feb 3–Mar 9)
Presidents Day (3rd Mon, Feb)
Memorial Day (end May)
Independence Day (Jul 4)
Labor Day (1st Mon, Sep)
Columbus Day (2nd Mon, Oct)
Veterans Day (Nov 11)
Thanksgiving (4th Thu, Nov)
Christmas Day (Dec 25)

Fireworks at the traditional Countdown on New Year's Eve

NEW ORLEANS AREA BY AREA

A View of Bourbon Street

Tile street sign on Bourbon Street

Today Bourbon Street, rather than Basin Street, is synonymous with sin. The name has nothing to do with bourbon, despite the string of bars that line this legendary street; it is named after the French royal family of Bourbon. One bar after another proffers vats of such lethal concoctions as Nuclear Kamikaze, Brain Freeze, and Sex on the Bayou, most often to the accompaniment of blasting rock or blues. Other emporiums offer everything from peep shows and topless and go-go dancers, to drag shows and gay action. During Mardi Gras, the lacy balconies above the sidewalks sag from the weight of drinking revelers.

The Famous Door
This nightclub lives with the beat of live 1970s and 1980s rock music.

Arnaud's
Count Arnaud Cazenave opened the original Arnaud's in 1918. There are 17 dining rooms with mosaic tiles, mirrored walls, and paddle fans (see p176).

Galatoire's
Run by the Galatoire family since 1905, this restaurant has the ambience of a perpetual cocktail party.

Old Absinthe House
This building is notable for its entresol, the half-story between the first and second floors.

The World Jeweler
Lafcadio Hearn, the famous American journalist, once rented a room here.

◁ **The bustling Central Business District**

Chris Owen's Club
The legendary Owens has been on Bourbon Street for decades. Dynamic shows include Las Vegas-style cabaret.

Preservation Hall
An aptly named music venue, Preservation Hall has helped preserve traditional New Orleans jazz. It opened in 1961, and still provides top-quality jazz.

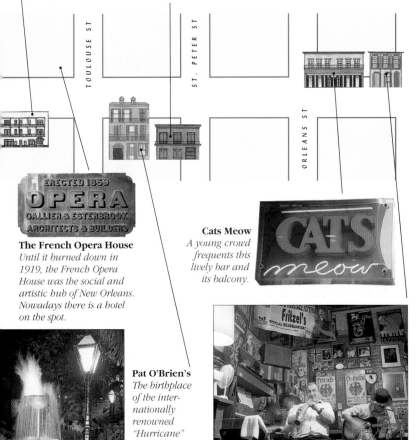

The French Opera House
Until it burned down in 1919, the French Opera House was the social and artistic hub of New Orleans. Nowadays there is a hotel on the spot.

Cats Meow
A young crowd frequents this lively bar and its balcony.

Pat O'Brien's
The birthplace of the internationally renowned "Hurricane" cocktail, O'Brien's has a spectacular fire fountain in the main courtyard.

Fritzel's
Fritzel's is the only traditional European live jazz club in the city.

A View of Royal Street

Tile street sign on Royal

This is the most fetching street in the French Quarter. It is lined with antique shops that are filled with beautiful, often French, treasures associated with an opulent Southern lifestyle; crystal chandeliers, massive inlaid armoires, ormolu furnishings, and more. In the early colony this was the city's financial center and its main and most fashionable street. Today, many stores occupy handsome landmarks.

Street musicians provide open-air entertainment on Royal Street

CONTI ST

Louisiana State Bank (# 403)

Built in 1821, this building was designed by Benjamin Latrobe (right), who also designed the US Capitol's south wing.

Brennan's (# 417)

Built around 1802 for a Spanish merchant, this building later became a bank and the property of Judge Alonzo Morphy. Brennan's restaurant moved here in 1954 (see p176). Its balcony seal is made of cast iron.

0 meters   10

0 yards   10

ST. LOUIS ST   TOULOUSE ST

The Historic New Orleans Collection (# 533)

Occupying a complex of houses built in 1792 for Jean-François Merieult and his wife, this museum boasts a magnificent collection of art and artifacts (see pp60–61).

Galerie d'Art Français

This art gallery features a range of works by contemporary French artists and highlights New Orleans' long-standing connection to French culture.

A Street of Living Tradition

Royal Street is the pride of the French Quarter. Its beautiful buildings have been carefully maintained and are today occupied by fine stores and restaurants.

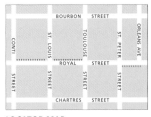

LOCATOR MAP

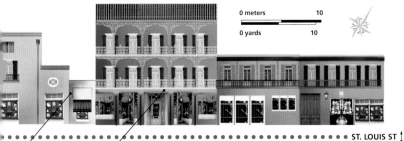

0 meters 10

0 yards 10

● **ST. LOUIS ST**

Moss Antiques offers a fine range of French antiques.

0 meters 10

0 yards 10

Antoine Peychaud's Pharmacy (# 437)

The cocktail was born here when pharmacist Antoine Peychaud mixed brandy with his bitters and served the potion in a coquetier (see p174). Today it is an antique shop.

↕ ST. PETER ST ● **ORLEANS ST ↕**

St. Anthony's Garden

This beautiful garden (see p55) stands at the back of St. Louis Cathedral. Its serenity hides the fact that it was a staging ground for duels in the 18th century.

The La Branche Buildings (# 700)
Embellished with fine oak-leaf ironwork, these buildings were constructed in 1835 for sugar planter Jean Baptiste LaBranche.

UPPER FRENCH QUARTER

The French Quarter is synonymous with New Orleans. The original 20 blocks were laid out around present-day Jackson Square in 1721. The Upper French Quarter runs from Iberville Street to St. Ann and includes the busiest blocks of Decatur, Chartres, Royal, and Bourbon streets. The last of these is particularly lively, offering several bars that promise rollicking good times. Architecturally,

Cupid statue in Le Petit Théâtre

the Vieux Carré (meaning Old Square) is quintessential New Orleans. The colorful Creole-style cottages featuring jalousie-shuttered windows stand flush along the sidewalks. There are also several Spanish-style buildings decorated with lacy iron galleries. This iconic neighborhood escaped with very little wind damage from Hurricane Katrina and experienced no flooding in the days that followed.

SIGHTS AT A GLANCE

Historic Buildings
Louisiana Supreme Court Building ⓫
Napoleon House ⓬
Père Antoine Alley and St. Anthony's Garden ❼
Pirate's Alley ❻
Pontalba Buildings ❹
St. Louis Cathedral, Cabildo, and Presbytère pp56–7 ❷

Museums and Galleries
The 1850 House ❸
Hermann-Grima Historic House ❾
Historic New Orleans Collection pp60–61 ❿
Jean Lafitte National Historical Park Visitor Center ⓮
Musée Conti Wax Museum ❽
New Orleans Pharmacy Museum ⓭

Theaters
Le Petit Théâtre du Vieux Carré ❺

Parks and Gardens
Jackson Square ❶

Boat Trips
Steamboat *Natchez* ⓯

KEY

	Street-by-Street map *See pp52–3*
	Streetcar stop

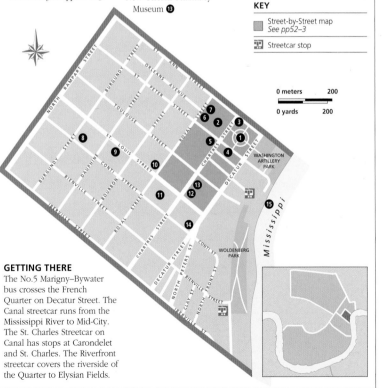

0 meters   200

0 yards   200

GETTING THERE

The No.5 Marigny–Bywater bus crosses the French Quarter on Decatur Street. The Canal streetcar runs from the Mississippi River to Mid-City. The St. Charles Streetcar on Canal has stops at Carondelet and St. Charles. The Riverfront streetcar covers the riverside of the Quarter to Elysian Fields.

◁ **St. Louis Cathedral in Jackson Square**

Street-by-Street: Upper French Quarter

**Leech jar,
Pharmacy
Museum**

This is the heart of the French Quarter, containing a striking and harmonious collection of buildings. The lively Jackson Square initially served as a military parade ground, or *place d'armes*, where troops were trained and drilled, executions carried out, and public meetings held. The Cathedral, Cabildo, and Presbytère face the square. It was redesigned in 1848, when Baroness Pontalba built the two elegant apartment buildings on the upriver and downriver sides of the square. An impressive statue of General Jackson was also unveiled in the center of the square, where artists now display their work.

**Père Antoine Alley and
St. Anthony's Garden**
*This garden was a favorite
local dueling place in the
19th century* ❼

Tennesee Williams wrote *A Streetcar Named Desire* in an apartment at 632 St. Peter Street.

Le Petit Théâtre du Vieux Carré
*This theater, established in 1916,
moved to its current location in
1919. The building is a replica
of the original* ❺

TOULOUSE ST

CHARTRES STREET

**The Omni Royal
Orleans** hotel *(see
p162)* is constructed
on the site of the
1836 St. Louis Hotel.

KEY

— — — Suggested route

DECATUR STREET

Napoleon House
*The most beloved bar in the French Quarter is
devoted to Napoleon's memory. His portraits
and other memorabilia adorn the walls* ⓬

STAR SIGHTS

★ The 1850 House

★ Jackson Square

★ St. Louis Cathedral,
Cabildo, and
Presbytère

★ **St. Louis Cathedral, Cabildo, and Presbytère**
These were the most important religious and administrative buildings in the French and Spanish periods **2**

Street musicians play in front of the cathedral.

LOCATOR MAP
See Street Finder maps 4 and 5

ST. ANN STREET

ST. PETER ST.

★ **The 1850 House**
This small museum displays opulent furniture and decorations that convey the middle-class lifestyles of the antebellum era **3**

★ **Jackson Square**
A magnificent statue of General Jackson takes center stage in the square, where artists hang their works "on the fence" **1**

Pontalba Buildings
The handsome Pontalba apartments, built in 1848 for $302,000, are located on the upriver and downriver sides of the square **4**

| 0 meters | 30 |
| 0 yards | 30 |

Jackson Square ❶

Map 5 D2. 🚋 *Riverfront*. 🚌 *5, 55*.

Today an attractive and lively meeting place, this square was named the *Place d'Armes* in the early French colony, when it was little more than a muddy field. Here the troops were drilled, criminals were placed in the stocks, and executions were carried out. In 1850, it was renamed for the hero of the Battle of New Orleans *(see p17)*, after the Baroness Pontalba paid for its beautification and laid out the gardens and pathways of the square as they exist today. Under her auspices, the Pelanne brothers designed the handsome wrought-iron fence that encloses the square. At the center stands a statue of General Andrew Jackson astride a rearing horse, which was sculpted by Clark Mills for $30,000. The inscription, "The Union must and shall be preserved," on the plinth was added by Union General Benjamin "Beast" Butler, when he occupied the city during the American Civil War *(see p18)*.

Jazz band playing in Jackson Square

Water vessel in The 1850 House

The park is landscaped in a radial pattern, with walkways stemming out from the center and there are plenty of benches to sit and enjoy the charm of the historical houses.

Outside the park, diverse artists rent space and hang their works on the enclosing fence, and there are plenty of artists waiting to draw your portrait or caricature. On the flagstones around the square, tarot card readers, jazz musicians, and clowns entertain visitors throughout the week. There are also shops on the ground level of the Pontalba Apartments, selling gifts, clothing, candy, and ice cream.

St. Louis Cathedral, Cabildo, and Presbytère ❷

See pp56–7.

The 1850 House ❸

523 St. Ann St. **Map** 5 D2. *Tel* 568-6968. 🚌 *5, 55*. ⬤ *10am–4:30pm Tue–Sun*. ⬤ *public hols*. 🎟️ 📷

In the Lower Pontalba Building, this museum recreates an antebellum apartment. The three-story residence above the ground-floor space is accessed by a dramatic circular staircase. The bedrooms contain all the innovations of their day, including walk-in closets and private bathrooms.

The Pontalba Buildings, the upriver side of Jackson Square

Also displayed are decorative arts and everyday artifacts of the period. A gift shop occupies the ground floor.

Pontalba Buildings ❹

St. Peter and St. Ann Sts. **Map** 5 D2.
🚋 *Riverfront*. 🚌 *5, 55*. ▣ ▥

In 1848, Baroness Micaela Pontalba supervised the building of these block-long apartments flanking the up-town and downtown sides of Jackson Square. They were erected for over $300,000, and at the time they were considered the best and the largest apartments of their kind.

At the age of 15, Micaela had married the foppish aristocrat Celestin Pontalba, a distant cousin, and moved to Paris. There, her father-in-law tried to force her to sign over her entire estate. When she refused, he attempted to kill her, but succeeded only in shooting off two of her fingers.

She courageously separated from her husband in 1848 and returned to New Orleans. The baroness, like her father the philanthropist Don Andrés Almonester y Rojas, was a developer. With plans brought back from Paris, she proceeded to build apartments like the ones she had seen in Paris. Architects James Gallier and Henry Howard drew up the plans. The design of the initials A and P (for Almonester and Pontalba) in the cast-iron railings of the galleries and balconies is attributed to one of the baroness's sons, an artist.

Le Petit Théâtre du Vieux Carré ❺

616 St. Peter St. **Map** 5 D2.
Tel 522-2081. 🚌 *5, 55*. **Box Office**
◻ *10:30am–5:30pm Tue–Sat.*
● *public hols.* ▨

This small theater was the brainchild of a group of actors called the Drawing Room Players, who came together in 1916 under the management of Mrs. Oscar

Interior of Le Petit Théâtre du Vieux Carré

Nixon. Their first theater was located in the Lower Pontalba Building, but in 1922 the current site was bought and was used for the first American productions of Eugene O'Neill's *Beyond the Horizon* and Oscar Wilde's *Lady Windermere's Fan*. It is a pretty building with a beguiling courtyard and fountain.

In 2011, the board of directors decided to convert part of the building into an eatery due to the severe financial problems faced by the theater. The restaurant is run by the famous Dickie Brennaan (*see p176*).

The theater hosts an annual season of performances from September to June; it is advised you call ahead if you wish to buy tickets. It also acts as a headquarters during the Tennessee Williams New Orleans Literary Festival and Writers' Conference.

Pirate's Alley ❻

Map 5 D2. 🚌 *5, 55*.

Although it is named after the famous pirate brothers, Jean and Pierre Lafitte (*see p17*), there is no evidence here that this was once a pirates' haunt or a slave market. Today, the alley's classic bohemian atmosphere and open-air cafés are what make it worth seeking out.

The Faulkner House, a bookstore where the shelves are lined with William Faulkner first editions as well as works by other

major Southern authors, is located in the building where Faulkner wrote his first novel, *Soldier's Pay*, in 1925.

Père Antoine Alley and St. Anthony's Garden ❼

Map 5 D2. 🚋 *Riverfront*. 🚌 *5, 55*.

This alley is named for one of the city's most beloved clergymen, Father Antonio de Sedella (Père Antoine), who served as pastor of St. Louis Cathedral for 40 years. He was loved for his compassionate ministry to the poor, whom he assiduously fed and clothed.

The fenced garden, once a popular dueling ground, features a great sculpture of the Sacred Heart. In the early morning and evening the scent of sweet olive lingers in the air.

Faulkner House, a bookstore in Pirate's Alley

St. Louis Cathedral, Cabildo, and Presbytère ❷

This complex of buildings was the most important ensemble in the early colony. The Cabildo, designed by Guilberto Guillemard, was built and financed in 1795 by Don Andrés Almonester y Rojas. It served as a capitol for the legislative assembly of the Spanish colonial government, and subsequently as the City Hall. From 1853 to 1911 it housed the state Supreme Court. The Casa Curial, or Presbytère, was built between 1794 and 1813, and served as a courthouse until 1911. Today, both buildings are flagship properties of the Louisiana State Museum. Two earlier churches on the site of the St. Louis Cathedral were destroyed, the first by a hurricane in 1722, the second by a fire in 1788. The current building was begun in 1789 and dedicated as a cathedral in 1794. It has been substantially modified since then.

★ **Main Altar**
The carved-wood Baroque altars were constructed in Ghent, Belgium, and brought to the cathedral in pieces.

Cathedral Dome
A great mural of St. Louis announcing the Seventh Crusade was painted above the altar.

Napoleon's Death Mask
The museum's collection includes a casting of Napoleon's face made after the French emperor's death in 1821.

Cabildo

★ **Sala Capitular**
The Louisiana Purchase (see p17) was signed in this room; this desk set was in place at the time.

Ceiling Murals
Painted by Alsatian artist Erasme Humbrecht in 1872, the murals portray different biblical stories.

Stained-glass windows
with figures of Catholic saints adorn the cathedral's interior.

VISITORS' CHECKLIST

Jackson Square. **Map** 5 D2. **Tel** 525-9585 (St. Louis Cathedral); 568-6968 (Cabildo and Presbytère). St. Charles Ave and Canal streetcars. 5, 55, 81. 10am–4:30pm daily (St. Louis Cathedral); 10am–4:30pm Tue–Sun (Cabildo and Presbytère). all major holidays (Cabildo and Presbytère). Cabildo and Presbytère. St. Louis Cathedral, regular services daily.
www.saintlouiscathedral.org
www.lsm.crt.state.la.us

Presbytère

Mardi Gras Exhibits
Pieces of floats, colorful costumes, and historic photos bring Mardi Gras to life all year round.

St. Louis Cathedral

The steeples,
the portico, and the pilasters were added in 1851.

The clock bell, given the name "Victoire" by Père Antoine, was cast in Paris. It has tolled hourly since 1819.

STAR FEATURES

★ Main Altar

★ Living with Hurricanes

★ Sala Capitular

★ Living with Hurricanes: Katrina and Beyond
The Presbytère houses exhibits and artifacts on Hurricane Katrina and storm science.

For hotels and restaurants in this region see pp162–3 and pp176–7

Master bedroom, the Hermann-Grima Historic House

Musée Conti Wax Museum ⓫

917 Conti St. **Map** 4 C2. **Tel** 525-2605. 🚌 5. ◯ 10am–4pm Mon, Fri, Sat. ● Thanksgiving, Dec 25, Mardi Gras. ▨ ▨ ♿ ⬚ **www.** neworleanswaxmuseum.com

The major part of this museum's space is taken up with a series of 25 vivid tableaus featuring lifelike historical figures. The museum presents the tempestuous story of New Orleans' development, from its founding in the 18th century to the lynching of 11 Italians accused of gunning down the police chief in 1891. One of the most imaginatively conceived scenes depicts Napoleon in his bathtub gesticulating madly as he informs onlookers of his

Recreation of America's purchase of Louisiana, Musée Conti

decision to sell Louisiana to America *(see p17)*. The museum also features wax representations of political figures such as the legendary governor of Louisiana, Huey Long (1893–1935). Also present is four-time Governor Edwin Edwards, who was found guilty of racketeering.

The tour ends with a series of tableaus featuring stock horror figures such as Dracula and Frankenstein in dungeon-like surroundings. Statues of Andrew Jackson, the pirate Jean Lafitte, and Marie Laveau also compete for your attention.

Hermann-Grima Historic House ⓭

820 St. Louis St. **Map** 4 C2. **Tel** 525-5661. 🚌 5. ◯ 10am–3:30pm Mon–Tue, Thu–Sat. ● public hols. ▨ ▨ ♿ **www.**hgghh.org

This gabled brick house stands out from those around it because it is one of the few examples of American Federal-style architecture in the French Quarter. William Brand built it in 1831 for Samuel Hermann, a German-Jewish merchant. Unfortunately, he lost his fortune in 1837 and had to sell the house to Judge Felix Grima. The house features a central doorway with a fanlight and

marble steps; another window with a fanlight graces the second floor.

Inside, the floors and doors are made of cypress, and the rooms feature elegant marble fireplaces. The three-story service quarters, located in a separate building off the parterre behind the house, are also striking. They feature slave quarters and a kitchen containing a rare four-burner wood-fired stove with a beehive oven.

Historic New Orleans Collection ⓯

See pp60–61.

Louisiana Supreme Court Building ⓱

400 Royal St. **Map** 4 C2. **Tel** 310-2300. 🚌 5. 🚊 Riverfront. ◯ 9am–5pm Mon–Fri. ● public hols. **www.**lasc.org

When this massive granite and marble structure was built in 1908–10, the French Quarter was on the downslide. Erecting this splendid Beaux Arts court building was an early exercise in urban renewal. Despite a few protests, an entire block of historic 18th- and early 19th-century buildings was razed to make way for it. The Louisiana Supreme Court occupied it

Façade of the Louisiana Supreme Court Building

Napoleon House, surmounted by its landmark cupola

from 1910 to 1958. Thereafter, the courthouse began to decline and massive trees were planted on the site to hide the dazzling white marble exterior. It was home to a string of state agencies, none of which took on the maintenance necessary for such an architecturally intricate structure. In the 1990s the state finally launched a renovation program and since 2004 the building has once again served as the home of the Louisiana Supreme Court, the Louisiana Law Library, and various other state legal offices. A small museum on the first floor includes exhibits on the development of Louisiana law.

Marble detail from the Supreme Court Building

Together, they were the home of Mayor Nicholas Girod, who planned to free Napoleon from imprisonment on St. Helena Island. With the help of Dominique You and a pirate band (*see p17*), Girod intended to bring Napoleon to this refuge, but Napoleon died before the mission could be undertaken. Today, the walls of the house are adorned with all kinds of Napoleonic decor and memorabilia. Both buildings are attributed to Hyacinthe Laclotte, and the balcony railings were crafted by William Malus. The cupola on the roof is a New Orleans landmark.

Napoleon House ⓬

500 Chartres St. **Map** 5 D2. **Tel** 524-9752. 🚌 5, 55, 81. ◯ 11am–5:30pm Mon, 11am–10pm Tue–Thu, 11am–11pm Fri–Sat. 🔲 🍽 💻 🍸 www.napoleonhouse.com

One of the city's most atmospheric bars, Napoleon House is famous for its Pimm's Cup and for a warm version of the *muffaletta* (*see p172*), a traditional New Orleans deli sandwich. It occupies two buildings, one of which is a two-story structure, built in 1798, facing St. Louis Street; the second, built in 1814, is a three-story building with a mezzanine.

New Orleans Pharmacy Museum ⓭

514 Chartres St. **Map** 5 D2. **Tel** 565-8027. 🚌 5, 55, 81. ◯ 10am–2pm Tue–Sat (to 5pm Sat). ◯ public hols. 📷 🎥 ♿ www.pharmacymuseum.org

This museum is located on the site of the first licensed pharmacy in the United States, operated by Louis Joseph Dufilho from 1823 to 1855. The original display cases and mahogany cabinets contain some gruesome-looking early surgical tools – saws, knives, and bloodletting

instruments – as well as early herbal remedies, many of which were forerunners of today's drugs. These include a bottle of salicin, an early form of aspirin produced by Bayer & Co. from black willow bark. The museum also features a splendid 1855 marble soda fountain at which appealing sodas were first concocted to help the medicine go down. The second floor features a 19th-century sick room, a fine collection of eye glasses, plus homeopathic remedies and an impressive collection of 19th-century dental instruments. The walled courtyard garden is filled with medicinal herbs.

Jean Lafitte National Historical Park Visitor Center ⓮

419 Decatur St. **Map** 4 C3. **Tel** 589-2636. 🚌 5, 55, 81. ◯ 9am–5pm daily. ◯ Dec 25, Mardi Gras. 📷 🎥 ♿ 🎵 www.nps.gov/jela

This visitor center has some excellent displays on the geography, history, and culture of the Mississippi River Delta region. It also offers slide shows and ranger-led walking tours of the French Quarter at 9:30 every morning.

The Jean Lafitte National Historical Park comprises six sites in all, including three in Cajun Country (*see p152 and p157*) and the Chalmette Battlefield (*see p88*).

A 19th-century soda fountain at the Pharmacy Museum

Historic New Orleans Collection ⑩

Spanish coat of arms

This massive collection, born of one couple's interest in the Battle of New Orleans, is housed in several 18th- and 19th-century structures. The Merieult House (1792) features more than 10 galleries displaying historical artifacts, ranging from maps and paintings to furnishings and decorative objects. Free changing exhibitions are held in a gallery on the first floor. The Williams residence, at the rear of the courtyard, was the home of the collectors, General and Mrs. L. Kemper Williams, who lived here from the 1940s to the 1960s. The Williams Research Center, at 410 Chartres Street, holds the archives of the collection.

Williams Research Center
This facility houses the largest private collection of historical documents in the city.

Old courtyard

Williams Residence

20th-Century Gallery
On display here are books and artworks depicting the city in the 1900s, such as this Brulator Courtyard *by C. Bennette Moore.*

The Counting House, once used for banking activities, is now a lecture hall and portrait gallery

Plantation Gallery
Plantation life was often captured in art. This collage portrays the hauling of cotton.

STAR EXHIBITS

★ Antebellum Gallery

★ Spanish Colonial Gallery

★ Victorian Gallery

★ Victorian Gallery
This gallery features elaborate furniture, and smaller objects, such as this teapot.

Slave Funeral
One of a series of paintings by John Antrobus evokes life on a Louisiana plantation in the Plantation Gallery.

VISITORS' CHECKLIST

533 Royal St. **Map** 4 C2. *Tel* 523-4662. St. Charles Ave. 55, 81, 82. 9:30am–4:30pm Tue–Sun (10:30am Sun). main hols. www.hnoc.org

French Colonial Gallery
French period items such as this refectory table, used in the Old Ursuline Convent, are displayed here.

★ Spanish Colonial Gallery
Portraits of residents during the Spanish colonial era are shown here.

Louisiana Purchase Gallery
With its message of prosperity, this image presents a rare welcome to the Americans after the Purchase (see p17).

★ Antebellum Gallery
On display in this gallery are items related to the city prior to the Civil War, including this painting of a fleet of frigates off the Louisiana coast.

The Shop at The Collection

Main entrance

Visitor welcome center

The French Quarter, open for business at dusk ▷

Steamboat *Natchez* ⓯

Upper deck light

For a reminder of the old days of river travel, visitors can take a two-hour cruise on the Steamboat *Natchez*. In the 19th century, steamboats traveled the length of the Mississippi, taking between three and five days to get from Louisville, Kentucky, to New Orleans. The boatmen were notorious brawlers who went looking for women and liquor at the end of a trip and established New Orleans' reputation as the "City of Sin." In their heyday, from 1830 to 1860, some 30 steamboats lined up at the levee. The steamboat era ended by the close of the 19th century as railroads and highways replaced them.

Steam Whistle
The genuine copper-and-steel steam whistle is a treasured antique.

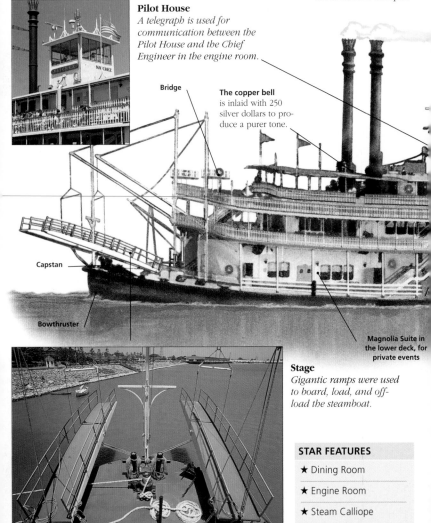

Pilot House
A telegraph is used for communication between the Pilot House and the Chief Engineer in the engine room.

Bridge

The copper bell is inlaid with 250 silver dollars to produce a purer tone.

Capstan

Bowthruster

Magnolia Suite in the lower deck, for private events

Stage
Gigantic ramps were used to board, load, and off-load the steamboat.

STAR FEATURES

★ Dining Room

★ Engine Room

★ Steam Calliope

★ **Dining Room**
A casual buffet dinner is served on the second deck, featuring live jazz music by the Dukes of Dixieland.

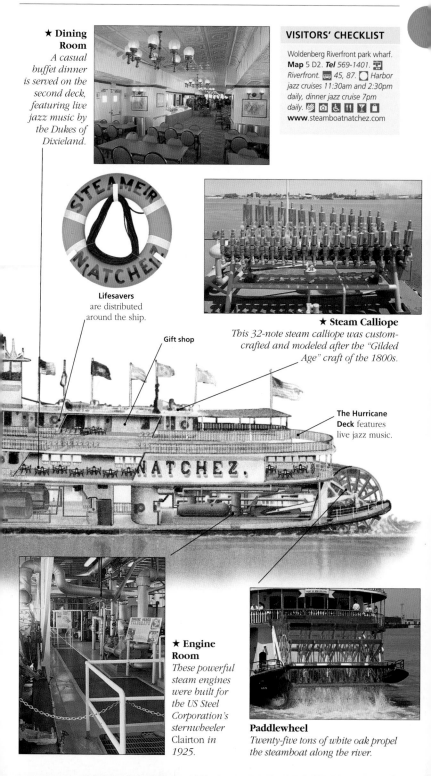

Lifesavers
are distributed around the ship.

Gift shop

★ **Steam Calliope**
This 32-note steam calliope was custom-crafted and modeled after the "Gilded Age" craft of the 1800s.

The Hurricane Deck features live jazz music.

★ **Engine Room**
These powerful steam engines were built for the US Steel Corporation's sternwheeler Clairton *in 1925.*

Paddlewheel
Twenty-five tons of white oak propel the steamboat along the river.

LOWER FRENCH QUARTER, MARIGNY, AND TREME

Extending from beyond St. Ann Street to Esplanade Avenue is the more residential part of the French Quarter. Within this area the busiest sidewalks are those around the French Market, where stalls display hot sauces, strings of garlic and peppers, and other Creole and Cajun specialties. The surrounding streets are lined with handsome Creole-style cottages. Esplanade Avenue divides the French Quarter and the Faubourg Marigny. Soon after the

Louis Armstrong statue

Louisiana Purchase *(see p17)*, the Marigny Plantation was subdivided, and the area was settled. Today, the Marigny is a lively place with restaurants and clubs. The area just west of the French Quarter is the Faubourg Treme, which was settled largely by free people of color. This area was moderately affected by Hurricane Katrina: the Old US Mint's roof was torn off by high winds, and the Mahalia Jackson Theater of the Performing Arts suffered flood damage.

SIGHTS AT A GLANCE

Museums and Galleries
Beauregard-Keyes House ❻
Gallier House Museum ❽
Madame John's Legacy ❶❺
New Orleans Jazz National
   Historical Park ❹
Old US Mint pp74–5 ❶

Parks and Gardens
American Aquatic Gardens ❷⓿
Armstrong Park ❷❶
Congo Square ❷❷
Washington Artillery Park &
   Moon Walk ❶❼
Washington Square ❶❾

Cemeteries
St. Louis Cemetery #1 ❷❺
St. Louis Cemetery #2 ❷❻

Historic Buildings
Cornstalk Fence ❶❻
Gauche Villa ❶❶

Lafitte's Blacksmith Shop ❶❽
Lalaurie House ❾
Latrobe House ❶⓿
Old Ursuline Convent ❺
Soniat House ❼

Landmarks
Café du Monde ❶❹
Central Grocery ❶❸
Esplanade
   Avenue ❶❷

Flea Market ❷
French Market ❸

Churches
Our Lady of Guadalupe ❷❹

Theaters
Mahalia Jackson Theater of
   the Performing Arts ❷❸

GETTING THERE
The 48 bus runs from Mid-City to Esplanade; the 3 circles the Quarter on Dauphine and Chartres. The Riverfront Streetcar has two stops here.

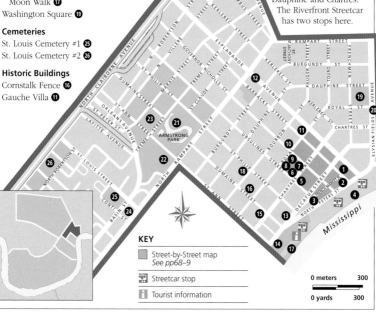

KEY

Street-by-Street map
See pp68–9

Streetcar stop

Tourist information

0 meters 300
0 yards 300

◁ Lacy, New Orleans ironwork, Royal Street

Street-by-Street: Lower French Quarter

The area surrounding the French Market is loaded with atmosphere. It has long been a place for meeting and mixing. In the city's early days, Native Americans came to this area to sell wild herbs, and today the district still offers a range of exotic goods. French Market Place, formerly Gallatin Street, was once the most notorious street in the Quarter, populated by prostitutes, rowdies, criminals (like the Black Hand Gang), and visiting sailors, who ventured here at their peril. It was lined with so many brothels and bars that it was dubbed "Louisiana's Barbary Coast." Today, it still has plenty of bars, and some of the oldest and most important buildings in the French Quarter.

Gallier House Museum
Set in a former residence, this is an informative showcase of 19th-century life ❽

Soniat House
This residence has been restored to its original splendor, and serves as a lovely small hotel (see p164) ❼

Beauregard-Keyes House, former home of Frances Parkinson Keyes, is now a museum ❻

★ **Old Ursuline Convent**
Designed in 1745, and built in 1752, this is the oldest building in the Mississippi Valley ❺

CHARTRES STREET

GOV. NICHOLLS ST

★ **Farmers Market at the French Market**
A New Orleans institution since 1791, the Farmers Market is the place to visit to stock up on fresh produce ❸

KEY

- - - - Suggested route

Gauche Villa
*Built in 1856, this house is notable for
its beautiful cast-iron balcony. Architect
James Freret designed the house* ⓫

LOCATOR MAP
See Street Finder maps 4 and 5

**Esplanade
Avenue**
*This beautiful
avenue was the
aristocratic resi-
dential street of the
Creole community
in the 19th century.
It marks the divi-
sion between the
French Quarter
and the Faubourg
Marigny* ⓬

0 meters 30
0 yards 30

DECATUR STREET

ESPLANADE AVENUE

BARRACKS ST

★ Old US Mint
*Coins were minted here until
1909. Today the building is a
state museum with extensive
exhibits on Louisiana music* ❶

**Flea Market
at the French
Market**
*Handcrafts,
souvenirs, and
curiosities can
be found at
this popular
flea market* ❷

STAR FEATURES

★ French Market

★ Old Ursuline
  Convent

★ Old US Mint

Old US Mint ❶

See pp74–5.

Flea Market ❷

French Market, North Peters St,
between Gov. Nicholls and Barracks
Sts. **Map** 5 E1. 🚊 *Riverfront.* 🚌 *55.*
⏰ *7am–7pm daily.* ♿ 🏧 🖥 🍴
www.frenchmarket.org

At stalls and tables inside and
outside the French Market
buildings, all kinds of items
can be bought, from jewelry
and pottery to African arts
and crafts. The flea market
stands on the site of the notorious neighborhood once called
the "port of missing men,"
because so many men who
visited the local bars and brothels were shanghaied or killed.

**Colorful wares for sale at New
Orleans' Flea Market**

French Market ❸

North Peters St to Barracks St.
Map 5 E1. 🚊 *Riverfront.* 🚌 *5, 48.*
⏰ *10am–6pm daily (some parts are
open later).* 🏧 🖥 🍴 🍷

Despite its name, this spot
has been a gathering place
for many different ethnic
groups. Originally, Native
Americans came here to sell
their baskets, beads, and *filé*
(ground sassafras leaves used
in gumbo). Later, African-
American women sold various
wares including *calas* (hot
rice cakes). German farmers
from upriver sold agricultural
produce, and Italians operated
most of the stalls in the late
1800s. Today, the French Market officially covers the five
blocks between St. Ann and

Typical French Market stand displaying fresh garlic and vegetables

Barracks streets, but in daily
use, it usually denotes the
open-air markets starting at St.
Philips Street. At the Farmers'
Market (starting at Ursulines
St) you can still find fresh
produce and walk-up food
stands. The Flea Market sells
a diverse range of clothing,
antiques, and art.

New Orleans Jazz National Historical Park ❹

916 N Peters St. **Map** 5 D1.
Tel 589-4841. 🚊 *Riverfront.*
🚌 *5, 82.* ⏰ *9am–5pm Tue–Sat.*
🚫 *Jan 1, Thanksgiving, Dec 25.* 📷
www.nps.gov/jazz

The National Park Service
offers seminars and jazz
concerts at this small visitors'
center; ranger-guided walking
tours also depart from here.
Other NPS venues in town
include Perseverance Hall in
Armstrong Park *(see p79)* and
a performance center at the
Old US Mint *(see pp74–5).*

Old Ursuline Convent ❺

1100 Chartres St. **Map** 5 D1. *Tel*
529-3040. 🚊 *Riverfront.* 🚌 *55.*
⏰ *10am–4pm Mon–Sat.* 📷 📷

Dating from 1752, this is
the oldest building in the
Mississippi Valley. With its
steep-pitched roof punctuated
by a row of dormers and tall
chimneys, it is typically
French Colonial.
    In the 1820s, when the nuns
departed to new quarters, the
convent became the first
official residence for the
bishops and archbishops of
New Orleans, and the home
of the archdiocesan archives.
Later, the convent became
part of a parish complex and
the old nuns' kitchen and
laundry became (as it remains
today) the rectory for Our
Lady of Victory Church.
    The current chapel, conse-
crated in 1845, was originally
known as St. Mary's, but
today it is called Our Lady of
Victory. Inside, visitors can

Main façade, Old Ursuline Convent

Beautiful ironwork adorning the Soniat House

a famous Civil War hero his name is still associated with the building.

Novelist Frances Parkinson Keyes, who wrote many of her 51 novels here, including *Dinner at Antoine's*, restored the property. Today, many of her personal possessions are on display, including all of her novels, plus a collection of dolls from all over the world. The rooms are arranged around an attractive courtyard, which contains a fountain that Mrs. Keyes brought from Vermont, her home state.

Soniat House **❼**

1133 Chartres St. **Map** 5 D1.
Tel 522-0570. 🚋 *Riverfront.*
🚌 5, 55. **www**.soniathouse.com
See Where to Stay, p164.

This historic residence was built in 1829 as a townhouse for wealthy sugar planter Joseph Soniat Dufossat and his family. Joseph was the second son of Chevalier Guy Saunhac du Fossat, who had been sent to Louisiana by Louis XV of France in 1751 to help the fight against the Native Americans.

The house combines Creole style – the flagstone carriage-way, a courtyard, an external spiral staircase, and lacy iron galleries – with Greek Revival detail in the mantels and moldings. In the 1940s, the Nathaniel Felton family restored it completely. Today it is a small hotel, exquisitely furnished with authentic antiques and decoration.

admire the splendid pine and cypress ceiling, two fine Bavarian stained-glass windows, and a window depicting the Battle of New Orleans *(see p17)* beneath an image of Our Lady of Prompt Succor.

A formal French garden containing a handsome iron gazebo lies in front of the building. It is accessed via the porter's lodge.

Beauregard-Keyes House **❻**

1113 Chartres St. **Map** 5 D1. *Tel* 523-7257. 🚋 *Riverfront.* 🚌 5, 55.
🕐 *10am–3pm Mon–Sat.* 📷 📹 *hourly.* **www**.bkhouse.org

Twin staircases lead up to this Federal-style townhouse, designed by François Corre-jolles in 1826. It is associated with several famous New Orleanians, including master chess player Paul Morphy who was born here in 1837, when it was the residence of his grandfather, Joseph Le Carpentier. General P. G. T. Beauregard lived here briefly for 18 months in 1866–7, and because he was such

Grand entrance to the Beauregard-Keyes House

Gallier House Museum **8**

1132 Royal St. **Map** 5 D1. *Tel 525-5661.* 5, 55, 81. ○ *10am–3:30pm Mon & Thu–Sat.* ● *public hols.* www.hgghh.org

In 1857, James Gallier, Jr. designed this attractive residence, which combines architectural elements of the Creole, with great height and verticality, and the American townhouse, with Federal-style windows and doorways *(see pp34–5)*. The interior incorporated many innovations of its time, including an ingenious hot-water and ventilation system. The kitchen was also inside the house, which was unusual for the period because of the danger of fire. On the exterior, the rosebud design of the railings is striking.

Inside, visitors can view the "isolation room," a sparsely furnished room designed for the sick. Many households had such a room, which was not surprising in a city that experienced 23 yellow fever epidemics between 1718 and 1860.

James Gallier, Jr. was the son of the city's renowned architect James Gallier, Sr., who designed Gallier Hall *(see p95)*. Gallier Hall served as the City Hall until the 1950s. James Gallier, Jr. also designed the portico of the Louisiana State Bank building *(see p48)*.

Lalaurie House, associated with ghostly visions

Lalaurie House **9**

1140 Royal St. **Map** 5 D1. 5, 55. ● *to the public.*

Residents of the French Quarter still hurry past this otherwise lovely building because of its grim associations and reputation for ghosts. It was built in 1832 for a distinguished couple, Dr. Leonard Louis Nicolas Lalaurie and his wife, Delphine, who were well known for their fashionable and lavish parties.

At these social events, though, guests could not help but notice the condition of the servants, who were painfully thin and seemed to be terrified of their mistress. The gossip about how she treated her slaves was confirmed on April 10, 1834, when a fire broke out at the residence. When neighbors rushed in to extinguish the fire and save the contents, they found seven half-starved and manacled slaves. A story in the local press further fueled the outrage,

Front door at Lalaurie House

and a mob arrived intent on destroying the place. During the melee, Madame Lalaurie and her husband escaped unharmed. After she died in 1842, it is believed that her body was secretly returned from Paris and was buried in St. Louis Cemetery #1 *(see p82)* or #2 *(see p83)*. During the Civil War *(see pp18–19)* the house served as a Union headquarters; later it was used variously as a school, conservatory of music, and gaming house.

A private residence now, some locals still swear that the house is haunted, and that the clanking of chains can be heard.

Latrobe House **10**

721 Governor Nicholls St. **Map** 5 D1. 5, 55. ● *to the public.*

When Benjamin Henry Latrobe designed this building in 1814, with its sturdy Doric columns, he helped launch the mania in New Orleans for Greek

Gallier House, an innovative 19th-century residence

Revival-style architecture. Known as the first professional architect in the US, Benjamin Henry Latrobe (1764–1820) was born in England, and after working as a professional architect for several years in Europe he came to the United States in 1796. Latrobe was highly influential, and built a variety of private residences and public buildings, the latter ranging from waterworks to cathedrals. He is largely responsible for the interior of the US Capitol Building, and for the East Portico of the White House. He died in New Orleans of yellow fever while supervising the building of a new waterworks.

Gauche Villa ⓫

704 Esplanade Ave at Royal.
Map 5 D1. 🚌 5. 🚋 Riverfront.
🚫 to the public.

The beautiful ironwork of this residence is uniquely integral to the villa's overall design, which accounts for the building's harmonious appearance. Little of the cast ironwork in New Orleans was constructed at the same time as the building – mostly it was added as an after-thought. Numerous patterns are used on the fence, the gate, the balconies, and the parapet, casting lovely shadows on the stucco exterior on sun-filled days. A bacchant

Gauche Villa, with its superb original ironwork

surrounded by grapevines adorns the balcony, cast in Saarbrucken, Germany, and shipped to New Orleans. Rows of anthema and other Greek floral motifs decorate the edge of the roof and the fence posts. Architect James Freret designed the house for crockery merchant John Gauche in 1856.

Esplanade Avenue ⓬

Maps 2 B2/C2–3 and 3 D3/E4.
🚌 46, 48.

Today, Esplanade Avenue acts as the dividing line between the French Quarter and Faubourg Marigny, and extends from the Mississippi to Bayou St. John. As early as the 1830s, this broad,

tree-lined 3-mile (2-km) long street cut through what was the most aristocratic Creole neighborhood of impressive villas and townhouses. The fashionable elite paraded in their carriages past the many elegant residences, some of which have survived to this day.

Many of these homes were designed by the city's fore-most architects, including Henry Howard, James Gallier, Sr., and William and James Freret. Their styles range from Greek Revival to Italianate and Queen Anne. Most are still private residences, but some have been converted into handsome bed-and-breakfasts. A stroll along this street will reveal over 190 homes that were built before 1900. Every block contains numerous architectural gems.

Elegant residences lining Esplanade Avenue

Old US Mint ❶

Fort St. Charles was the original occupant of this site in the Lower French Quarter; it was here that Andrew Jackson reviewed his troops before the Battle of New Orleans *(see p17)*. The Greek Revival building seen today was built in 1835 by William Strickland, and functioned as a mint until 1909. In 1931, it was converted into a federal prison; later, it was used by the Coast Guard. Today the Mint houses a permanent exhibition on coins and coin-making, as well as displays on Louisiana music, from opera to zydeco, and a $4-million, 4,000-sq-ft (371-sq-m) performance space.

Trombone slide detail

★ History of the Old US Mint Exhibition
A selection of the gold and silver coins formerly minted here are displayed in this glittering exhibit.

Early Jazz
Vintage photographs depict the early bands with their jug and tin drums, washboards, kazoos, and other homemade instruments.

Ironwork
The balconies and railings display some of the city's beautiful wrought iron.

Ebony Clarinet
George Lewis, who was most popular during the 1950s and 1960s, played this clarinet.

★ New Orleans Jazz Collection
Original musical instruments, vintage photographs, and historic documents show the evolution from Dixieland to modern jazz music.

Cornet
Louis Armstrong learned to play jazz on this horn.

Conference room

New Orleans-style Band
Murals such as this, showing the traditional jazz line-up, formed of cornet, clarinet, trombone, drums, string bass, and banjo, are part of the Jazz Museum at the Mint.

Louisiana State Museum Archive

Daniel Dana fashioned this spear-pointed fence in the 1850s.

Jazz Origins
A selection of photographs of early jazz bands and musicians, as well as a steamboat scale model, are displayed at the Jazz Collection entrance.

Main Façade
Visitors enter the Old US Mint through a grand Neo-Classical portico, which has been carefully restored along with the rest of the building.

STAR EXHIBITS

★ History of the Old US Mint Exhibition

★ New Orleans Jazz Collection

Central Grocery ⓭

923 Decatur. **Map** 5 D2.
Tel 523-1620. 🚌 5, 55.
🚋 *Riverfront.* ⭘ 9am–5pm Tue–Sat.
🖻 🍴

This historic store, one of the
few Italian delis left in the
city, sells all kinds of Italian
food, from pasta, provolone,
and mozzarella, to sausages,
parmesan, and olive oil. In
the 1890s many Italians began
to move to the French
Quarter, and became major
stallholders at the nearby
French Market *(see p68)*.
Today, customers gather at the
counters at the back of the
store to order another specialty,
the *muffaletta (see p172)*,
which is a sizable sandwich
filled with deli meats and
cheeses. The most vital
ingredient, however, is the
olive salad – a blend of olives,
celery, carrots, cauliflower,
and capers, which can also be
purchased at the store.

Olive salad and other deli
specialties at the Central Grocery

Café du Monde ⓮

800 Decatur. **Map** 5 D2. *Tel* 525-
4544. 🚌 5, 55. 🚋 *Riverfront.*
⭘ 24 hours daily. ⭘ Dec 25. ♿
🖻 🍴 www.cafedumonde.com

Everyone who visits New
Orleans stops here for a plate
of sugar-dusted *beignets*
(square French donuts)
accompanied by *café au lait*
or the famous chicory-flavored
version, iced coffee or a glass
of milk. This coffeehouse,
which was established in 1862,
is perfect for relaxing at a
table under the arcade and
listening to the street musicians

Taking a break at Café du Monde, with *beignets* and coffee

entertain. During the mid-19th
century there were as many
as 500 similar coffeehouses in
the French Quarter. Coffee
was one of New Orleans'
most important commodities,
and the coffee trade helped
the economy recover after the
Civil War, when New Orleans
vied with New York City to
control coffee imports. During
the Civil War, locals drank
coffee flavored with peanuts
and pecan shells, to make the
coffee supply last.

Madame John's Legacy ⓯

632 Dumaine St. **Map** 5 D2. *Tel*
568-6968. 🚌 5, 55. 🚋 *Riverfront.*
⭘ 10am–4:30pm daily. ⭘ public
hols. 🎦 🎟 www.crt.state.la.us/
museum/properties/
madamjohnslegacy.aspx

Dating from 1789, this is
one of the oldest surviving
residences in the Mississippi
Valley. It is a typical
Creole plantation-
style house,
supported on brick piers
which rise some 9 ft (3m)
off the ground. A veranda,
accessible via French windows
from all the rooms, extends
around the first floor.

The name Madame John's
Legacy refers to George
Washington Cable's famous
story *Tite Poulette* (1873), in
which the hero leaves a
residence as a legacy to his
quadroon mistress, who sells
the building, deposits the cash
in a bank, and loses it all when
the bank fails. Cable used this
residence as a model of the
home in his story. In the late
19th century, the house was
converted into rental apartments, which were occupied
by a mixture of immigrants.

Today, exhibits in the first-
floor galleries relate the history
of the house and its many
owner-residents. Among them
were Jean Pascal, a Provençal
sea captain who built the
original house on this site
before being killed by Natchez
Indians in 1729; pirate-admiral
René Beluche,
who was

Madame John's Legacy, the oldest residence in the Mississippi Valley

born here and later served in the Venezuelan Revolutionary Navy; and the Segher family, whose household inventory featured four slaves, including a mulatto, valued at $2,500, and his daughter, who was valued at only $1,200, because she had been promised her freedom at age 30. The second-floor galleries are now used for contemporary art exhibitions.

Cornstalk Fence ⓰

915 Royal St. **Map** 5 D2. 🚃 5, 55.

This handsome cast-iron landmark fence is one of three remaining in the city (see p106). It was erected around 1850, when cast iron began replacing wrought iron (see pp38–9). The cornstalks are entwined with morning glories, and each element is painted in its natural color – yellow for the ears of corn, green for the stalks, and blue for the morning glories. A butterfly decorates the central portion of the gate, and a spray of holly adorns the bottom. It was cast by the prestigious Philadelphia company, Wood & Perot.

View of Artillery Park and Moonwalk on the Mississippi River

Washington Artillery Park and Moon Walk ⓱

Decatur Street (between St. Ann and St. Peter sts). **Map** 5 D2. 🚃 5, 55. 🚋 Riverfront.

Washington Artillery Park faces Jackson Square from across Decatur Street. Inside the park is an austere concrete amphitheater with a central staircase leading to the Moon Walk. This community boardwalk was named after former New Orleans Mayor Maurice "Moon" Landrieu, who approved the construction of a boardwalk that made the riverfront area accessible to the public in the 1970s. For decades, it had been walled off by port authorities, so the public was able to re-establish its historic relationship with the riverfront. Today Moon Walk is favored by street performers. Crowds often gather to witness impromptu performances by solo musicians, including guitarists, clarinetists, saxophonists, trombonists, and steel drummers, who play with an open music case at their feet to collect donations.

Standing on the Moon Walk, the audience can enjoy a welcome break from the city's humidity, as a constant breeze along the waterfront makes temperatures feel several degrees cooler than in the rest of the city. It also provides an excellent vantage point from which to view the river, Jackson Square, and the surrounding area.

Stone steps lead right down from the boardwalk to the Mississippi River where you can sit and dangle your feet in the whiskey-colored water, or watch the steamboats, ocean-going barges, and other river traffic float past. Do not attempt to stand in the river, however, as the current is deceptively rapid and powerful.

If you do want to get closer to the water, there are plenty of river cruises – from 1-hour sightseeing trips to romantic night-time dinner cruises (see p217).

Cast-iron Cornstalk Fence and hotel

Tree-shaded passage in Washington Square

Lafitte's Blacksmith Shop ⑱

941 Bourbon St. **Map** 5 D1.
Tel 593-9761. 🚌 55, 89.
🕐 10am–4am daily. ♿ 🍸 ♫
www.lafittesblacksmithshop.com

This is the oldest bar in New Orleans. It is an example of the brick between posts *(see p34)* French-style building, and was constructed sometime before 1772, although the precise date is unknown. Inside, several small fireplaces warm the place on cool evenings, and there is also a small patio containing a sculpture of Adam and Eve embracing on a bed of ivy. The sculpture was created by an artist as payment for his bar bill.

Despite its name, there is no proof that the pirate brothers, Jean and Pierre Lafitte, operated a smithy here as a front for their smuggling activities. Very little documentation of their lives exists, so that many myths have been woven around these two legendary figures. They operated as smugglers and were prominent slave traffickers, selling all manner of contraband, including seized slave ships, when the importation of slaves into the United States was forbidden in 1808. They earned local gratitude by warning the Americans of the planned British attack on

New Orleans, and with their band they fought bravely in the ensuing battle *(see p17)*. Regardless of whether this shop was indeed occupied by the Lafitte brothers, the building certainly existed to witness Jean Lafitte brazenly walking the streets when posters calling for his capture were plastered all over town.

Just up Bourbon Street from Lafitte's stands another bar, called Lafitte's in Exile. It is so called because, until the early 1950s, gays frequented the old Lafitte's; when the bar changed hands, its new owner refused to renew the lease, and in 1953 its gay patrons were driven into exile. They established their new quarters just up the street at Lafitte's in Exile, making it the oldest gay bar in the US.

Washington Square ⑲

Frenchman between Royal and Dauphine. **Map** 5 E1. 🕐 9am–6pm *daily.* 🚌 5, 55. ♿

Washington Square, one of the earliest parks to be laid out in New Orleans, was created in 1808. It lies at the center of the Faubourg Marigny, today the most "bohemian" part of the city and home to most of the city's gay community. The park is a good place to throw a frisbee and for ball games, or just to relax on the vast green areas it offers. There are also open-air concerts here in summer and caroling in December.

Water lily at the American Aquatic Gardens

American Aquatic Gardens ⑳

621 Elysian Fields. **Map** 5 E1.
Tel 944-0410. 🚌 5, 55. 🕐 9am–4pm daily. ● major holidays. 📷
www.americanaquaticgardens.com

This delightful "store," which occupies half a city block, is the largest – and widely considered the best – aquatic plant nursery and garden supply

The historic Lafitte's Blacksmith Shop

Main entrance to Armstrong Park

store in the United States. It is worth visiting for its glorious display of aquatic and exotic plants in the outdoor gardens, which include an Asian garden complete with decorative Buddhas and Oriental lanterns. The water gardens contain exquisite water lilies, and there are also spectacular sculpted fountains, handsome statuary, attractive pond designs, and ornamental wall planters. The gardens were quite badly damaged by Hurricane Katrina, but they have now been repaired.

Armstrong Park ㉑

Rampart St between St. Peter St and St. Ann St. **Map** 4 C1.
5, 48, 88, 89.

Named for the legendary trumpeter Louis "Satchmo" Armstrong (see pp20–21), this spacious park stands on hallowed jazz ground. It is situated near what used to be Storyville (see p81), the legal red-light district that nurtured so many of the early jazz artists.

Armstrong's statue stands in the park, and his name is emblazoned on the arch at St. Ann Street. He was born in New Orleans on August 4, 1901, and as a boy he spent his time singing on the streets

in a quartet until he was sent to the Colored Waifs' Home after firing a pistol in public. It was there that he learned to play the trumpet, and soon he was talented enough to challenge such leading players as Joe "King" Oliver and Freddie Keppard. He left New Orleans in 1922 to join King Oliver in Chicago, and went on to build an international career, entertaining audiences

until his death in 1971. The park features an artificial lake, the Mahalia Jackson Theater of the Performing Arts (see p80), and Congo Square (see p80). The National Park Service opens its historic Perseverance Hall in the park from 9am until 5pm on Saturdays. The venue hosts educational concerts, including a traditional music workshop for children.

WOMEN IN JAZZ

Jazz was not solely a male preserve; many noted female singers and musicians also made their names in New Orleans. Blanche Thomas declined the life of endless one-night stands and stayed in the city singing the blues with such artists as Al Hirt and Pete Fountain. She could be heard in the bars along Bourbon Street in the early 1970s, where her command of traditional jazz and big blues voice made her a particular favorite. Singer Louise "Blue Lu" Barker is said to have influenced

Blanche Thomas

both Billie Holiday and Eartha Kitt. Lizzie Miles dazzled the crowds in the 1920s, and Esther Bigeou was dubbed the "Creole songbird" in the 1930s. There were also some prominent female instrumentalists in the early jazz bands – pianists like Sweet Emma Barrett and Lil Hardin. The most famous female jazz musicians to emerge from New Orleans were the Boswell Sisters (see p21), a trio of middle-class white girls who learned jazz from growing up in a mixed-race neighborhood. Their close harmonies and up-tempo tunes propelled them out of New Orleans and on to a national weekly radio program in the 1930s, and then into movies.

Congo Square ❷

N Rampart St, between St. Peter St and St. Philip St. **Map** 4 C1.
🚌 5, 48, 88, 89. ♿

Under the *Code Noir* (an edict concerning the treatment of slaves), slaveholders were forbidden to work slaves on Sunday in order to encourage them to attend church and become good Roman Catholics. Such minimal amounts of freedom allowed the slaves of New Orleans to retain more of their African heritage than those in other parts of the South. On Sunday afternoons, during the 18th and early 19th century, slaves and free people of color would gather in Congo Square (also known as *Place des Nègres*), part of Armstrong Park *(see p79)*, to speak in their native African tongues. They would sing and dance, and perform the *calinda*, an African line dance, and the *bamboula*. These dances were one of the chief origins of jazz, and Congo Square is thus remembered as one of the birthplaces of jazz music. The infamous Marie Laveau *(see p83)* is said to have performed voodoo rituals here.

Sidney Bechet's statue

Congo Square, home of the calinda and bamboula dances

Mahalia Jackson Theater of the Performing Arts ❸

Armstrong Park, Rampart St between St. Peter St and St. Ann St. **Map** 4 C1. **Tel** 525-1052. 🚌 48, 46, 52, 57. 📷 ♿ **www**.mahaliajackson theater.com

Named for the celebrated gospel singer Mahalia Jackson (1911–72), this theater is used by local and visiting dance, music, and theater companies.

A New Orleans native, Jackson began her career singing in the local church, where her father was a pastor. At the age of 16 she moved to Chicago and opened first a beauty shop, then a flower store. Despite her strict upbringing, she fell in love with the syncopated rhythms of blues but never sang the more bawdy songs in its repertoire. Jackson was discovered in the 1930s and made her first recording in 1934. Her career took her to Carnegie Hall, the Newport Jazz Festival, and other major music venues. Jackson was also active in the civil rights movement and was a supporter of Martin Luther King, Jr.

The theater suffered flood damage after Hurricane Katrina but has been restored.

The Mahalia Jackson Theater of the Performing Arts

Stained-glass window, Our Lady of Guadalupe

Our Lady of Guadalupe ㉔

411 N. Rampart St. **Map** 4 B2.
Tel 525-1551. 🚌 48, 46, 52, 57.
🕐 9am–5pm daily. ♿

Renamed Our Lady of Guadalupe in 1875, when it served an Italian congregation,

St. Anthony's Chapel was built on the outskirts of the French Quarter in 1826, when funerals were no longer being held in St. Louis Cathedral, for fear of spreading yellow fever *(see p18)*. It was originally known as "Mortuary Chapel" because all the bodies were taken directly from the chapel to St. Louis Cemetery #1 *(see p82)*, via the back entrance. It displays several brilliantly colored stained-glass windows, representing different saints honored by devoted New Orleanians.

The most visited altar is dedicated to St. Jude, the "patron saint of hopeless causes," but a more light-hearted one stands to the left of the exit; this is dedicated to New Orleans' very own St. Expedite, whose name is not in any official dictionary of saints. According to apocryphal legend, a crate marked with the word "Spedito!" (meaning "rush") arrived in the chapel one day. The statue inside it was removed and mounted on the wall, and its name was confused with the word on the box. To this day,

New Orleanians visit the altar to pray for help when they need something in a hurry. St. Expedite is also associated with voodoo *(see p83)*, which is why the church is called the "voodoo church." Guadalupe is the official place of worship for the police and fire departments, whose altar stands to the right of the main altar.

Our Lady of Guadalupe

STORYVILLE

From 1897 to 1917 the 38 blocks roughly bounded by Iberville, Basin, Robertson, and St. Louis streets were set aside as a legal red-light district *(see p22)*. Saloons and high-class brothels lined Basin Street, cheap bawdy houses clustered along Dauphine, Burgundy, St. Louis, Conti, and Bienville streets, while the poorest huts, called cribs, were found along Rampart and Iberville streets. Names and addresses of 700 prostitutes were listed in the Blue Book, which was available at bars like the Annex, which was operated by state legislator and political boss Tom

Anderson, the informal "Mayor" of Storyville. Many of the brothels were quite luxurious, furnished with velvet drapes, gilt-framed paintings and leopard-skin fabrics. At No. 317 Basin Street, Countess Willie Piazza held court. She regularly employed pianist Jelly Roll Morton, who played behind a screen, as did most musicians at these establishments, so they were not able to observe the patrons. The district was officially closed in 1917 by the Navy Department *(see p22)*. In the 1940s, the Federal government leveled Storyville to make way for low-income housing.

Mahogany Hall in Basin Street, one of Storyville's notorious bordellos

Poignant statue atop an above-ground tomb at St. Louis Cemetery #1

St. Louis Cemetery #1 ㉕

Basin St between St. Louis and Conti.
Map 4 B2. **Tel** 482-5065. 🚌 48, 46, 52, 57. ⏰ 8:30am–4pm Mon–Sat, 8:30am–3pm Sun. ♿ 📷

This cemetery opened in 1789 and is the oldest in the city. Because of its age, it is one of the most fascinating to visit. However, this cemetery and its neighbor, St. Louis Cemetery #2, should not be visited alone; both are ideal places for muggers and pickpockets to operate. By 1829 St. Louis #1 was already filled,

mostly with victims of yellow fever. Today, the narrow alleyways are full of mausoleums, many in advanced stages of decay. Although Catholic, it at one time accepted Protestants (although these graves were later moved). There are numerous legendary local figures buried here, including Homer Adolph Plessy (1862–1925), who challenged the segregation laws in the 1890s (see p19); and Bernard de Marigny (1788–1871), who inherited $7 million at age 15 and squandered it playing craps (dice), the game he introduced to the United States (see p102). Daniel Clark (1766–1813), the wealthy Irish merchant who challenged Governor Claiborne (see p17) to a duel and wounded him in the leg, lies here, along with his daughter Myra Clark Gaines (1803–85). She fought for 65 years to secure her father's estate, in a case that generated 8,000 pages of court documents. Jean Etienne Boré (1741–1820), the plantation owner who

was the city's first post-colonial mayor, is buried in a low brick vault. Boré contributed much to the city's prosperity as he was the first to granulate sugar on a commercial scale in 1796. Boré's grandson, the historian Charles Gayarré, is also buried here, as is Paul Morphy (1837–84), the genius chess player who was a world champion at age 13 but who later went mad. Most famous of all is probably Marie Laveau (see box, opposite), known as the voodoo queen. Crowds visit her tomb (though some believe it is not the correct one) to leave unusual voodoo "gifts" or mark it with X's, which symbolizes a request that she grant a particular wish. A more recent figure is Ernest "Dutch" Morial (1929–1989), the first black mayor and the father of another former mayor, Marc Morial. The largest tomb belongs to the Société Française de Bienfaisance, which contains 70 vaults. The tallest monument, sculpted by Pietro Gualdi in 1857 for $40,000, belongs to the Italian Society. It was the background in psychedelic scenes in the film Easy Rider. A plaque memorializes Benjamin Henry Latrobe (see p72), the architect who came to New Orleans to build a waterworks and died in 1820 of yellow fever (see p18). No one knows where his remains are. Many bodies were moved from the St. Louis Cemetery #1 in 1823 to Lafayette Cemetery (see p102) and from there to Metairie Cemetery (see p127) in the 1950s. Somehow, Latrobe's body got lost in the shuffle.

Recommended tours (see p198) are given by the Save Our Cemeteries organization, and by New Orleans Tours, Inc. Both provide plenty of excellent local information.

A beseeching angel

Ornate family mausoleums in St. Louis Cemetery #1

VOODOO WORSHIP

Voodoo arrived in New Orleans from Africa, via the Caribbean, where it originated as a form of ancestor worship among the West African tribes who were brought to North America as slaves. With the revolution in Saint Domingue in 1793, slaves and free people of color arrived as refugees and increased the practice in the city. Voodoo enabled those slaves to preserve their African culture and roots alongside the Roman Catholic religion, for it mixed both traditions. The most famous of all 19th-century voodoo leaders was Marie Laveau (c.1794–1881), a mulatto and a great marketer. She used such Catholic elements as prayer, incense, and saints in her rituals, which she opened to the public for an admission fee. The high point of the voodoo calendar was the celebration she held along the Bayou St. John on St. John's Eve. She is believed to be buried at St. Louis Cemetery #1.

Portrait of Marie Laveau

The Barelli tomb

St. Louis Cemetery #2 ㉖

Iberville to St Louis St, between N Claiborne Ave and N Robertson St. **Map** 4 B1. *Tel* 482-5065. 📠 48, 46, 52, 57. ⏰ 8:30am–4pm Mon–Sat, 8:30am–3pm Sun. ⚞ ⚐

By the end of the colonial period, and mostly because of a devastating series of epidemics, this cemetery was established as the natural extension of St. Louis Cemetery #1 around 1823. The final resting place for much of New Orleans' 19th-century Creole aristocracy, it contains remarkably ornate mausoleums. Many of them were designed by Jacques Nicholas Bussière De Pouilly, who arrived in New Orleans from France in

Tree-shaped statue

the 1830s. His plans were inspired by the tombs in Paris's Père Lachaise Cemetery. Grand in design and scale, and modeled on Greek, Egyptian, and other Classical styles, the patterns for these ambitious mausoleums became very popular in New Orleans. The tombs are like impressive residences, often enclosed within beautiful wrought-iron gates, featuring such motifs as lyres, winged hourglasses, hearts, inverted torches, and urns with arrows. The fences around the tombs are some of the finest wrought-iron work in the city. The intricate immortelles made of wire, beads, and glass are also unique and represent everlasting tributes to the dead.

Among the notables buried here are General Jean Baptiste Plauché, who fought with Andrew Jackson at the Battle of New Orleans *(see p17)*. J. N. B. DePouilly himself is humbly buried in a modest wall vault with his brother, who was also an architect. Other famous New Orleans figures buried here include jazz musician Danny Barker, and the pirate Dominique You *(see p17)*, who rests in the main aisle in a tomb marked with a Masonic emblem and the inscription: "This New Bayard could have witnessed the

end of the world without fear or trembling." Near the cemetery office, the Barelli tomb recalls the tragedy that occurred on November 15, 1849, when the steamer *Louisiana* exploded, killing 86 people, including the young son of Joseph Barelli, who erected the memorial in 1856. Five sculpted angels hover around the tomb and a bas-relief depicts the explosion.

A common legend says that Napoleon Bonaparte's followers were waiting for his arrival in New Orleans from his exile in St. Helena, but since he died beforehand on December 20, 1821, a funeral service for him was held here.

Guided tours, available from several organizations *(see p198)*, will help visitors get the most out of their time at this fascinating site.

Creole family mausoleum, fallen into disrepair

WAREHOUSE AND CENTRAL BUSINESS DISTRICTS

When the Americans arrived after the Louisiana Purchase (see p17) they developed a community of their own on the upriver side of Canal Street. It was called the Faubourg St. Mary and extended from Canal Street to Louisiana Avenue. Between 1820 and 1860 the waterfront was developed, and behind it grew a

Louisiana State Seal at the Spanish Plaza

commercial and residential district that matched the Creole district downriver. Today the CBD incorporates narrow streets lined with Victorian warehouses, banks, and office buildings, as well as such broad thoroughfares as Poydras, which is lined with skyscrapers belonging to oil companies, hotels, and financial institutions.

SIGHTS AT A GLANCE

Museums and Galleries
Confederate Memorial Hall **16**
Custom House/Audubon
  Insectarium **9**
Gallier Hall **11**
Louisiana Children's Museum **18**
The National WWII Museum **19**
New Orleans Contemporary
  Arts Center **17**
Ogden Museum of
  Southern Art **15**

Shopping Areas
Canal Place **8**
Riverwalk
  Marketplace **4**

Entertainment
Audubon Aquarium of the
  Americas pp90–91 **7**
Harrah's Casino **6**
Louisiana Superdome **12**
Saenger Theatre **13**

Landmarks
World Trade Center **5**

Churches
St. Patrick's Church **10**

Parks and Squares
Lee Circle **14**
Spanish Plaza **3**
Woldenberg Riverfront Park **1**

Boat Trips
Ferry to Algiers **2**

KEY

	Street-by-Street map See pp86–7
🚉	Railroad station
🚌	Bus station
🚃	Streetcar stop
⛴	Ferry boarding point
⊠	Post office

0 meters 500
0 yards 500

GETTING THERE
RTA routes 10, 16, and 91 run from the Lakefront, Mid-City, and Uptown to this area. The Canal Street, St. Charles Avenue, and Riverfront streetcars have stops in the area.

◁ Canal Street at dusk

Street-by-Street: CBD

Spanish coat
of arms

When the Americans arrived from the North in the early 1800s they developed the uptown side of Canal Street. It is still the city's commercial area, where the headquarters of oil, energy, and banking corporations and many public institutions are located. The median running through the middle of Canal Street was the neutral ground separating the English-speaking Americans from the French-speaking Creole community. Today, Canal Street is lined with hotels, restaurants, and stores. A casino and the ferry to Algiers are located at the riverfront end. During the last three decades the riverfront has been totally redeveloped with parks, walks, and such major attractions as the Aquarium and Riverwalk Marketplace.

Harrah's Casino
This enormous casino, with its garish over-the-top decor, is open 24 hours a day, 365 days a year ❻

World Trade Center
Built in the shape of a Greek cross, this 1960s skyscraper towers over the river, port, and Warehouse District ❺

Riverwalk Marketplace
Containing more than 120 stores, including a huge food court, this is one of the largest malls in the city ❹

TCHOPITOULAS

Ferry to Algiers
A free ferry takes visitors across the Mississippi to Algiers ❷

MISSISSIPPI RIVER

Spanish Plaza
Located next to the Riverwalk Marketplace, this plaza was dedicated by Spain to the City of New Orleans in 1976. It has a beautiful fountain at its center ❸

★ River Cruises
The Creole Queen paddlewheeler offers narrated tours of the New Orleans riverfront (see p217).

Canal Place

The city's most upscale shopping mall features big names such as Saks, Gucci, and Williams-Sonoma. There is also a theater and a cinema on the third floor **8**

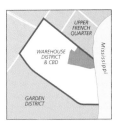

LOCATOR MAP
See Street Finder, maps 4, 5, and 8.

0 meters	100
0 yards	100

★ **Audubon Aquarium of the Americas**
Marine life sculptures by Ida Kohlmeyer are at the entrance **7**

Woldenberg Riverfront Park
Named for local businessman Malcolm Woldenberg, the park contains a charming statue of Woldenberg, but the most notable sculpture is the 16-ft (5-m) tall kinetic steel Ocean Song, *by John Scott* **1**

STAR SIGHTS

★ Audubon Aquarium of the Americas

★ River Cruises

KEY

– – – Suggested route

Woldenberg Riverfront Park ❶

2 Canal St. **Map** 5 D3.
🚋 *Riverfront.* 🚌 *3, 55, 57.* ♿

The 16-acre Woldenberg Park extends all the way along the riverfront from St. Peter Street to the Riverwalk Marketplace, providing a pleasant garden setting studded with contemporary sculpture. From Jackson Square, visitors can access Woldenberg Riverfront Park via Washington Artillery Park and the Moon Walk. Here, many of the city's street performers can be found; the latter is named after Moon Landrieu, who is widely regarded as paving the way for the first black mayor, "Dutch" Morial, to be elected in 1978 *(see p23)*. The park is open from dawn till dusk daily.

River view from the Woldenberg Riverfront Park

Ferry to Algiers ❷

The ferry is at the end of Canal St.
Map 5 D4. 🚋 *Riverfront.* 🚌 *55, 57.*
www.friendsoftheferry.org

From the foot of Canal Street, a free ferry crosses the Mississippi to the historic neighborhood of Algiers on the West Bank, offering spectacular views of the New Orleans skyline on the short journey.

Algiers was established in 1719 and is the second oldest part of the city. For over a century it was used as a depot for imported slaves,

who were held here before being sold on. It is possible that Algiers is the site of the origins of jazz, as single-line melodies were probably used by the slaves to communicate and to comfort themselves and their families.

The area was not connected directly to the rest of the city until a bridge was built in the late 1950s, so it has a separate, small-town feel. It has beautiful late-Victorian churches, homes, parks, and businesses, and at the heart is the Romanesque Revival-style Algiers Courthouse dating from 1896, which can be seen from the French Quarter across the river. It continues to serve the residents of the entire city as a courthouse, and is home to various municipal offices.

The courthouse is also the setting for much of the Old Algiers RiverFest, a weekend-long festival celebrating

the role of the area in the development of jazz. Visitors can enjoy great live music, various arts and crafts, and sample typical New Orleans cuisine. The festival takes place in April each year.

Spanish Plaza ❸

2 Canal St. **Map** 5 D4. 🚋
Riverfront. 🚌 *3, 55, 57.* ⏰ *24 hrs daily.* 🅿 🍴 📷

This small plaza at the entrance to the Riverwalk Marketplace is a good place to take a rest and enjoy an uninterrupted view of the river. A fountain stands at its center, surrounded by a circular mosaic bench on which the coats of arms of Spain are depicted.

The *Creole Queen* paddle-wheeler departs from the Plaza and takes passengers downriver to the Chalmette Battlefield Park, the site of Andrew Jackson's victory at the Battle of New Orleans *(see p17)*. Rangers provide a 40-minute tour of the site. Adjacent to the battlefield is Chalmette National Cemetery, where thousands of Union soldiers are buried. An antebellum house, the Malus-Beauregard home stands on park property. This residence was built in 1833 and purchased in 1880 by the son of General P. G. T. Beauregard *(see p71)*.

Fountain at the center of the Spanish Plaza

Riverwalk Marketplace ❹

1 Poydras St. **Map** 5 D4. **Tel** 522-1555. 🚊 *Riverfront*. 🚌 *3, 55, 57, 65*. ⏰ *10am–7pm Mon–Sat, noon–6pm Sun.* 🚻 🅿 ♿
www.riverwalkmarketplace.com

This massive riverside shopping mall, designed by the same company that developed Boston's Faneuil Hall, contains more than 140 stores, including brand-name favorites like Ann Taylor, Brookstone, Nine West, and Gap. The entire top floor is the food court, while a highlight of the ground floor is the Creole Delicacies Gourmet Shop *(see p189)*, which offers a 2-hour course in cooking.

In addition to shopping opportunities, the mall has an outdoor walkway that runs along the Mississippi River, giving visitors one of the best views of the river and river traffic in the city. International and other cruise ships dock alongside the marketplace, the most notable being those operated by the Delta Queen Steamboat Company, which was established in 1890. A number of information plaques attached to railings along the walkway describe everything from the types of boats plying their trade on the river to the seagulls that drift up from the Gulf of Mexico.

Entrance to the Riverwalk Marketplace

World Trade Center ❺

2 Canal St. **Map** 5 D4. **Tel** 529-1601. 🚊 *Riverfront*. 🚌 *57, 65*.
www.wtcno.org/

The World Trade Center building was designed by Edward Durrell Stone in the 1960s. Originally called the International Trade Mart Building, it housed the headquarters of various mercantile companies and consulates. Architecturally, it has little to recommend it; however, being built in the shape of a Greek cross, it serves as a useful landmark. Currently, the building is mostly vacant. The City of New Orleans, as its owner, is exploring ways to redevelop the building to take advantage of its prime location at the foot of Canal Street.

Riverside view of the WTC Building

Harrah's Casino ❻

228 Poydras St. **Map** 5 D4. **Tel** 533-6000. 🚊 *Riverfront*. 🚌 *3, 57, 65*. ⏰ *24 hrs daily.* 🅿 🍴 🍸
www.harrahsneworleans.com

This casino is close to the riverfront, just a block away from the Mississippi. Covering 100,000 sq ft (9,290 sq m) of floor space, Harrah's offers a vast ballroom in addition to a wide range of games, including 2,900 slot machines and 117 table games featuring baccarat, blackjack, craps, and roulette.

Masquerade is a state-of-the-art entertainment venue set at the heart of the casino. It features a four-storey tower surrounded by a stage for the free nightly shows. There is also an ice-topped bar and exclusive lounge area.

Audubon Aquarium of the Americas ❼

See pp90–91.

The modern and lively Harrah's, a popular New Orleans casino

Audubon Aquarium of the Americas ❼

Concentrating on the waters around New Orleans, from the Mississippi and the swamps to the Gulf of Mexico and the Caribbean, this aquarium complex features some 500 species of marine life. Highlights include a tank containing a Caribbean reef, and a replica of an oil rig. The aquarium lost much of its sea life due to generator failures in the aftermath of Hurricane Katrina. It reopened in 2006.

Seahorses
The Seahorse Gallery features a collection of creatures raised here at the aquarium.

Shark cove

The Amazon Rainforest
Piranhas lurk in the waters that flow under the forest canopy, which is inhabited by tropical birds and wild orchids.

Food court
with several different kinds of restaurants.

Main entrance and information center

Gift shop

★ The Caribbean Reef
An acrylic tunnel underneath a 132,000-gallon tank provides a startling perspective from which to view the rays, angelfish, and other denizens that float above.

Jellyfish
These transparent, fluid creatures sway and dance in eight specially designed exhibits, some of the aquarium's most colorful.

★ The Gulf of Mexico
A 400,000-gallon tank holds a replica of an offshore oil rig, around which swim the species that share the waters – sharks, tarpon, sting rays, and sea turtles.

VISITORS' CHECKLIST

Canal St at Mississippi River.
Map 5 D3. **Tel** 581-4629.
Riverfront. 5, 55, 57.
10am–5pm Tue–Sun. Dec 24 and 25, Thanksgiving, Mardi Gras.

Adventure Island
This interactive play area gives kids the chance to learn about sharks and stingrays, and to explore a pirate ship.

Frogs! has poison dart frogs and other amphibians from around the world.

The Entergy IMAX Theater
This cinema adds a high-tech dimension to the complex. The screen is 5 ½ stories high.

Sea Otter Gallery
A lovable pair of sea otters frolic in this exhibit where a waterfall creates waves for their amusement.

★ The Mississippi River and Delta Habitat
Check out the blue-eyed, white alligator that hangs suspended in the water along with some other Mississippi regulars – catfish, gar, and turtles.

STAR FEATURES

- ★ The Caribbean Reef
- ★ The Gulf of Mexico
- ★ The Mississippi River and Delta Habitat

Main entrance to Canal Place and its many luxury stores

Canal Place ❽

Canal and N Peters Sts. **Map** 4 C3.
🚌 5. 🚋 Canal. ⬤ 10am–7pm
Mon–Sat, noon–6pm Sun. ♿ 🏠 📷
📶 www.theshopsatcanalplace.com

Downtown's most upscale shopping mall is anchored by Saks Fifth Avenue, and contains fashionable stores such as Brooks Brothers, Williams-Sonoma, Anthropologie, Banana Republic, and Coach. The third floor features the food court, plus the only cinema in the city that shows foreign, arthouse, and independent films.

The third floor also houses the Southern Repertory Theater, which stages cutting-edge productions and provides a showcase for local playwrights. There are spectacular views of the Mississippi River from the fourth floor.

Custom House/ Audubon Insectarium ❾

423 Canal St. **Map** 4 C3.
🚌 5. 🚋 Canal. **Audubon**
Insectarium _Tel_ 861-2537.
⬤ 10am–5pm Tue–Sun.

This architectural landmark is home to the Audubon Insectarium, a state-of-the-art interactive museum with fascinating displays of termites,

butterflies, and roaches. Two of the highlights are the cooking show, which illustrates the art of cooking with insects, and Metamorphosis, a lab where visitors can observe insect courtship, mating, and life cycles.

Alexander Thompson Wood was the original architect of the Custom House, though he was succeeded by James Dakin, Confederate General Beauregard _(see p71)_, and Thomas K. Wharton. Construction began in 1847 and was completed in 1881.

Inside, the Marble Hall is a dramatic space under a ground-glass ceiling with a decorative stained-glass border and a skylight above. Juno and Mercury embellish the capitals of the marble columns that support the structure. Over the years the building has served as a post office, armory, and prison.

St. Patrick's Church ❿

724 Camp St. **Map** 4 C4. **Tel** 525-4413. 🚌 11, 41. 🚋 St. Charles. ⬤ 11am–1pm Mon–Sat, 9am–1pm Sun. (Guided tours only.) ♿ 📷 www.oldstpatricks.org

Old St Patrick's Church was completed in 1841 to minister to the Irish Catholic population at the urging of Father James Ignatius Mullon. The brothers Charles and James Dakin were the original architects, but James Gallier, Sr. replaced them. It is an impressive church with a 185-ft (60-m) high tower, a Gothic-inspired interior, and splendid stained-glass vaulting in the sanctuary.

Behind the altar are three paintings by the French artist Leon Pomarede. At the center is a copy of _Raphael's Transfiguration of Christ_, flanked by _St. Patrick Baptizing the Irish Princesses_ and _Christ Walking on Water_. Each of these works dates from 1841. Although the Irish community has largely moved away from the neighborhood, the congregation still draws loyal followers from other districts. Father Mullon is still remembered as an ardent Confederate. He prayed publicly for a Confederate victory, and when General Benjamin "Beast" Butler _(see pp18–19)_ accused him of refusing to bury a Union soldier, he volunteered that he would be "very happy to bury them all." At noon on St. Patrick's Day, a mass is attended by most Catholics as an important part of the festivities held all over the city.

The impressive tower of St. Patrick's Church

Greek Revival-style façade of Gallier Hall

Gallier Hall ⓫

545 St. Charles Ave. **Map** 4 B4.
Tel 565-7457. ⬚ *St. Charles.*
◯ *for tours only: 10am, 11am, noon, 2pm, 3pm.*

James Gallier, Sr.'s master-piece was built between 1845 and 1853, at a cost of $342,000. Constructed of bricks that were plastered and scored to look like stone, the building is 215 ft (65.5 m) deep, extending behind a façade only 90 ft (27 m) wide. Six fluted Ionic columns support the tympanum on the façade, which is decorated with bas-reliefs of Justice and Commerce created by Robert A. Launitz.

Gallier Hall was built to serve as the headquarters of the Second Municipality when the city was briefly served by three separate governments. In 1852 it became City Hall, when the three "cities" (or districts) were reunited. Many great historical figures have lain in state here, including Jefferson Davis, president

of the Confederacy, and General Beauregard.

The building faces Lafayette Square, which was laid out in 1788 as Place Gravier, and renamed in 1824. The square contains statues of statesman Benjamin Franklin by Hiram Powers, and famed Senator Henry Clay by Joel T. Hart. John McDonogh, the great benefactor of the New Orleans public schools, is remembered with a statue by Atallio Piccirilli. Today, the building is a popular vantage point during the famous Mardi Gras parades *(see pp28–9)*.

Louisiana Superdome ⓬

Sugar Bowl Drive. **Map** 4 A3.
Tel 587-3663. ⬚ 16. ⬚ *St.Charles.*
◯ *for sporting events only.* ♿ ◨
www.superdome.com
New Orleans Arena 1501 Girod St. **Map** 4 A3. *Tel* 587-3663.
www.neworleansarena.com

This flying saucer-shaped land-mark is home to local football teams the Saints and Tulane University's Green Wave. It is also the venue for the annual Sugar Bowl, and other sports and entertainment events.

The Superdome has become synonymous with the suffering of those affected by Hurricane Katrina. It was here that many thousands sought refuge from the flood waters. The building was severely damaged by wind, flooding, and the frustra-tions of the desperate people it harbored. In September 2006, the Superdome reopened after a $193 million restoration.

As the world's largest steel-constructed stadium that is unobstructed by posts, it has hosted the Super Bowl more times than any other facility: Super Bowl XXXVI in 2002 was the sixth to be held here. The stadium will again host the game in 2013. It was built between 1971 and 1975; it occupies 52 acres, and stands 27 stories high.

The New Orleans Arena, the "babydome," opened in 1999. In 2002 the Charlotte, North Carolina, Hornets professional basketball team moved to New Orleans and became the home team. The Arena is also home to the Tulane University basketball team.

Saenger Theatre ⓭

143 N Rampart St. **Map** 4 C1. *Tel* 525-1052. ⬚ 3, 41. ⬚ *St. Charles.*
www.thesaengertheatre.com

This beautiful Italian Renaissance theater opened in 1927 as a cinema. Designed by Emile Weil, it features an elegant mezzanine and towering arcade, while the main theater space is made to look like the courtyard of an Italian villa, with archways and statuary decorating the walls. The ceiling is accented by some 150 tiny lights, which resemble stars in the night sky. Heavily damaged by the flood of 2005, the Saenger sat empty for years. New owners have pledged to return this landmark building to its former glory, and the theater is set to reopen in 2013 to host touring Broadway shows.

Louisiana Superdome, one of the world's largest indoor stadiums

Memorial to Robert E. Lee at Lee Circle

Lee Circle ⓮

St. Charles Ave & Howard Ave. **Map** 4 B5. 🚌 *11, 41.* 🚋 *St. Charles.* ♿

The towering 60-ft (18-m) column at the center of Lee Circle, topped by a 16-ft (5-m) statue of Confederate general Robert E. Lee, is one of the city's key landmarks. For many years the Lee Circle area was merely a grubby intersection favored by homeless people. Since the 1990s, however, it has become the anchor of an attractive and growing museum district. The Ogden Museum of Southern Art opens on to the circle and the National WWII Museum is just a block away. Meanwhile, these additions have boosted the regeneration of existing museums nearby, such as the New Orleans Contemporary Arts Center and the Confederate Memorial Hall.

The statue of Robert E. Lee is one of three prominent tributes to Confederate leaders in New Orleans, the others being of Jefferson Davis and Gen. P.G.T. Beauregard, located in separate parts of Mid-City. However, the city was not an especially staunch rebel stronghold. It was evenly split over the secession issue, and it fell early in the Civil War due to poor defenses and an unwillingness to see the city burned down.

Ogden Museum of Southern Art ⓯

Camp St at Howard Ave. **Map** 4 B5. **Tel** 539-9600. 🚌 *11.* 🚋 *St. Charles.* ◷ *10am–5pm Wed–Mon (to 8pm Thu).* 📷 📎 ♿ **www.**ogdenmuseum.org

Opened in 2003, this museum is named for Roger H. Ogden, a philanthropist who donated the core collection of some 1,200 works by more than 400 Southern artists. The museum displays its artworks in a two-building complex connected by a corridor gallery. The Romanesque-style Howard Memorial Library was designed by native-born Henry Hobson Richardson in 1888. This architectural masterpiece, with its splendid wood-paneled rotunda, is incorporated into the very contemporary Goldring Hall. These two structures are designed to wrap around the Confederate Memorial Hall, so that the complex fronts both Camp Street and Lee Circle.

The museum contains works from the 18th to the 21st century, and portrays the diversity of urban and rural life in the South from the Depression to the modern day. The collection includes works by William Henry Buck, Clarence Millet, John McCrady, George Dureau, Robert Gordy, Clementine Hunter, and Ida Kohlmeyer.

On Thursdays, the Ogden After Hours features live music, refreshments, and special exhibits.

Confederate Memorial Hall ⓰

929 Camp St at Howard Ave. **Map** 4 B5. **Tel** 523-4522. 🚌 *11, 41.* 🚋 *St. Charles.* ◷ *10am–4pm Tue–Sat.* ● *major holidays.* 📷 📎 **www.**confederatemuseum.com

One of the oldest museums in the city, Confederate Memorial Hall offers a moving experience. The memorabilia on display tell the often tragic, personal stories of the many young men who fought in the Civil War. Some were teenagers, like Landon Creek, who had fought in seven battles and was wounded three times by the age of 15.

The Howard Memorial Library, now part of the Ogden Museum

Several display cases contain objects relating to the occupation of the city by General "Beast" Butler *(see p18)*, including the document ordering that all women who insulted Union officers, wore Confederate colors, or sang Southern songs, were to be locked up as if they were common prostitutes.

The museum also possesses a large collection associated with the Confederate president Jefferson Davis, from his cradle to his military boots. Several interesting exhibits are devoted to the black regiments, which served on both sides during the Civil War. The cypress hall of the museum was originally constructed in 1891 as a meeting place for Confederate veterans to reflect on their Civil War experiences and to house and protect their relics.

Replica of one of the Higgins boats in The National WWII Museum

Modern art bench, at the Contemporary Arts Center

New Orleans Contemporary Arts Center ⑰

900 Camp St. **Map** 4 C5. **Tel** 528-3805. 🚌 11. 🚃 St. Charles. 🕐 11am–4pm Thu–Sun. 🌑 public hols. 📷 📷 ♿ **www**.cacno.org

This warehouse-style center is the city's premier space for all of the contemporary arts, from dance, painting, film, and video, to performance art, theater, and music. The museum combines the original structure with modern designs to its full advantage, presenting a unique, modern space mostly illuminated with natural light that houses four galleries and two theaters. The rotating shows in the galleries usually remain for four to eight weeks. The café provides free Internet access.

Louisiana Children's Museum ⑱

420 Julia St. **Map** 4 C5. **Tel** 523-1357. 🚌 10, 11. 🚃 St. Charles. 🕐 9:30am–4:30pm Tue–Sat, noon–4:30pm Sun. 🌑 public hols. 📷 📷 ♿ 📷 **www**.lcm.org

This activity-oriented museum allows children to entertain themselves with a variety of role-playing games, plus other interactive exhibits with a didactic focus. Kids can anchor their own news show in the TV studio, go shopping in the supermarket, or pilot their own tugboat, and there is an area designed specifically for one- to three-year-olds. One of the museum's newest exhibits is a child-sized replica of the Port of New Orleans.

The Louisiana Children's Museum, playground for children of all ages

The National WWII Museum ⑲

945 Magazine St and Howard Ave. **Map** 4 C5. **Tel** 528-1944. 🚌 11, 41. 🕐 9am–5pm daily. 🌑 Thanksgiving, Dec 24 and 25, Mardi Gras. 📷 📷 ♿ **www**.nationalww2 museum.org

This museum honors the veterans of World War II and celebrates New Orleans shipbuilder Andrew Higgins, who played a major role in many events, including D-Day in June 1944 *(see p22)*. More than 20,000 of Higgins's crafts were deployed in US landings on all fronts during the war, from North Africa to the Pacific Islands. The museum is in the middle of a $300-million expansion that will quadruple its original size by 2015. Its state-of-the-art Solomon Victory Theater, opened in 2009 as part of this expansion, uses a 120-ft (36-m) screen, moving props, and rattling seats to immerse viewers in the war experience. In the Restoration Pavilion, visitors can watch as staff refurbish a range of World War II artifacts that will join the museum's growing collection of planes, tanks, and boats. Future halls will focus on each branch of the US military service.

Loyola University

SIGHTS AT A GLANCE

Historic Buildings
Brevard-Wisdom-Rice House ⓭
Briggs-Staub House ❹
Carroll-Crawford House ❼
Claiborne Cottage ❸
Colonel Short's Villa ⓫
Louise S. McGehee School ❻
Musson-Bell House ⓬
Payne-Strachan House ⓮
Robinson House ❺
Toby's Corner ❾
Women's Guild Opera
    House ❿

Museums and Galleries
Amistad Research Center ⓱
Mardi Gras World ❽
Newcomb Art Gallery ⓲

Cemeteries
Lafayette Cemetery ❷

Universities
Loyola University ⓯
Tulane University ⓰

Entertainment
Audubon Park ⓳
Audubon Zoo pp112–13 ⓴
Riverbend ㉑

Landmarks
St. Charles Avenue Streetcar
    pp104–5 ❶

GARDEN DISTRICT AND UPTOWN

In 1832 a residential quarter was established uptown on the former Livaudais Plantation. The land was subdivided and developed to create the city of Lafayette, which was incorporated into New Orleans in 1852. Here, between Jackson and Louisiana Avenues, and St. Charles Avenue and Magazine Street, wealthy merchants, planters, and bankers built mansions in a variety of styles, ranging from Greek Revival to Italianate and

Stone sculpture at Tulane University

Queen Anne. The area became known as the Garden District because of the lush gardens that were laid out around the mansions. Settlement continued across Uptown as New Orleans annexed Jefferson City and Carrollton. Fears were high that these architecturally and historically significant neighborhoods would be damaged in the aftermath of Hurricane Katrina, but they were spared by the waters and remain as beautiful as ever.

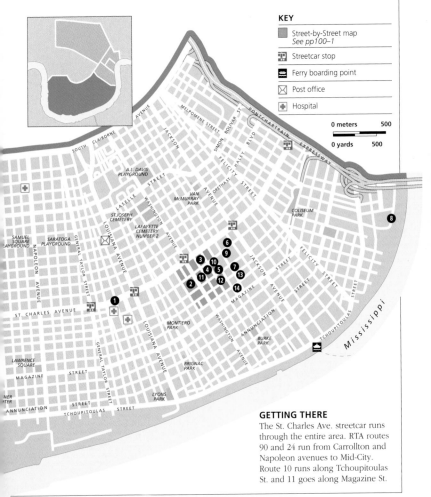

KEY

- ▬ Street-by-Street map
  See pp100–1
- 🚋 Streetcar stop
- ⛴ Ferry boarding point
- ⊠ Post office
- ✚ Hospital

0 meters 500
0 yards 500

GETTING THERE

The St. Charles Ave. streetcar runs through the entire area. RTA routes 90 and 24 run from Carrollton and Napoleon avenues to Mid-City. Route 10 runs along Tchoupitoulas St. and 11 goes along Magazine St.

Street-by-Street: Garden District

When the Americans arrived in New Orleans, they
settled upriver from the French Quarter. The plantations
that lined St. Charles Avenue in the 1820s were subdivided and the city of Lafayette established. It was
incorporated into the city of New Orleans in 1852.
Today, this area is referred to as the Garden District,
a residential neighborhood filled with grand Victorian
mansions built by wealthy city merchants and
planters. The gardens, planted with magnolia,
camellia, sweet olive, jasmine, and azalea, are
as stunning as the residences themselves.

LOCATOR MAP
See Street Finder maps 6 and 7

★ Lafayette Cemetery
*Confederate General Harry T.
Hays and Samuel Jarvis Peters,
a wealthy 19th-century developer
of the Garden District, are buried
in this cemetery, which often
appears in Anne Rice's books* **2**

Commander's Palace
*Excellent Creole food is the
specialty of this landmark
restaurant, one of the best
in the US (see p182).*

KEY

- - - Suggested route

★ Colonel Short's Villa
*Built in 1859 for Colonel Robert Short of
Kentucky and designed by Henry Howard,
the house has an exquisite morning glory
and cornstalk fence (see p39)* **11**

Briggs-Staub House
This handsome Gothic Revival mansion was designed by James Gallier, Sr. in 1849 4

Claiborne Cottage
This cottage was built in 1857 for the daughter of the first American governor of Louisiana. It has served as a school and a convent 3

Women's Guild Opera House
This Greek Revival mansion was designed in 1858 by William Freret 10

0 meters   40

0 yards   40

ST CHARLES AVENUE

STREET

3RD STREET

★ **Robinson House**
One of the grandest residences in the Garden District, Robinson House was built between 1859 and 1865 for Virginia tobacco merchant Walter Robinson 5

Musson-Bell House
This was the home of Michel Musson, uncle of artist Edgar Degas; an iron merchant added the lacy galleries later 12

STAR SIGHTS

★ Colonel Short's Villa

★ Lafayette Cemetery

★ Robinson House

St. Charles Avenue Streetcar ❶

See pp104–5.

Lafayette Cemetery ❷

1400 block of Washington Ave. **Map** 7 F3. 🚋 *St. Charles.* 🚌 *11, 14.* 🕐 *7am–2:30pm Mon–Fri, 7am–noon Sat.* ⬤ *public hols.* 📷 www.lafayettecemetery.org

This walled cemetery was laid out in 1833 by Benjamin Buisson to accommodate the residents of the adjacent Garden District. The second Protestant cemetery to open in New Orleans, it is the resting place of many German and British Protestants, as well as numerous Americans who had migrated here from the east coast. By 1840 it was full, mostly with yellow fever victims, and a new cemetery was needed.

Among the notables buried here are Confederate general Harry T. Hays and Samuel Jarvis Peters (1801–85), an influential city politician and land developer. A Canadian,

Peters arrived in New Orleans and ascended to a powerful position by the time he was 30. He was one of the movers and shakers who developed the area above Canal Street, fashioning it into a Second Munici- pality comparable to the downtown Creole community below Canal Street. It had its own fashionable hotel, the St. Charles, which was equal to the St. Louis and mirrored its Creole counterpart in other ways.

One of the most striking memorials in this cemetery is the one built in 1852 to commemorate the Jefferson Fire Company #22. It is embellished with a typical pumper. In her book *Interview with the Vampire* Anne Rice often gives Lestat and Claudia free rein to wander around this cemetery. The author herself staged a mock burial here in 1995 to promote her book, *Memnoch the Devil*.

The wall vaults were added to the cemetery in 1858.

Angel statue at Lafayette

Greek columns, Claiborne Cottage

Claiborne Cottage ❸

2524 St. Charles Ave. **Map** 7 F3. 🚋 *St. Charles.* 🚌 *11, 14.* ⬤ *to the public.*

The history of this Greek Revival-style cottage is disputed, but the plaque in front states that it was built in 1857 for Louise Claiborne, the daughter of the first governor of Louisiana. She was married to Mandeville Marigny, the youngest son of Bernard de Marigny *(see p82)*, who introduced dice to the United States. His gambling friends thought he resembled a frog, and so he was nicknamed "Le Crapaud," after which the game "craps" takes its name.

Some experts date the house to 1860 and claim that it was built for a Virginian, James Dameron.

Briggs-Staub House ❹

2605 Prytania St. **Map** 7 F3. 🚋 *St. Charles.* 🚌 *11, 14.* ⬤ *to the public.*

A rarity in New Orleans, this Gothic Revival home was built for gambler Cuthbert Bullitt in 1849. The Gothic style is uncommon in this part of the city, because

Above-ground vaults at Lafayette Cemetery

Gothic arched windows, Briggs-Staub House

many Protestant Americans claimed it reminded them of Roman Catholic France. After James Gallier, Sr. had designed the building, Bullitt refused to pay for it, perhaps because of a gambling loss, and the house subsequently became the property of Charles Briggs, an English insurance executive.

The second-floor galleries at Robinson House

Robinson House ❺

1415 3rd St. **Map** 8 A3. 🚋 *St. Charles.* 🚌 *11, 14.* 🚫 *to the public.*

One of the grandest and largest residences in the Garden District, this house was built for the Virginia tobacco merchant, Walter Robinson. Designed by Henry Howard, it was built between 1859 and 1865. The galleries of this Italian-style villa are supported with Doric columns on the first floor and Corinthian on the second. Domenico Canova, a famous European craftsman, was hired to decorate the interior, which boasts elaborate

painted ceilings. It was one of the first buildings in the city to have indoor plumbing. An unusual feature of this mansion is the curved portico.

Louise S. McGehee School ❻

2343 Prytania St. **Map** 8 A3. 🚋 *St. Charles.* 🚌 *11, 14.* 🚫 *to the public.*

James Freret designed this elaborate French Second Empire home in 1872 for sugar planter Bradish Johnson, for $100,000. Freret had recently returned from Paris and was enamored of the École des Beaux-Arts, which is evident in this mansion's Renaissance Revival style. When it was built, the house incorporated all of the fashionable interior design elements and conveniences

of the day: a conservatory, a marble pantry, a passenger elevator, and a magnificent circular staircase. It is one of the few houses in the city to have a basement.

Since 1929 it has served as a private school for girls. The cafeteria was once a stable, and the gym is a refurbished carriage house. Note the steep mansard roof with its wrought-iron parapet and the unique bull's-eye window on the façade. The gardens contain some magnificent magnolias and ginger trees.

Carroll-Crawford House ❼

1315 First St. **Map** 8 A3. 🚋 *St. Charles.* 🚌 *11, 14.* 🚫 *to the public.*

This broadly proportioned house was designed by Samuel Jamison in 1869 for Joseph Carroll, a cotton merchant from Virginia. The surrounding gardens include venerable live oaks and other lush plantings. A two-story home with octagonal wings, the house is Italianate in design with fine cast-iron galleries, made in New Orleans by Jacob Baumiller.

The original carriage house can still be seen around the corner on Chestnut Street. Jamison also constructed an identical building at 1331 First Street for cordage dealer Joseph C. Morris.

The ornate façade of the Carroll-Crawford House

St. Charles Avenue Streetcar ❶

For a slow-moving romance, take a ride on the St. Charles Avenue streetcar, which passes many of New Orleans' most famous landmarks. It was this type of streetcar that inspired Tennessee Williams's drama *A Streetcar Named Desire*. It travels 6.5 miles (10 km) from Canal Street through the Central Business District, along tree-shaded St. Charles Avenue to Carrollton Avenue. It began operating in 1835 under steam power; in 1867 mule power took over, then, in 1893, it was electrified. Due to electrical damage sustained during Hurricane Katrina, the St. Charles Avenue streetcar was out of commission for more than two years. The return of its familiar green cars was greeted with delight by New Orleanians during the holiday season of 2007.

Statue of John McDonogh, Lafayette Square

A metal pole conducts power from an overhead cable.

ST. CHARLES · 06 · 922

Claiborne Cottage
This classic raised cottage was built in 1857 for the daughter of the first American Louisiana governor (see p102).

Touro Synagogue
This building is named after Judah Touro, who came to New Orleans from Newport, Rhode Island, and donated the money for its construction.

Lee Circle
This 60-ft (18-m)- tall Doric column supports a statue of General Robert E. Lee, looking north (see p96).

Christ Church
This bulding is one of the few examples of Gothic Revival style in the city.

ST. CHARLES AVENUE SIGHTS

Christ Church ④
Claiborne Cottage ③
Lafayette Square ①
Lee Circle ②
St. Charles House ⑦
The Columns ⑤
The Latter Public
 Library ⑧
Touro
 Synagogue ⑥

0 kilometers 2

0 miles 1

KEY

🚋 Streetcar stops

– – Streetcar route

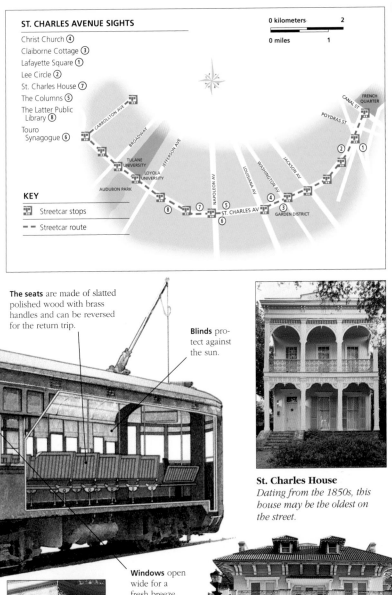

The seats are made of slatted
polished wood with brass
handles and can be reversed
for the return trip.

Blinds pro-
tect against
the sun.

Windows open
wide for a
fresh breeze.

St. Charles House
*Dating from the 1850s, this
house may be the oldest on
the street.*

The Columns
*Built for a
wealthy cigar
manufacturer, this
imposing building
was used by
director Louis
Malle as one of the
sets for his movie*
Pretty Baby *(1978).*

The Latter Public Library
*One of the most elegant library buildings,
the Latter Public Library started life in 1907
as a private mansion and was donated to
the city in the 1940s.*

One of the impressive floats at Mardi Gras World

Mardi Gras World ❽

1380 Port of New Orleans Place. **Map** 8 C3. **Tel** 361-7821. 🚋 *Riverfront.* ⏱ *9:30am–4:30pm daily.* 📷 🎫 🚻 **www**.mardigrasworld.com

Blaine Kern is often called "Mr. Mardi Gras" because so many of the massive floats that roll through the streets during Carnival *(see pp28–9)* are constructed here in the 20 warehouse-dens of his company.

A tour of Mardi Gras World begins with a short film showing the floats in the parades and the stages of their production, from the original drawings to the manufacture of the final pieces. Visitors are then free to don some of the costumes that krewe members have worn in past parades. Many of these are very heavy and ornate. Visitors can also wander through the warehouses and view gigantic decorative figures, made of either fiberglass or Styrofoam overlaid with papier-mâché. It is also possible to climb on to the floats to get an idea of what it is like to ride them. The cost of the floats is borne by the krewes themselves, with contributions from their members.

Toby's Corner ❾

2340 Prytania St. **Map** 8 A3. 🚋 *St. Charles.* 🚌 *11, 14, 27.* ⭘ *to the public.*

Built around 1838, this house was constructed for Thomas Toby and is believed to be the oldest residence in the Garden District. Toby was a native Philadelphian, who moved to New Orleans and became a very successful wheelwright. He amassed a huge fortune but lost it financing Sam Houston and the cause for Texas independence from Mexico. It was, in fact, his wife who paid for the construction of the house. Subsequently, Toby worked as a plantation manager until he died.

After the Civil War *(see pp18–19)* the house was foreclosed and sold at auction for $5,000. Nowadays, it is privately owned and closed to the public. However, its façade is an impressive example of the Greek Revival style.

Women's Guild Opera House ❿

2504 Prytania St. **Map** 8 A3. **Tel** 899-1945. 🚋 *St. Charles.* 🚌 *11, 14, 27.* ⭘ *for tours by appointment only.* 📷 🎫

William Freret designed the original Greek Revival section of this house in 1858 for a wealthy merchant. In 1996 the house was bequeathed to the Women's Guild of the New Orleans Opera Association, and it is now used for meetings and receptions. It also features some exhibits relating to the history of opera in the city; in the 19th century New Orleans was a major opera center, although the original opera house burned down in 1919.

It is open to the public for guided tours for 20 or more people with reservations.

Colonel Short's Villa ⓫

1448 Fourth St. **Map** 7 F3. 🚋 *St. Charles.* 🚌 *11, 14, 27.* ⭘ *to the public.*

Henry Howard designed this large Italian-style residence in 1859 for native Kentuckian Colonel Robert Short. The veranda, with fine iron railings, extends around three sides of the house. An exquisite

The Women's Guild Opera House, combining an octagonal tower and a Greek Revival main house

Colonel Short's Villa, with its remarkable cornstalk fence

ironwork fence, incorporating a morning glory and cornstalk motif, encloses the gardens (see pp38–9). The story goes that the Colonel had it installed to please his wife. Unlike a similar fence on Royal Street in the French Quarter (see p77), famous for its detailed ironwork, this one has not been painted and shows its original colors. In September 1863, the Union troops seized the residence. It was returned to the family after the Civil War (see pp18–19). Although closed to the public, the famous cornstalk fence is much visited.

Musson-Bell House ⑫

1331 Third St. **Map** 8 A4.
🚋 St. Charles. 🚌 11, 14, 27.
⬤ to the public.

When this handsome Italianate villa was built in 1853 for Michel Musson (1812–85), he was a successful cotton merchant and prominent Creole, and was also the New Orleans postmaster (see p126). Musson had close ties with his extended family, including his sister Celestine Musson Degas, who lived in France. Celestine's son, Edgar Degas, was to become one of the world's great artists.

After the Civil War Degas came to visit Louisiana but it is unlikely he ever saw this house. The war had dealt Musson's fortunes a severe

blow and he sold the house in 1869, moving his family to a rented home on Esplanade Avenue (see p126).

Brevard-Wisdom-Rice House ⑬

1239 First St. **Map** 8 A3.
🚋 St. Charles. 🚌 11, 14, 27.
⬤ to the public.

Fans of the Gothic author Anne Rice stop to gawk at the Brevard-Wisdom-Rice House, where she lived from 1989 to 2003. The house was designed by James Calrow for merchant Albert Hamilton Brevard in 1857 and cost $13,000, at the time a formidable sum. It is adorned with ornate ironwork, including a fence incorporating a charming rose motif, for which reason the house is referred to as "Rosegate." Ionic and Corinthian columns support the galleries. The second owners of the property, the Clapp family, added the hexagonal wing in 1869. The gardens are splendid and feature some stunning camellias.

Anne Rice, who was

born in New Orleans and grew up in the Irish Channel, has portrayed the city in many of her best selling *Vampire Chronicles,* which began with the *Interview with the Vampire,* published in 1976. She and her husband, poet-scholar Stan Rice, returned to New Orleans from San Francisco in 1988. Rice used this house as the setting for her book *The Witching Hour* (1990). Rice spent her teenage years at 2524 St. Charles Avenue, which inspired much of her novel *Violin.* The author has restored several historic buildings. After Stan died in 2003, Anne began to sell her New Orleans properties.

Payne-Strachan House ⑭

1134 First St. **Map** 8 A4.
🚋 St. Charles. 🚌 11, 14, 27.
⬤ to the public.

This grand home was built in the 1850s by Judge Jacob U. Payne, who brought slaves from his plantation in Kentucky and had them construct it. The two-story Greek Revival residence features Ionic columns on the first gallery and Corinthian on the second. The house passed to Payne's son-in-law, Charles Erasmus Fenner, a close friend of Jefferson Davis, United States senator and president of the Confederacy (see pp96–7). Davis died here on December 6, 1889, in the first-floor guest room.

Musson-Bell House, in the Italianate style

A side window of Loyola University's chapel

Loyola University ⓯

6363 St. Charles Ave. **Tel** 865-3240. **Map** 6 B3. St. Charles. 15, 22. 9am–7pm daily.

The Jesuit Order established the College of the Immaculate Conception downtown in 1840. It merged with Loyola College in 1912, and together they became Loyola University. The Tudor-Gothic buildings house the largest Catholic university in the South. The three buildings facing St. Charles Avenue are Marquette Hall, the adjacent Thomas Hall, and the Most Holy Name

of Jesus Roman Catholic Church, the design of which was inspired by Canterbury Cathedral in the UK.

The statue of Jesus with uplifted arms in front of Marquette is referred to locally as "Touchdown Jesus," for obvious reasons.

Tulane University ⓰

6823 St. Charles Ave. **Map** 6 B2. **Tel** 865-5000. St. Charles. 15, 22. 9am–5pm daily.

Founded in 1834 as a medical college, the precursor of Tulane University was given its present name in 1882 after it received a substantial gift from Paul Tulane, a native of Princeton, New Jersey. He made a fortune from a merchandising business, which he launched in New Orleans in 1822. Tulane's School of Business is the oldest college of commerce in the country.

The University moved to its current location in 1894. The 110-acre campus has 79 buildings, designed in a variety of styles. The Howard Tilton Memorial Library houses the Hogan Jazz Archive, plus other special collections. About 12,000 students attend the university.

Amistad Research Center ⓱

Tilton Hall, Tulane University. **Map** 6 B3. **Tel** 862-3222. St. Charles. 15, 22. 8:30am–4:30pm Mon–Fri.

This research center is named for the famous slave mutiny aboard the Cuban slave ship *Amistad* in 1839. After a trial in Hartford, Connecticut, the slaves were acquitted and allowed to return home. The American Missionary Association, an organization formed to defend the slaves, established the center's archive, which moved to New Orleans in 1969. It consists of documents, photos, pamphlets, and oral history records. A small gallery shows the works of artists including such names as Henry O. Tanner and Elizabeth Catlett.

Newcomb Art Gallery ⓲

Tulane University. **Map** 6 B2. **Tel** 865-5328. St. Charles. 15, 22. 10am–5pm Tue–Fri, 11am–4pm Sat & Sun. public hols and summer months.

In 1886 Josephine Le Monnier Newcomb founded a women's college that was allied with Tulane University. Initially she

Stately Tulane University's Gibson Hall, built in Richardson-Romanesque style

For hotels and restaurants in this region see pp166–7 and pp180–82

Taking a rest on a hot day in Audubon Park

donated $100,000 in memory of her daughter Harriot Sophie Newcomb, who died at the age of 15 in 1870. When Josephine herself died, she left an additional estate of more than $2.5 million to the college.

The Woldenberg Art Center houses the Newcomb Art Gallery and a smaller space to display student and faculty works. The Newcomb Gallery focuses on presenting traveling shows and also curates its own exhibitions.

The name of Newcomb is more familiarly associated with the arts-and-crafts style of pottery that was made at the Newcomb College of Art from 1895 to 1940. The gallery has some typical pieces on display.

Audubon Park ⑲

6500 Magazine St. **Map** 6 B3.
St. Charles. 11, 22.
www.auduboninstitute.org

This park was carved out of the plantations owned by the Foucher and Boré families in 1871. The 1884 World's Industrial and Cotton Exposition was held here. New Orleans was still recovering from the double devastations of the Civil War and Reconstruction (see pp18–19), and the exposition helped boost the city's morale. The main building

alone covered almost four times the surface of the Superdome (see p95). The first streetcar was introduced at the Expo, and it so entranced Thomas Lipton of tea company fame that he became a motorman. The Mardi Gras Krewe of Rex (see pp28–9) arrived at the Expo aboard a yacht, establishing a tradition that survives to this day. Inside the park there is a fine executive golf course, several ponds, recreation areas, sport facilities, and the Audubon Zoo, which occupies 58 acres of the grounds. The park was named for naturalist John James Audubon, whose statue stands in its grounds. Audubon, the artist of *Birds of America*, was born in the West Indies. He came to New Orleans and rented his first studio in 1821 at 706

Bronze statue in Audubon Park

Barracks Street. He stayed only four months before taking off for another brief sojourn as tutor to a young girl at Oakley Plantation in West Feliciana Parish (see p151). Here, in this rich ornithological environment, he began many of his bird portraits, but he stayed only a short time because of a dispute with his employer. He returned to New Orleans and took up residence at a studio at 505 Dauphine Street.

Audubon Zoo ⑳

See pp112–13.

Riverbend ㉑

Riverfront of St. Charles Ave.
Map 6 A1. St. Charles. 34.

With more than 300 billion gallons of water flowing by the city each day, New Orleans lives under the constant threat of flood. A system of spillways, pumps, and levees, like this one along the St. Charles Avenue Riverfront, forms a line of defense against the Mississippi. Still, certain sections of the city are prone to flooding, particularly after heavy rains. The pumping system was installed soon after 1927 when the city was so threatened that the authorities cut the levee below the city in St. Bernard Parish to forestall urban flooding. This part of the levee has been adapted as a recreation area, where visitors can enjoy a beautiful view of the river.

Riverbend, a popular place for outdoor recreation

Audubon Zoo ⑳

Elephant giving a show

This appealing 58-acre zoo, landscaped with fountains and water gardens, can be toured easily in a few hours. It opened in 1938 but was completely redesigned in the 1980s; today most of the animals are living in open paddocks that replicate their natural habitats. Only a few of the 1930s buildings remain. The swamp exhibit is one of the most engaging, showcasing Louisiana white alligators, as well as Acadian culture and music. The world-class zoo is part of Audubon Park (see p111), one of the loveliest urban parks in the country. Originally, the 340-acre park was the sugar plantation of Jean Etienne Boré, who developed the commercially successful sugar granulation process. It was also the location of the 1884 World Exposition.

★ **Louisiana Swamp**
Alligators bask along the banks or float like logs in the muddy lagoon.

Primates, such as orangutans and gorillas, play here.

The African Savannah
Rhinos, hippos, zebras, African wild dogs, and white pelicans all live together with a host of opportunistic visitors such as ibis, heron, and egrets.

Tropical Bird House

Sea Lions
The sea lion pool is one of the oldest features of the zoo. Feeding time draws the crowds.

Reptile Encounter
King cobras, rattlesnakes, many amphibians, and the impressive Komodo dragon hold court here.

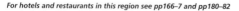

★ Jaguar Jungle
Sloths, spider monkeys, and anteaters cohabit with jaguars in this exhibit, which is built around a replica of Mayan ruins set in a super-lush jungle.

VISITORS' CHECKLIST

6500 Magazine St. **Map** 6 B3.
Tel 581-4629. 🚌 11. 🚋 St.
Charles. ⬜ 10am–4pm Tue–Sun
(to 5pm Sat, Sun). ⬤ first Friday
in May, Thanksgiving, Dec 24–25,
Mardi Gras. 🖼 ♿ 📷 🍴

Flamingos
A peaceful lake is home to dozens of beautiful flamingos.

Cool Zoo
This animal-themed splash park is especially popular with young visitors.

Main entrance

St. Charles Streetcar free shuttle stop

Elephant Plaza
An elephant show is presented in front of the plaza, while children are able to enjoy the unique experience of touching one.

STAR FEATURES

★ Jaguar Jungle

★ Louisiana Swamp

Evocative statue at the New Orleans Botanical Garden

SIGHTS AT A GLANCE

Museums & Galleries
Degas House ❿
Longue Vue House and
    Gardens ⓭
New Orleans Museum of Art
    pp120–23 ❶
Pitot House ❼
Storyland and Carousel
    Gardens ❸

Parks and Gardens
Bayou St. John ❻
Dueling Oaks ❷
New Orleans
    Botanical Garden ❹

Cemeteries
Cypress Grove
    Cemetery ⓫
Metairie Cemetery ⓬
St. Louis Cemetery
    #3 ❽

Entertainment
Fair Grounds ❾
Sports Facilities
    in City Park ❺

KEY

▨ Street-by-Street map
  See pp116–17

🚉 Streetcar stop

⊠ Post office

✝ Church

GETTING THERE
Routes 22, 46, 48, 54, 90.
The Canal Streetcar runs from
the Mississippi River to City
Park Ave. A spur line goes to
City Park itself.

Rose garden entrance, Botanical Garden

MID-CITY

Extending from the French Quarter toward Lake Pontchartrain, Mid-City is the greenest part of New Orleans, with the largest swath of land taken up by City Park. This is carved out of an old plantation that was donated to the city in 1850 by bank director John McDonogh on the provision that the funds from its sale be used for public schools. The city bent the rules a little and created a park instead. The other green areas in Mid-City are given over to various cemeteries such as Greenwood, Metairie, St. Louis

Angel statue in Greenwood cemetery

Cemetery #3, and Cypress Grove. The major streets in the area are Canal Street and Esplanade Avenue. Canal connects downtown with the cemeteries, while Esplanade is lined with Creole mansions. Mid-City suffered from flooding in the aftermath of Hurricane Katrina. While portions of it are above sea level, other areas were under water for weeks. Tremendous strides have been made toward reconstruction, and today the bright-red Canal streetcar rumbles through this charming area once again.

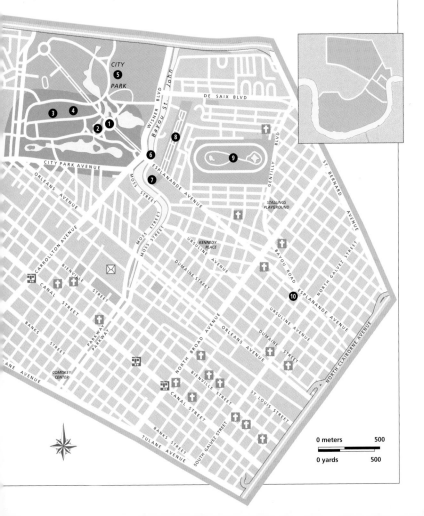

Street-by-Street: City Park

Sculpture at NOMA

This 1,300-acre park is among the ten largest urban parks in the US. Hurricane Katrina caused damage to the grounds, trees, infrastructure, and facilities, but most of the park has now reopened and is thriving. Visitors flock to the spectacular Botanical Garden and the New Orleans Museum of Art, while kids love the carousel and Storyland, a theme park with rides and fairy tale exhibits. Eight miles of lagoons allow for fishing and boating. The park's Besthoff Sculpture Garden showcases 30 major 20th-century sculptures.

Storyland and Carousel
The wooden carousel is one of the main attractions in the amusement park ❸

The Goldring/ Woldenberg Great Lawn
This landscaped area hosts many concerts ❺

VICTORY AVENUE

Popp's Bandstand
Playgrounds surround this bandstand, named after lumber magnate John Popp.

DREYFOUS DRIVE

CITY PARK AVENUE

0 meters	100	**KEY**
0 yards	100	- - - Suggested route

The Peristyle
Situated by a pretty lagoon, the Peristyle has been a popular gathering spot for more than a century.

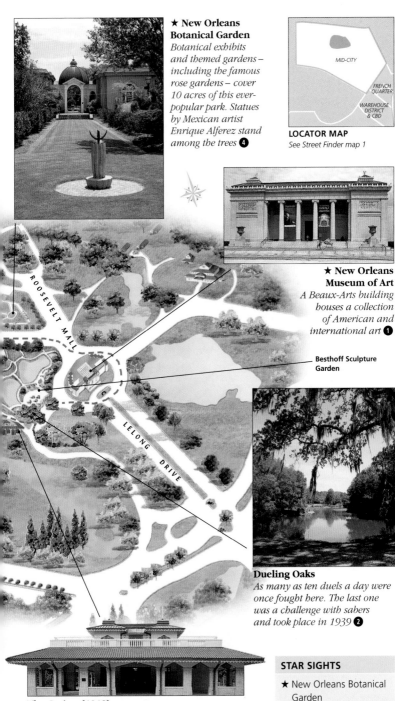

★ **New Orleans Botanical Garden**
Botanical exhibits and themed gardens – including the famous rose gardens – cover 10 acres of this ever-popular park. Statues by Mexican artist Enrique Alferez stand among the trees ❹

LOCATOR MAP
See Street Finder map 1

★ **New Orleans Museum of Art**
A Beaux-Arts building houses a collection of American and international art ❶

Besthoff Sculpture Garden

Dueling Oaks
As many as ten duels a day were once fought here. The last one was a challenge with sabers and took place in 1939 ❷

ROOSEVELT MALL

LELONG DRIVE

The Casino (1912)
This Mission Revival building houses a gift shop and food concessions. It is often used as a venue for weddings.

STAR SIGHTS

★ New Orleans Botanical Garden

★ New Orleans Museum of Art

The Flute Player, by Enrique Alferez, at the Botanical Garden

New Orleans Museum of Art ❶

See pp120–23.

Dueling Oaks ❷

City Park. **Map** 2 A1. 🚌 46, 48, 90. 🚋 Canal. ♿

Behind the famous statue of Confederate General P. G. T. Beauregard *(see p71)*, which guards the entrance to City Park, Lelong Avenue approaches the New Orleans Museum of Art. To the left is a grand, solitary oak, still commonly called the Dueling Oaks although there is now only one.

Many duels were fought in New Orleans, and most of these took place in the bosky acres of what has since become City Park. Under the massive branches of live oaks, as many as ten duels a day were fought. Reports indicate that one particular dueler called for the use of whaling harpoons, after which the offended party decided he wasn't so offended after all. The last duel was fought in 1939 between two students from a local fencing academy. The owner of the original plantation from which City Park was carved, Louis Allard, is rumored to be buried at the foot of the oaks.

Storyland and Carousel Gardens ❸

City Park. **Map** 2 A1. **Tel** 482-4888. 🚌 46, 48, 90. 🚋 Canal. ◯ 10am–4pm Tue–Fri, 11am–6pm Sat & Sun. ● Dec 25. 📷 ♿ www.neworleanscitypark.com

Storyland, a beguiling theme park for children, is filled with all kinds of entertainments derived from traditional folk tales and well-known nursery rhymes. Kids can enjoy Jack and Jill's slide, climb around Miss Muffet's spider web, or challenge Captain Hook to a duel. Along the way, they may also encounter fairytale characters such as Jack (of the Beanstalk), Puss in Boots, Rapunzel, and many others. There is also story reading, puppet shows in the Puppet Castle, and face painting.

The carousel, situated in the southwest corner of the gardens, was built in 1906 and is one of the few antique wooden carousels left in the US. Nearby, visitors can climb aboard a miniature train, which has run around the park since 1896. A large Ferris wheel offers a birds-eye view of the park.

New Orleans Botanical Garden ❹

Victory Ave, City Park. **Map** 2 A1. **Tel** 483-9386. 🚌 46, 48, 90. 🚋 Canal. ◯ 10am–4:30pm Tue–Sun. ● Jan 1, Dec 25, Mardi Gras. 📷 📷 ♿ www.neworleanscitypark.com

This 10-acre public garden was created in the 1930s. Back then, it was mainly a rose garden, but today there are also spring and perennial gardens featuring azaleas, camellias, and magnolias, as well as tropical plants and trees. Several statues by Mexican artist Enrique Alferez, including his *Women in Huipil* and *The Flute Player*, stand among live oaks.

The Garden Study Center and the Pavilion of the Two Sisters are reminiscent of European garden architecture. The Conservatory houses orchids and two major exhibits: Living Fossils, showcasing plants that grew on the earth before flowering plants, and the impressive Tropical Rainforest exhibit.

Much of the plant collection was lost as a result of Hurricane Katrina, but the gardens have now been completely rebuilt.

The carousel in City Park, one of the oldest enclosed carousels in the United States

For hotels and restaurants in this region see pp167–8 and pp183–4

Sports Facilities in City Park ❺

Map 2 A1 B1. *Riverfront*. **Tel** *482-4888*. 🚌 *46, 48, 90*. 🚋 *Canal*. **www**.neworleanscitypark.com

The majestic City Park contains many excellent sports facilities. The Wisner Tennis Center has 34 lighted courts, which can be reserved by phone 30 days ahead of time. The City Park Practice Center has a 74-tee lighted driving range. Its 18-hole North Course has been rebuilt since Hurricane Katrina and has water features on eight holes.

The park's 8 miles (13 km) of lagoons provide ample opportunities for boating, and for fishing for bass and trout. Egrets, heron, and the occasional alligator also inhabit the lagoons. Fishing permits can be obtained at the Administrative Center. There is also a stable, offering riding lessons and trail rides.

Bayou St. John ❻

Map 2 B1. 🚌 *46, 48, 90*. 🚋 *Canal*.

The French recognized this bayou as a key strategic asset, providing access to the Gulf of Mexico via Lake Pontchartrain.

The Wisner Tennis Center, City Park

As New Orleans grew, so did plantations along the bayou and a canal was dug, linking it to the downtown, ending in Basin Street at Congo Square. Today, the canal is filled in, but the name Basin Street survives.

In the 18th and 19th centuries the bayou was the scene of voodoo ceremonies. Marie Laveau *(see p83)* was the most infamous practitioner.

Pitot House ❼

1440 Moss St. **Map** 2 B2. **Tel** *482-0312*. 🚌 *46, 48, 90*. 🚋 *Canal*. ⬤ *10am–3pm Wed–Sat*. ⬤ *major hols*. 🚫 **www**.pitothouse.org

This classic West Indian-style raised house was built in 1799, on the banks of Bayou St. John. Once a working plantation, it was carefully moved in the 1960s a block upstream to this location. In 1810, the house was purchased by James Pitot, who had been the second mayor of the city five years earlier. He had arrived from Haiti in 1796 after the slave uprising led by Toussaint L'Ouverture. Pitot went on to direct a bank and run the New Orleans Navigation Company before being appointed to a judgeship.

In 1904, the house was bought by Mother Cabrini, who was later to become America's first saint, and converted into a convent. It is now a museum and contains the original antiques and furnishings from the house.

Bayou St. John, where plantations developed a unique way of life

New Orleans Museum of Art ●

Aztec maize goddess

Together, the New Orleans Museum of Art (NOMA) and the adjacent Sydney and Walda Besthoff Sculpture Garden comprise one the most important cultural destinations in the Gulf South. Housed in a classic Beaux-Arts building, NOMA's impressive collections include the Fabergé gallery; works by Picasso, Degas, Miró, Rodin, and Pollock; a 7,000-piece photography collection; and Asian, African, and American art. In a beautiful 5-acre site, the sculpture garden showcases pieces by world-renowned artists, such as Henry Moore and Barbara Hepworth.

Third floor

Japanese Suit of Armor
This 18th-century Domaru-style one-piece body armor manifests the moral and spiritual traditions of the Samurai warriors.

Stairs to third floor

Stairs to first floor

← To sculpture garden

★ **Portrait of a Young Woman** (1918)
This is one of Italian Expressionist Amadeo Modigliani's most famous paintings, and the oval face and elongated lines are typical of his style.

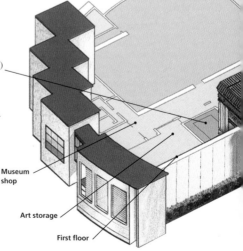

Museum shop

Art storage

First floor

STAR EXHIBITS

★ Portrait of a Young Woman

★ Reclining Mother and Child

★ Serpent about to Strike

Melanesian Ancestor Figure
This carved-wood figure from the Abelan peoples in Papua New Guinea is one of the finest representations of the religious art of Melanesia.

VISITORS' CHECKLIST

1 Collins Diboll Circle, City Park.
Map 2 A1. *Tel* (504) 658-4100.
46, 48. 10am–5pm Tue–Sun (to 9pm Fri). public hols.

Lousiana Indians Walking Along the Bayou (1847)
Alfred Boisseau portrayed the Choctaw Indians engaged in everyday activities.

Stairs to third floor

★ **Serpent about to Strike**
(1889–1908)
This Fabergé silver snake rests on a piece of Persian turquoise. It was created by Johan Aarne, one of the firm's talented work-masters, and is regarded by many as his masterpiece.

Second floor

GALLERY GUIDE
The main entrance leads to three European art collections. The second floor houses the American Art, the Fabergé, and three further European collections. The third floor offers African, Oceanic, and Native American exhibits.

KEY TO FLOOR PLAN

	African and Oceanic Art
	American Art
	Asian Art
	Contemporary Art
	Decorative Arts
	European Art
	Prehispanic/Native American Art
	Photography and Graphics
	Non-exhibition space

★ **Reclining Mother and Child** (1975)
A gift of the Sydney and Walda Besthoff Founda-tion, this Henry Moore sculpture depicts the bond between mother and child.

Main entrance

Stairs to second floor

Exploring the New Orleans Museum of Art

The major collections displayed in the museum's 46 galleries include a vast selection of European art, from 12th-century Italian Florentine to 20th-century French and Spanish works. There are specialized collections of Latin American and Prehispanic art; Native and modern American works; arts of Africa and Asia; photography; and decorative arts. The Sydney and Walda Besthoff Sculpture Garden displays an eclectic array of works in a landscaped park.

AFRICAN AND OCEANIC ART

This is one of the finest African art collections in the country.

Established in 1953, it now represents Sub-Saharan Africa's five major art-producing regions, including works by the Baman and Dogon peoples of Mali and the Benin, the Yoruba, the Ibo, and the Ekoi peoples of Nigeria, Cameroon, and the Ivory Coast.

Among the highlights is a rare palace veranda post carved in the shape of an equestrian warrior figure by Yoruba artist Olowe of Ise.

Yoruba mounted warrior

Another gem is a terra-cotta head from the Nok culture dating from around 500 BC– AD 200. *The Head of an Oba* (late 18th century) is a striking bronze funerary portrait, which might have been placed on an altar in the Benin royal palace to commemorate the deceased.

The Oceania gallery includes wooden figures from Papua New Guinea; nephrite (a hard green jade-like stone) weapons, tools, and ornaments from the Maoris; and a standing Malanggan figure, also from New Zealand.

AMERICAN ART

This collection includes some fine examples of early American artists such as John Singleton Copley, Gilbert Stuart, Charles Willson

Peale, Benjamin West, and John Singer Sargent. An entire gallery is devoted to a collection of Louisiana paintings, including *Louisiana Indians Walking Along the Bayou (see p121)* by Alfred Boisseau, *Back of Algiers* (1870–73) by Richard Clague, and *Blue Crab and Terrapins* (1880) by Achille Perelli. The *Portrait of Mme. René de Gas, née Estelle Musson*, painted in 1872–3 by Edgar Degas during a visit to New Orleans, is also displayed.

ASIAN ART

One of the finest collections of Edo (1600–1868) Japanese paintings can be seen in these galleries. All the major Japanese schools are represented, and it is particularly strong on the Nanga, Zenga, and Maruyama-Shijo schools. The collection also includes a wide variety of ceramics, lacquer, textiles, prints, photographs, and armor. The Chinese collection

Portrait of a Bijin (courtesan), Yamaguchi Soken (1800)

has ceramics from the Neolithic to the modern era. There are stone, wood, and bronze sculptures, plus miniatures, and religious art from India.

CONTEMPORARY ART

A great variety of sculpture, paintings, and mixed- media works, such as Joseph Cornell's intricate small-scale shadow boxes, are included in the Contemporary Art collection, which is divided into Contemporary European Art and the American Art exhibits. The European collection features works from such artists as Miró and Picasso. The American exhibit ranges from Georgia O' Keefe's *My Back Yard* (1937) and Hans Hofmann's *Abstraction with Chair and Miró* (1943), to Jackson Pollock's *Composition (White, Black, Blue, and Red on White)* (1948) and Roger Brown's *California Hillside* (1988).

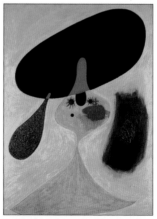

Portrait of a Young Girl, Joan Miró (1935)

DECORATIVE ARTS

The museum has a fabulous glass collection consisting of more than 6,000 items, including ancient glass and Tiffany vases. The pottery collection features a large group of pieces from New Orleans' own Newcomb Pottery. There is also a rare collection of "Old Paris" porcelain, plus examples of Sevres and Limoges. The silver collection contains some lustrous pieces by English silversmith Paul Storr.

EUROPEAN ART

The European collection spans a period of 600 years and features examples from the major national schools.

The Kress Collection, donated to the museum by the American philanthropist Samuel H. Kress, includes sublime Italian Old Master paintings from the early Renaissance to the 18th century.

Morning Glory Tiffany vase

French art is also well represented, with works from the 17th to the 20th centuries. The Hyams Gallery features lesser-known 19th-century Salon and Barbizon painters, in contrast with the more familiar Impressionist and Post-Impressionist painters

represented in the adjacent Forgotston Gallery.

Other highlights include gems such as Picasso's *Woman with Tambourine* (1938), Miró's *Lady Strolling on the Rambla in Barcelona* (1925), Degas' *Dancer in Green* (1878), Rodin's *The Age of Bronze* (1876), and works by other European masters.

PREHISPANIC/ NATIVE AMERICAN ART

These galleries display a strong collection of material from Mayan culture, including some impressive sculptures and ceramics. Artifacts from Central American cultures are also represented, such as Olmec and Mixtec, along with the later Aztec civilization.

The Native American collections include Kachina dolls from the Hopi and Zuni, pottery from the Acoma Santo Domingo and San Ildefonso pueblos, Apache and Pima baskets, and Percé beadwork and textiles from the northwest coast.

The museum also has a special collection of Latin American colonial art, much of it from Cuzco in Peru. It includes an early 18th-century portrait of an archangel with a musket.

Native American kachina dolls representing a family (1958)

PHOTOGRAPHY AND GRAPHICS

This collection of more than 7,000 vintage photographs is one of the finest of its kind in the Southeast. It includes works by all the known masters, such as William Henry Fox Talbot's *View of the Paris Boulevards* (1843), André Kertész's *Théâtre Odeon* (1926), Man Ray's *Portrait of Berenice Abbott in front of Man Ray Composition* (1922), and Diane Arbus's *A Young Brooklyn Family Going on a Sunday Outing* (1966). In his 1946 *Elegy for the Old South (No. 6)*, Clarence John Laughlin captures the nostalgia of the old South in surrealistic images of decay. His photographs of abandoned plantation homes and the South in the early 20th century are justly famous.

SCULPTURE GARDEN

The dynamic sculptures of Henry Moore, Barbara Hepworth, Louis Bourgeois, George Segal, and other renowned artists are displayed among the ancient oaks, magnolias, and tranquil lagoons of the Sydney and Walda Besthoff Sculpture Garden.

This five-acre site, adjacent to the museum building, was opened in 2003 to provide a beautiful natural space for more than 50 modern and contemporary sculptures. Visitors are free to wander around the park, or join one of the daily tours.

The Cardinal's Friendly Chat, Jehan Georges Vibert (1880)

Miniature train passing through the oaks at City Park ▷

Some of the city's most poignant tombs at St. Louis Cemetery #3

St. Louis Cemetery #3 ❽

3421 Esplanade Ave.
Map 2 B1. **Tel** 482-5065.
🚌 48, 90. 🕐 8am–4:30pm daily.
⚫ Mardi Gras.

This pristine cemetery, with its beautiful wrought-iron gates, opened in 1856. Among the notables buried here is Antoine Michoud, the original owner of a plantation which is now the site of the NASA plant where the Saturn rockets were built in the 1960s. There is also a memorial to architect James Gallier, Sr. (see p95) and his wife, who are buried in Metairie Cemetery. Both were killed when the steamer Evening Star sank en route from New York to New Orleans in October 1866.

Other famous figures here include Father Rouquette, missionary to the Choctaw, and black Creole philanthropist Thomy Lafon, owner of the old Orleans Ballroom,

where the famous "quadroon balls" were held. Lafon also sponsored an orphanage for African-American children.

Fair Grounds ❾

1751 Gentilly Blvd. **Map** 2 C1.
Tel 944-5515. 🚌 48. 🅿 ♿
www.fairgroundsracecourse.com

In the mid-1800s, New Orleans was a leading center for horse racing. The Creole Racecourse operated during the 19th century on what is now the Fair Grounds. When Metairie Racecourse closed, the Louisiana Jockey Club took over and purchased the Luling Mansion just off Esplanade as a clubhouse. The name change occurred when the Fair Grounds Corporation took over in 1940. Races are run here from November to March, and in April the Fair Grounds host the New Orleans Jazz Fest (see p41). The track also has a slot machine casino that is open year round.

Degas House ❿

2306 Esplanade Ave. **Map** 3 D3.
Tel 821-5009. 🚌 48.
🕐 by appointment only.
🅿 🅲 **www**.degashouse.com

Calling himself "almost a son of Louisiana," Impressionist painter Edgar Degas (1834–1917) visited his uncle, Michel Musson (see p107), at this house from October 1872

until March 1873. Degas was charmed with America and especially New Orleans. Several important paintings evolved from his sojourn here, despite the fact that he did not venture far from the house for fear of the intense New Orleans sun affecting his eyesight. The Cotton Buyer's Office (1873) shows his uncle with several members of his family, including the artist's own brothers René and Achille, who both worked in the cotton business.

The Esplanade house, which dates from 1854, has Greek Revival details and cast-iron balconies. The house is beautifully maintained throughout and offers bed and breakfast accommodations (see p167), as well as welcoming visitors during the day. Many reproductions of Degas' work are on display.

Cypress Grove Cemetery ⓫

120 City Park Ave. **Map** 1 C2.
Tel 482-3232. 🚌 40, 46.
🕐 8am–4:30pm daily. ♿

This cemetery, established by the Firemen's Charitable Association, was laid out in 1841. The impressive Egyptian-style gate leads into a graveyard filled with handsome memorials. Many of the tombs are dedicated to individual firefighters, such as Irad Ferry, who lost their lives in the line of duty. Ferry's tomb, which features a broken column, was designed by the famous architect J. N. B. de Pouilly (see p83).

The cemetery also contains a large number of rich Protestants, who were buried here after Girod Cemetery began to deteriorate. Many of the tombs have remarkable ironwork, like the weeping cupid gate which is crowned with lovebirds and set between inverted torches.

An extension to Cypress Grove was built right across the street to fulfil a need for

Marble statue at Cypress Grove

Period furniture in the dining room at Degas House

space after the yellow fever epidemic of 1853. Known as Greenwood Cemetery, it was the first in New Orleans to be built without a boundary wall. It is the site of the city's first Civil War Memorial.

Metairie Cemetery ⑫

5100 Pontchartrain Blvd. **Map** 1 B1.
Tel 486-6331. 🚌 40, 46.
🕐 8am–5pm daily. ♿

This is the most attractively landscaped cemetery in New Orleans, and the final resting place of many of its blue-bloods. In the 19th century, the city was the premier venue for horseracing, and the Metairie Racetrack was the most famous. After the Civil War, mismanagement afforded Charles T. Howard the opportunity to take revenge on the racetrack members who had refused him admission. He purchased it in 1872 and converted it into a cemetery. The oval racecourse became the cemetery's main drive.

Many magnificent tombs are located here, and near the entrance stands the massive 85-ft (26-m) high Moriarty monument, which required the laying of a special railroad to bring it into the cemetery. Daniel

Egan Family tomb, modeled after the ruins of an Irish chapel

Moriarty was an Irish immigrant and saloonkeeper who had succeeded financially but was scorned socially. He was determined to avenge his wife, Mary, and designed this tomb so that in death she could look down on all those who had snubbed her.

The tomb of legendary madam Josie Arlington bears a bas-relief of a young girl knocking on a door. Orphaned at the age of four, Josie went into business for herself as a teenager. She became a notorious whore and brawler, and once bit off half an ear and the lower lip of a fellow prostitute.

A large bell from his boat *America* marks the grave

of Captain Cooley, who ran several steamboats until his death in 1931. Other denizens include P. B. S. Pinchback, a free man of color who became Louisiana's only black governor in 1872–3, and William C. C. Claiborne (*see p17*), first governor of Louisiana. David C. Hennessy, the police chief who was assassinated in 1891, also has an impressive tomb.

Longue Vue House and Gardens ⑬

7 Bamboo Road. **Map** 1 A2.
Tel 488-5488. 🚌 34, 39.
🕐 10am–5pm Mon–Sat, 1–5pm Sun. ● public hols. 🎟️ 🔲 ♿ 🔲
www.longuevue.com

Cotton broker Edgar Stern and his wife Edith Rosenwald, heiress to the Sears fortune, established this estate between 1939 and 1942. The interiors are exquisitely decorated with antiques, Oriental carpets and fine art, including works by Jean Arp, Pablo Picasso, and Barbara Hepworth. The gardens, which contain 23 fountains created by Ellen Biddle, are exceptional examples of landscape design. The largest garden is modeled on Spain's 14th-century Alhambra gardens; others are inspired by French and English designs.

One of Ellen Biddle's fountains gracing the gardens of Longue Vue House

THREE GUIDED WALKS

These three walks take visitors through landmark districts and also into the heart of elegant residential areas that showcase the unique make-up of New Orleans' historic neighborhoods. The walk along the Mississippi riverfront has sweeping views of the city, and the short ferry ride to Old Algiers Point provides a fascinating glimpse of the workings of this powerful natural waterway. The Faubourg St. John walk explores an area with deep historic ties to the city's colonial origins, with its French West Indies-style raised houses and

Garden District ironwork detail

distinctive cemetery, circling around a lesser-known waterway, the Bayou St. John. The third walk heads uptown to the Lower Garden District, a diverse and bustling area full of interesting shops, historic churches, and fine architecture, with literary connections. In addition, each of the five neighborhoods covered in the *Area by Area* section of this book has a walk marked on its *Street-by-Street* map. Several organizations also offer guided walks through the French Quarter, Garden District, and other areas in the city *(see pp198–9).*

CHOOSING A WALK

The Three Walks
This map shows the location of the three guided walks in relation to the main sightseeing areas of New Orleans.

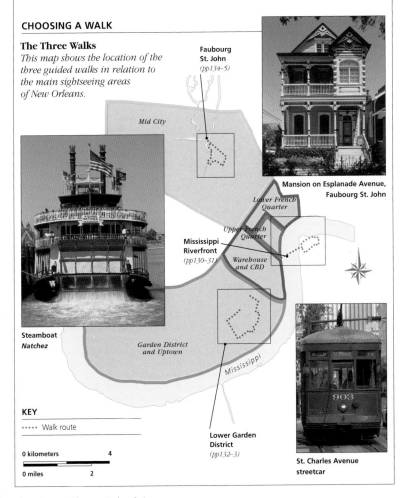

Faubourg St. John *(pp134–5)*

Mid City

Mansion on Esplanade Avenue, Faubourg St. John

Lower French Quarter

Upper French Quarter

Mississippi Riverfront *(pp130–31)*

Warehouse and CBD

Steamboat Natchez

Garden District and Uptown

Mississippi

Lower Garden District *(pp132–3)*

St. Charles Avenue streetcar

KEY

····· Walk route

0 kilometers 4

0 miles 2

◁ **An elegant residence on Esplanade Avenue**

A Walk Around the Mississippi Riverfront

New Orleans owes its very existence to the Mississippi River, one of the world's great waterways and an iconic feature on the cultural, historic, and economic landscape of America. This walk provides superb vistas from both sides of the river, explores a portion of the levee system and, thanks to a free ferry ride, gives you a chance to experience its swirling waters up close.

Cannon, Washington Artillery Park ①

The Steamboat *Natchez*, crossing the wide Mississippi River ④

Jackson Square to the Aquarium

Begin at Washington Artillery Park ① *(see p77)*. This raised platform features a 19th-century cannon and has excellent views of Jackson Square *(see p54)* and the river. Descend the stairs on the river side of the platform and cross the railroad tracks to

TIPS FOR WALKERS

Starting point: *Washington Artillery Park near Jackson Square.*
Length: *1 mile (1.6 km), plus the ferry ride.*
Getting there: *The riverfront area is within easy walking distance of downtown or French Quarter hotels. The Riverfront streetcar also runs along here.*
Stopping-off points: *The renovated Jackson Brewery has a coffee shop and food court. There are many outdoor vendors in the Spanish Plaza near the Canal Street ferry terminal. Adjacent to the plaza is the Riverwalk Marketplace, which has a large food court with a branch of the famous Café du Monde (see p76 and p176). Across the river in Algiers, drop into the Dry Dock Café and Bar opposite the ferry terminal for gumbo, or "po'boys" and plenty of atmosphere.*

reach the Moonwalk ②, a paved walkway named for former New Orleans mayor Maurice "Moon" Landrieu. Take the set of steps leading down to the water. This is a popular place for visitors to watch passing vessels, while street musicians performing for tips add to the ambience. Follow the Moonwalk upriver (toward Canal Street), passing the Jax Brewery ③, which at one time was the largest brewery in the South and is now a shopping mall. You also pass the berth for the Steamboat *Natchez* ④ *(see pp64–5)*, a paddle wheeler that offers river trips and enlivens the riverfront with music from its steam calliope prior to each departure. Just upriver is Woldenberg Riverfront Park ⑤ *(see p88)*, named for a local philanthropist. Once occupied by rusting river warehouses, the park now provides an open green area that's popular for picnics, outdoor games, and jogging, as well as a bandstand. The park is also the setting for a collection of sculptures and monuments, including the white marble *Monument*

Monument to the Immigrant, Woldenberg Riverfront Park ⑤

to the Immigrant and the city's Holocaust memorial. Coast Guard cutters or tugboats often temporarily tie up along this stretch of the river, giving walkers a close-up view of the vessels. Just past Woldenberg Park is the Audubon Aquarium of the Americas *(see pp90–91)* and Entergy IMAX Theater ⑥. This area is filled with whimsical sculptures of marine life, shady park benches, and outdoor vendors serving refreshments.

Canal Street Ferry to Old Algiers Point

Next to the aquarium is the terminal for the Canal Street Ferry ⑦ *(see p217)*, a state-run commuter ferry providing free rides for

The façade of St. Louis Cathedral

arms. The ferry ride is brief but offers excellent views of the New Orleans skyline, St. Louis Cathedral *(see pp56–7)*, as well as the various craft

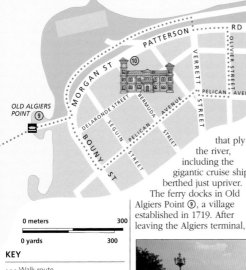

that ply the river, including the gigantic cruise ships berthed just upriver. The ferry docks in Old Algiers Point ⑨, a village established in 1719. After leaving the Algiers terminal,

turn left and follow the trail of crushed shells that top the grassy levee. This manmade embankment is part of a system of levees along thousands of miles of riverfront that protects communities from the Mississippi's floodwaters. On the right, you can see the Algiers Courthouse ⑩, a grand Romanesque Revival structure built in 1896 after a devastating fire wiped out much of the neighborhood. Looking toward the river, you can watch huge ships from around the globe make the dramatic hairpin turn round Algiers Point. This curve in the river suggested New Orleans' most enduring nickname, the Crescent City.

Follow the levee path for about 1,640 ft (500 m), then descend the set of colorfully painted concrete steps down to Patterson Road. Turn left on Patterson Road and continue walking one block to Olivier Street. Turn right and walk two blocks past some of the area's beautifully restored Creole townhouses and shotgun-style homes *(see p35)*. Turn right on Pelican Avenue, a tree-shaded residential street with more distinctive architecture. At the end you reach Bouny Street; turn right here and continue up the levee to the ferry terminal for the return trip.

KEY

• • • Walk route

🚉 Streetcar stop

⛴ Ferry boarding point

foot passengers across the Mississippi. If the ferry is not in dock at the terminal, you could use the waiting time to explore the adjacent Spanish Plaza ⑧ *(see p88)*. Dedicated in 1976, the plaza was a gift from Spain in a gesture of friendship to its one-time colony and features a fountain ringed by tile mosaics of Spanish coats of

The fountain at the center of the Spanish Plaza ⑧

A Walk Around the Lower Garden District

The Lower Garden District offers visitors a diverse sampling of the ethnic, historical, and economic dynamics at work in the area through the last two centuries. Although this area is not as opulent as the neighboring Garden District (*see pp100–1*), it has seen a tremendous amount of revitalization since the 1990s. The walk takes you past buildings with fascinating histories, ornate churches, an antebellum mansion, and a cut-down Eiffel Tower.

St. Charles Avenue fuses the old with the new

Interior of St. Mary's Assumption ⑤

Coliseum Square to Magazine Street

Begin at the streetcar stop at St. Charles Avenue and Melpomene Street ①, which is one of a collection of parallel streets in the area, named for the Nine Muses of Greek mythology. Walk two blocks toward the river to Coliseum Park ②, an irregular space that was laid out in 1806. The park's name refers to an outdoor arena that was planned here but never realized. Follow the path along Camp Street beneath the spreading branches of oak trees for three blocks and turn left on Race Street. Continue one block then turn right on Magazine Street.

Dominating the corner here is St. Vincent's Guesthouse, a sweeping structure with fanciful wrought-iron balconies ③. The inn was originally built as an orphanage in 1861, a time when yellow fever left many children without parents. The orphanage was a beneficiary of Margaret Haughery, an Irish immigrant and orphan herself who made an enormous fortune operating bakeries around the city. Continue up Magazine Street, where homes give way to rows of boutiques and restaurants with large balconies shading the sidewalks beneath. After four blocks on Magazine Street, turn left on St. Andrew Street and continue for one block before turning right on Constance Street.

St. Alphonsus and St. Mary's Assumption

This single block on Constance Street is home to two historic Catholic churches built in close proximity for separate Irish and German parishes during the immigration boom of the mid-19th century. The Irish worshipped at St. Alphonsus ④, located on the right side of the street. Now deconsecrated, St. Alphonsus is open as an arts and cultural center with tours available (Tuesday, Thursday, and Saturday) to view its frescoes, stained glass, and a small exhibit on the early Irish experience in New Orleans.

TIPS FOR WALKERS

Starting point: *The streetcar stop at the corner of St. Charles Avenue and Melpomene Street.*
Length: *1.75 miles (2.8 km)*
Getting there: *By streetcar to the Melpomene Street stop; or a cab ride from Canal Street.*
Stopping-off points: *Mojo Coffee House at Magazine and Race streets is a popular spot. Farther down Magazine, Jackson Restaurant serves lunch, dinner, and brunch, while Juan's Flying Burrito serves Tex-Mex fare with rock and roll flair. On St. Charles Avenue, near Jackson Avenue, Igor's Lounge and Game Room has big burgers.*

Former home of Anne Rice, a prominent New Orleans author ⑦

KEY

••• Walk route

🚊 Streetcar stop

It was consecrated on the same day in 1858 that the cornerstone was laid across the street for St. Mary's Assumption ⑤. This German Baroque Revival church has an altar, statues, and stained glass all imported from Munich and is considered one of the most ornate churches in New Orleans. Regular services continue at St. Mary's

The familiar sight of a St. Charles streetcar

Assumption, which is also home to the National Shrine of Blessed Francis Xavier Seelos. Known as "the Cheerful Ascetic," Father Seelos died of yellow fever in 1867 and was beatified by the Church in 2000. The shrine houses his remains, a collection of religious art, and a gift shop.

First Street to St. Charles Avenue

Leaving the church of St. Mary's Assumption, turn right on Josephine Street and continue for one block. Turn left on Magazine Street and continue for three blocks past more boutiques. Turn right on 1st Street, one of the first streets in the Garden District proper. On the left, at No. 1134, is the privately owned Payne-Strachan House ⑥ (see p107), where Jefferson Davis, president of the

American Confederacy, died in 1889. One block up at No. 1239 ⑦ (see p107), is the Brevard-Wisdom-Rice House, the private home previously owned by novelist Anne Rice and used as a setting for her book The Witching Hour.

Continue walking three blocks to St. Charles Avenue and turn right. This avenue is the main route for Mardi Gras parades (see pp28–9) and, if you look up, the remnants of colorful beads thrown from the floats can often be seen tangled in the branches of the oaks along the street.

One block down, at No. 2220 St. Charles Avenue, is the House of Broel ⑧, an antebellum mansion that is open to the public for tours.

A further two blocks down St. Charles Avenue you'll find the striking metal structure known locally as the Eiffel Tower building ⑨. It was built from pieces of the Paris landmark that were removed during its 1980 renovation and shipped here. The building houses a nightclub and restaurant called Eiffel Society.

On the same block is the visitors' center of the New Orleans Metropolitan Convention and Visitors' Bureau ⑩, which is a good place to pick up maps, and information on tours, restaurants, and attractions across the city. Outside, at the corner of St. Andrew Street, is a streetcar stop for the return trip downtown and the walk's end.

Louis Armstrong statue, outside the New Orleans Visitors' Bureau ⑩

A 90-Minute Walk Around the Faubourg St. John

This walk circles a portion of Bayou St. John, an historically strategic waterway where some of the city's earliest colonial development took place. It also showcases a beautiful residential neighborhood with original Creole mansions and the distinctive above-ground St. Louis Cemetery #3. The area is easily accessible from downtown via the Canal streetcar and is close to the attractions in City Park *(see pp116–17)*.

The banks of the Bayou St. John waterway

Pitot House, a West Indian-style raised house ②

Around the Bayou

Begin at Beauregard Circle ①, where a statue honors Confederate general P. G. T. Beauregard, nicknamed "the Mighty Creole" *(see p71)*, who directed the opening battle of the Civil War at Fort Sumter in South Carolina. Cross N. Carrollton Avenue to the Esplanade Avenue bridge and, once across, turn right on Moss Street. Follow the sidewalk or the grassy footpath around the bend of Bayou St. John *(see p119)*. Local Choctaw Indians first showed

this waterway to French explorers in 1699, and it quickly became an important shipping route that connected the early trading posts on the Mississippi River with Lake Pontchartrain and the Gulf of Mexico. Later, the bayou was extended to the French Quarter by a canal that has since been filled. Today, the bayou is an informal recreational area. The banks of the waterway have also historically been connected with voodoo rituals *(see p83)*, including those led by Marie Laveau in the 19th century. Although voodoo practice is much less in public evidence today, some practitioners still congregate at Bayou St. John on holidays, especially St. John's Eve on June 23.

In the 18th and early 19th centuries French colonists built country homes in this area and these can still be seen in the French West Indies-style houses here. An outstanding example is Pitot House ② *(see p119)*, a Creole raised country house that is

TIPS FOR WALKERS

Starting point: *Beauregard Circle, at the gates of City Park.*
Length: *2 miles (3.2 km).*
Getting there: *From Canal Street, take the Canal streetcar marked City Park to the end of the line. RTA bus #48 runs from N. Rampart Street at Esplanade Avenue to Beauregard Circle.*
Stopping-off points: *There are many casual and upscale restaurants and cafés clustered around Esplanade Avenue and Ponce de Leon Street, including the French bistro Café Degas, the Fair Grinds Coffeehouse, and the Spanish restaurant Lola's.*

KEY

••• Walk route

now a museum. Named for James Pitot, New Orleans' first American mayor, construction of the house started in 1799. It is filled with period antiques, and offers a glimpse of life in early 19th-century New Orleans.

Next to Pitot House is Cabrini High School ③, a private school named for Mother Frances Cabrini who had originally established an orphanage on the spot in 1905. Mother Cabrini later became America's first canonized saint.

Cross the bayou on the steel pedestrian bridge ④ directly across from the school, then turn left to wander along the grassy bank of the bayou until you arrive at the next bridge located at Dumaine Street ⑤. Take the bridge to the other side of the bayou and turn left again, continuing along the opposite bank. Small concrete embankments and steps here-abouts provide

One of several impressive Victorian mansions on Esplanade Avenue ⑦

good places to sit and admire the wildlife and views. Fish often leap from the water after insects and, in the cooler months, the bayou attracts large pelicans, which plunge down dramatically to scoop their own meals from the water.

From Ursulines to Esplanade

Strolling on along Moss Street, turn right on Bell Street, which becomes Ursulines Street ⑥ after one block. This broad avenue, named for the order of nuns who came to New Orleans from France in 1727, was laid out around 1860 after the marshy lands surrounding the bayou were drained. Today, all kinds of beautiful homes can be seen here, including Victorian houses, bungalows, and cottages trimmed with gingerbread woodwork. Three blocks down Ursuline Avenue, turn left on N. Lopez Street at a small triangular park and walk three blocks to Esplanade Avenue ⑦. Turn left here and walk up this impressive avenue, with its mansions that were built in the late 19th and early 20th

centuries. If you would like a break, on Ponce de Leon Street ⑧ you will come across a cluster of charming restaurants, cafés, and small boutiques. Near here, each spring, the New Orleans Jazz and Heritage Fest is held at the Fair Grounds Race Course ⑨ (see pp41 and 126). Two blocks farther on the left, is Our Lady of the Holy Rosary ⑩, a Catholic church built in 1925 with Classical columns and a dome that's visible from the bayou. One block further up on the right, is St. Louis Cemetery #3 ⑪ (see p126), which has well-maintained examples of New Orleans' distinctive tombs and funerary art. Continue along Esplanade Avenue, crossing Bayou St. John again, to end the walk back at Beauregard Circle.

An angel at prayer, St. Louis cemetery ⑪

MYSTERY STREET

⑨

MAUREPAS STREET

ESPLANADE

⑧ PONCE DE LEON STREET

RAND   ROUTE   ST JOHN

AVENUE

⑦

OTO STREET   HAGAN ST   N. RENDON STREET   N. LOPEZ STREET   DESOTO ST

URSULINE AVENUE

⑥   BELL STREET

KENNEDY PLACE

PHILIP STREET

0 meters   200

0 yards   200

A view of the altar, Our Lady of the Holy Rosary church ⑩

Old oaks line the road to Oak Alley Plantation ▷

BEYOND
NEW ORLEANS

BEYOND NEW ORLEANS

*T**he countryside around New Orleans is a land full of history and tradition. The beautiful plantations of the Mississippi River, Baton Rouge (the capital of Louisiana), and the famous Cajun Country are full of cultural and entertainment interest. Venturing beyond New Orleans allows you to experience the unique mixture of Louisiana's cultures in all their various accents.*

The lifeblood of New Orleans was, and still is, the Mississippi River. In the 18th and 19th centuries, the river banks were lined with large plantations producing all kinds of commodities, including sugar, tobacco, and cotton, which were shipped around the world via New Orleans. Today only a handful of plantation homes survive along the River Road, but many are open to visitors, and some offer accommodation.

Sculpture at the Louisiana State Capitol

Prior to Hurricane Katrina, the state capital, metropolitan Baton Rouge, had a population of about 600,000; however, as people resettled away from low-lying areas, numbers rose to close to 700,000. An oil-refining center, Baton Rouge has several attractions associated with its role in state government, including the State Capitol, the Old State Capitol, and the

Governor's Mansion. Other sights include the Rural Life Museum, the World War II destroyer the USS *Kidd*, and the Louisiana State University. To the west of Baton Rouge lie the massive Atchafalaya Swamp and Cajun Country. The latter is famous for its Francophone culture, Cajun and zydeco music, and its robust, spicy cuisine. Visitors can explore Cajun culture in a number of towns in this area – Eunice, Lafayette, and Opelousas – as well as along the bayous of New Iberia, and Avery Island. To get a feel for life on the bayous, you can attend a *fais do-do* (dance), try the local cuisine, or tour the McIlhenny Tabasco Sauce Factory. For an insight into the Cajun way of life, visitors can drift among age-old cypress trees in the swamps, or visit museums and historic villages.

Original Cajun house in the Acadian Village near Lafayette

◁ **St. John the Evangelist cathedral in Lafayette**

Exploring Beyond New Orleans

An excursion to the bayous and small towns a few hours away from New Orleans will show visitors just how different the city is from its Louisiana surroundings. Upriver, the Cajun heritage is evident in the architectural styles, the food, and even the language, since French is spoken almost everywhere. Only a few hours' drive from New Orleans, it is possible to visit more than a dozen Creole and American plantations along the Mississippi River and to get a taste of life as it used to be. The city of Baton Rouge, the state capital, makes an interesting modern counterpoint.

Vermilionville
This restored 19th-century Cajun-Creole settlement is peopled by costumed staff. Traditional ways of life are enacted.

KEY

═══ Interstate highway

═══ State highway

─── Major road

─·─ Main railway

─── Minor railway

SEE ALSO

• *Where to Stay* pp168–9

• *Where to Eat* pp184–5

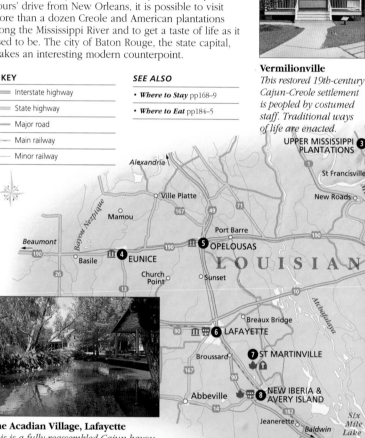

The Acadian Village, Lafayette
This is a fully reassembled Cajun bayou community, with houses boasting traditional Cajun furnishings.

GETTING AROUND

All of the sights can be reached easily by road from New Orleans. Interstate 10 (I-10) connects the city directly to Baton Rouge. Some exits from route I-10 also lead to the River Road Plantations and to Cajun Country. From New Orleans, several guided tours to the bayous are available *(see pp220–21),* which offer a convenient way to explore life on the bayous.

Cajun Music Hall of Fame, Eunice
A country store dating from the 1930s now houses a museum of local music.

Nottoway
Built in 1859, Neo-Classical Nottoway Planta-
tion has 64 rooms. Today it operates as a bed
and breakfast and has a fine restaurant.

Old State Capitol, Baton Rouge
This Gothic Revival castle, built
in 1847, was burned by the
Union Army and repaired in
1882. Today it houses a museum
of local political history.

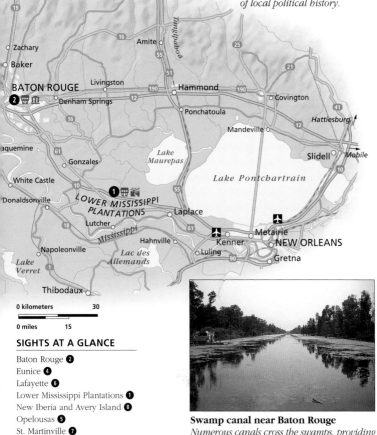

Swamp canal near Baton Rouge
Numerous canals cross the swamps, providing
access to the area.

SIGHTS AT A GLANCE

Lower Mississippi Plantations ❶

Old plantation water pump

The River Road meanders along both banks of the Mississippi River, changing route numbers as it goes. It runs behind the levee, past petro-chemical plants, towering live oaks draped with Spanish moss, and magnificent plantation homes. Creole families once owned and operated the plantations located between New Orleans and Baton Rouge. Some of the old plantation residences have been given a new lease of life as small museums.

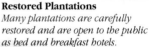

Restored Plantations
Many plantations are carefully restored and are open to the public as bed and breakfast hotels.

Nottoway
The largest plantation in the area, Nottoway boasts an impressive 65 rooms.

Baton Rouge

61

10

● GONZALES

1

70

● DONALDSONVILLE

70

1

Lafourche

1

Miss

| 0 kilometers | 20 |
| 0 miles | 10 |

Houmas House
The country's largest sugar plantation in the 19th century, this grand house now displays a fine antiques collection.

Madewood Plantation
This Greek Revival style plantation house is one of the best preserved in the area and is also a bed and breakfast.

For hotels and restaurants in this region see pp168–9 and pp184–5

Oak Alley
*A glorious double row of live oak trees lines the
drive to this mansion, which was built in 1837.*

LOCATOR MAP

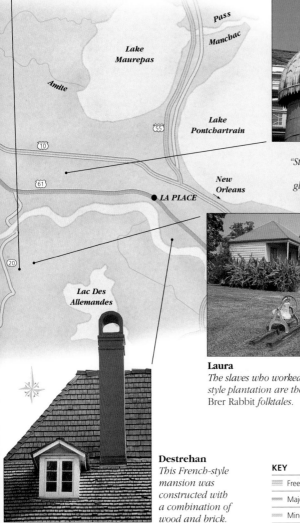

San Francisco
*"Steamboat Gothic" style
is displayed in all its
glory at this plantation.*

Lake
Maurepas

Pass
Manchac

Amite

Lake
Pontchartrain

55

10

61

New
Orleans

LA PLACE

20

Lac Des
Allemandes

Laura
*The slaves who worked this typical Creole-
style plantation are the source for the*
Brer Rabbit *folktales.*

Destrehan
*This French-style
mansion was
constructed with
a combination of
wood and brick.*

KEY

▬	Freeway
▬	Major road
▬	Minor road

Exploring Lower Mississippi Plantations

By 1850, two-thirds of America's millionaires lived on plantations located along the Great River Road. The economic relationship between the plantations' production and the trade from New Orleans to the rest of the world made it one of the wealthiest regions of the nation. The treasures of this glory are displayed in homes from New Orleans to Baton Rouge, with colorful French and Spanish Creole architecture and beautiful natural surroundings.

Destrehan plantation

🏛 Destrehan
13034 River Rd, Destrehan. **Tel** (985) 764-9315. ⭕ 9am–4pm daily. ⚫ major holidays. 🎟 🎦 ⭐
www.destrehanplantation.org
Charles Pacquet, a free man of color, built this home for Robert de Logny in 1787. The original Creole cottage was modified in 1810 and 1840. Union troops housed freed slaves here during the Civil War (see pp18–19).

🏛 San Francisco
2646 Hwy 44, River Rd, Garyville. **Tel** (985) 535-2341. ⭕ 10am–4pm daily. ⚫ Jan 1, Easter, Thanksgiving, Dec 25, Mardi Gras. 🎦 🎟
www.sanfranciscoplantation.com
The term "Steamboat Gothic" has been applied to this ornate plantation home built in 1856 for Edmond Bozonier Marmillion. Originally it was painted in flamboyant purples, blues, and greens, and the structure was decorated with plenty of ornate grillwork and gingerbread trim. The interiors feature some splendid ceiling paintings completed by Dominique Canova (cousin of the famous sculptor) featuring

cherubs, trailing vines, flying parrots, and exquisite faux marbling and graining. Commissioned by Edmond's son, Valsin, and his daughter-in-law in 1860, they were so expensive that Valsin named the house Saint Frusquin, from the French *sans fruscins*, meaning "without a penny." The name eventually became corrupted to "San Francisco." Valsin died before he could enjoy the house he had imagined, and shortly after the Civil War his widow sold

it to a Colonel Bougere. The grounds of the original plantation have been reduced by several levee setbacks over the years, and so today it stands very close to the road.

🏯 Laura
2247 Hwy 18, Vacherie. **Tel** (225) 265-7690. ⭕ 10am–4pm daily. ⚫ major holidays. 🎟 🎦 🎟
www.lauraplantation.com
Revolutionary War veteran Guillame Duparc was given a large land grant and built the classic raised Creole plantation house in 1805. After he died, four generations of women ran the plantation. In 1891, Laura Locoul sold the property in order to marry and move with her husband to St. Louis.

The plantation gained notoriety for the stories told by the French-speaking slaves, later tenant farmers, living there. Folklorist Alcée Fortier first translated these Senegalese stories about Brer Rabbit, which later inspired Joel Chandler Harris's *Uncle Remus* and *Brer Rabbit* books. After being devastated by fire in 2004, the house was meticulously rebuilt under the guidance of architectural historians. Guided tours are offered daily by reservation.

🏯 Oak Alley
3645 Hwy 18, Vacherie. **Tel** (225) 265-2151. ⭕ 9:30am–4:30pm daily (to 5pm Sat, Sun). ⚫ Jan 1, Thanksgiving, Dec 25, Mardi Gras. 🎟 🎦 ⭐ www.oakalleyplantation.com
Oak Alley's name comes from the 28 magnificent live oaks that line the entrance to this plantation home. They were planted about 300 years ago,

San Francisco plantation, the ultimate in "Steamboat Gothic" style

The Great White Ballroom at Nottoway plantation

even before the house was built for Jacques Telesphore Roman III in 1837. The house and grounds are so striking that it has been used as a location for several movies, including *The Long Hot Summer* (1985) and *Interview with the Vampire* (1994). A slave gardener developed the first commercial variety of pecan nut, the "Paper Shell," on the property.

🏛 Nottoway

30970 Hwy 405, White Castle. *Tel* (225) 545-2730. ☐ 9am–4pm daily. ● Dec 25. 🖋 🖾 www.nottoway.com

This is the largest plantation on this stretch of the Mississippi. It was designed by architect Henry Howard to accommodate John Hampden Randolph, his wife, and a family of 11 children, and completed in 1859. Randolph was a wealthy sugar planter originally from Virginia. The mansion occupies 53,000 sq ft (18,000 sq m), with 64 rooms, 16 fireplaces, 200 windows, and 165 doors. At the time it was built, it incorporated some innovative conveniences such as indoor plumbing, gas lighting, and coal fireplaces. In the Great White Ballroom, which is 65 ft (22 m) long, seven of Randolph's daughters celebrated their weddings. It is the largest and most impressive room in the house. It survived the Civil War due to the intervention of a Union

Antique clock at Nottoway

gunboat officer, who asked that it be spared because he had once been a guest of the Randolphs. It now operates as a bed and breakfast.

🏛 Madewood

4250 Hwy 308, Napoleonville. *Tel* (985) 369-7151 or (800) 375-7151. ☐ by appointment only. ● Jan 1, Thanksgiving, Dec 25. 🖋 🖾 www.madewood.com

Built in the prosperous times of pre-Civil War Louisiana, Madewood is unusual among south Louisiana plantation houses. It is a classic Greek Revival house, uninfluenced by the raised Creole villa style that predominates in the region. The first significant building by architect Henry Howard, it was erected between 1840 and 1848 for sugar planter Thomas Pugh using construction materials from his holdings. Bricks for the exterior were made on the plantation

and then covered with stucco to give the illusion of masonry. In 1964 New Orleans preservationist Naomi Marshall saved the house from ruins after it lay neglected for years. She and her family then spent 13 years restoring the building and grounds. It now serves as a bed-and-breakfast inn, and the site for many events, such as classical music recitals, art fairs, and holiday celebrations.

🏛 Houmas House

40136 Hwy 942, River Rd, Darrow. *Tel* (225) 473-9380. ☐ 9am–5pm Mon–Tue, 9am–8pm Wed–Sun. ● Jan 1, Dec 25. 🖾 🖋 www.houmashouse.com

With its grand two-story verandas and monumental Tuscan columns, Houmas House is one of the most recognizable plantation villas in the South. As well as sprawling gardens, there is also a second house, a two-story French Colonial-era structure, which is attached to the main house by a carriageway. The main house, dating from 1840, is furnished in high antebellum style

Embroidery stand

with a fine collection of period antiques. It survived the Civil War because its Irish owner, John Burnside, claimed immunity as a British subject. A wealthy merchant, Burnside amassed several sugar mills and at the end of the 19th century, this plantation was producing as much as 20 million pounds (9 million kg) of sugar each year.

Houmas House, a fine example of Greek Revival style

Baton Rouge ❷

In 1719, the French established Baton Rouge as a fort designed to control access to the Mississippi and the interior. It was so named by Jean Baptiste Le Moyne, Sieur de Iberville *(see p19)*, after he observed the spikes (red sticks) hung with bloody fish heads that were arranged along the river bluffs. In 1762, the French ceded it to the British. During the American Revolution, the Spanish took the opportunity to seize the garrison, which remained under their control until 1810. After that, the local American population took the fort and proclaimed the Republic of West Florida. The area was claimed for the United States and it was incorporated into the Union in 1817. It has been the state capital since 1849.

Lantern at LSU

The graceful interior of Louisiana Old State Capitol

🏛 Louisiana Old State Capitol

100 North Blvd. **Tel** (225) 342-0500. ◯ 9am–4pm Tue–Sat. ◉ public hols. 🖼 ♿

James Harrison Dakin designed this striking castle-like building in 1847. William Freret conceived the soaring iron spiral staircase, installed during a renovation in 1882, which winds from the foyer toward the stained-glass dome. It was here, in the House Chamber, that Louisiana's state representatives voted in 1861 to secede from the Union. Seven decades later, in 1929, impeachment proceedings were begun here against Huey "Kingfish" Long. Today, this magnificent building serves as the state's Center for Political and Governmental History. Visitors can view and listen to many of the state's colorful political orators expressing their views.

🏛 Louisiana State University

Nicholson Drive btw Highland Rd and W Chimes St. **Tel** (225) 578-8654. With its 31,000 students, this is the state's flagship university. The tree-shaded campus is attractively landscaped and boasts some unique features. In the northwest corner, for example, two mounds rise some 20 ft (6 m) high. Archaeologists believe that they are 5,000-year-old Native American mounds built before the first Egyptian pyramids.

The university's sports teams are some of the hottest tickets in college sports. In baseball, the Tigers have won national titles for several consecutive years, and the enthusiasm generated by the football team is legendary.

The university also has two cutting edge research facilities; the Pennington Biomedical Research Center, devoted to nutritional medicine, and the Center for Microstructures

and Devices. The collections at the Museum of Natural Science in Foster Hall (225-578-2855) are also worth seeing. The visitor information center is at Dalrymple Drive and Highland Road.

🏛 Magnolia Mound Plantation

2161 Nicholson Dr. **Tel** (225) 343-4955. ◯ 10am–4pm Mon–Sat, 1–4pm Sun. ◉ public hols. 🖼

John Joyce built this plantation home in 1791. In the 19th century it stood at the center of a 900-acre farm, producing indigo, cotton, perique tobacco, and sugarcane. The building has been carefully restored to reflect the antebellum era.

🏛 Old Governor's Mansion

502 North Blvd. **Tel** (225) 387-2464. ◯ 10am–4pm Tue–Fri. ◉ public hols. 🖼 🎫 only (last tour 3pm). ♿

Governor Huey Long had this mansion built in 1930. He modeled it on the White House, even down to the office, which is a smaller version of the Oval Office. The building has been carefully restored, and the rooms have even been repainted in their original colors, some of which are outlandish; Huey Long apparently loved hot pinks, purples, and greens, which appear in several bathrooms. Many of the furnishings in the library and the master bedroom are original to the house. There is also memorabilia from other governors, including the singing governor, Jimmie Davis, who wrote *You Are my Sunshine*.

Façade of the Greek Revival Old Governor's Mansion

The House Chamber, State Capitol

🏛 State Capitol

State Capitol Dr at N 3rd St.
Tel (225) 342-7317. ◯ *9am–4pm
daily.* ⬤ *Jan 1, Easter Sunday,
Thanksgiving, Dec 25.* &

Huey Long worked hard to
persuade the legislators to
approve the $5 million
funding for this Modernist
34-story building, erected in
1932. It is the tallest capitol
in the United States. Both
the House and Senate
chambers are impressive, as
are the murals in Memorial
Hall. Visitors can still see
the bullet holes in the
marble walls of the first-floor
executive corridor, where
Long was assassinated on
September 8, 1935, by Dr.
Carl A. Weiss, the son-in-law
of a political enemy, Judge
Benjamin Pavy. The grounds
contain Long's grave in a
sunken memorial garden.

There are excellent
views of the Mississippi
and the city from
the 27th-floor observa-
tion deck.

🏛 USS Kidd

305 S River Rd. *Tel (225)
342-1942.* ◯ *9am–5pm
daily.* ⬤ *Thanksgiving,
Dec 25.* 🎟 &

Commissioned in
1943, this World War
II destroyer saw action
in the Pacific, where she
suffered a kamikaze attack on
April 11, 1945, and 38 of the
crew were killed. She also
served in the Korean War and
other missions until 1964,
when she was decommi-
ssioned. Visitors can see the
anti-aircraft guns and
other equipment
on the ship, and
tour the cramped
quarters shared by
the 330-man crew
below decks.

🏛 Rural Life Museum and Windrush Gardens

4560 Essen Lane at I-10. *Tel (225)
765-2437.* ◯ *8:30am–5pm daily.*
⬤ *Jan 1, Easter Sunday, Thanksgiving, Dec 24 & 25.* 🎟 &

Ione Burden and her brother,
Steele, who landscaped
Louisiana State University,
assembled this collection of

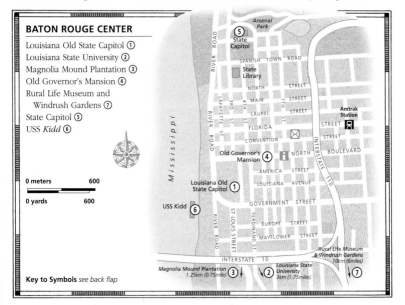

Old tractor at the Rural Life Museum

VISITORS' CHECKLIST

90 miles (144 km) NW of New
Orleans. 🚗 576,330. ✈ 9430
Jackie Cochran Drive, (225) 355-
0333. 🚌 Greyhound Bus Lines,
1001 Loyola Ave, (504) 524-7571.
ℹ 730 North Blvd, (800) 527-
6843. 🎪 Greater Baton Rouge
State Fair (for 10 days, mid-Oct).

buildings and 19th-century
tools and artifacts. Each building is filled with fascinating
objects – a washing machine
dating from 1900, pirogues
(a type of boat used on the
bayous), cockfighting spurs,
and a tobacco press, to name
a few. Steele Burden's paintings and ceramic figures are
also displayed,
along with other
collectibles. In
the time before it
was fashionable to
preserve African
American culture,
Steele also rescued
all the buildings from nearby
Welham Plantation and
re-erected them in a typical
plantation layout. Today,
visitors can gain some insight
into how such a plantation
functioned as a self-contained
community. Crape myrtle,
azaleas, and other plantings
fill the adjacent gardens.

BATON ROUGE CENTER

Louisiana Old State Capitol ①
Louisiana State University ②
Magnolia Mound Plantation ③
Old Governor's Mansion ④
Rural Life Museum and
   Windrush Gardens ⑦
State Capitol ⑤
USS *Kidd* ⑥

0 meters   600
0 yards   600

Key to Symbols *see back flap*

Arsenal Park
⑤ State Capitol
SPANISH TOWN ROAD
State Library
RIVER ROAD
NORTH STREET
LAFAYETTE
3RD ST.
4TH ST.
MAIN STREET
7TH ST.
LAUREL STREET
RIVER ROAD
FLORIDA STREET
Amtrak Station
CONVENTION STREET
INTERSTATE 110
Old Governor's Mansion ④
NORTH BOULEVARD
AMERICA STREET
Louisiana Old State Capitol ①
LOUISIANA AVENUE
USS Kidd ⑥
GOVERNMENT STREET
ST LOUIS STREET
FERDINAND ST.
EUROPE STREET
MAYFLOWER STREET
Mississippi
INTERSTATE 10
Magnolia Mound Plantation ③
1.25km (0.75mile)
Louisiana State University ②
3km (1.75miles)
*Rural Life Museum
& Windrush Gardens
10km (6miles)* ⑦

Upper Mississippi Plantations ❸

Weather vane

The West Feliciana Parishes, to the north of Baton Rouge, were not included in the Louisiana Purchase *(see p17)* and remained part of the Spanish domain until 1810. The plantations in this area differ from the southern Creole-style plantations. They were established by British immigrants or by Americans from North Carolina and Virginia, who made their fortunes here and brought their own culture and architectural styles. These beautiful plantations, with exceptional surrounding gardens, are well worth visiting.

Living Traditions
Many of the original work-shops and tools have been reconstructed and are in use.

Greenwood Plantation
One of the largest and most beautiful plantation houses in the area, Green-wood was built in 1830 by William Ruffin Barrow in classic Greek style.

Butler Greenwood
Built in 1796, this house is thoroughly Victorian, both in its architecture and furniture.

Mississippi

← *Alexandria*

NEW ROA

The Myrtles
Built between 1796 and 1830, The Myrtles plantation is exceptionally well preserved. Its 120-ft (40-m)-long cast-iron gallery is its most extravagant exterior feature.

For hotels and restaurants in this region see pp168–9 and pp184–5

Cottage Plantation
With its original 14-karat gold wallpaper in the parlor, this offers one of the best stays in the area. Andrew Jackson stayed here after the Battle of New Orleans (see p17).

LOCATOR MAP

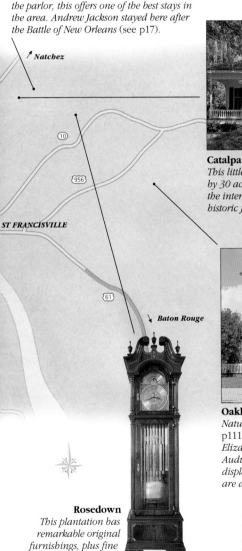

↑ Natchez

⑩

☖956

ST FRANCISVILLE

☖61

↘ *Baton Rouge*

Rosedown
This plantation has remarkable original furnishings, plus fine formal gardens.

Catalpa
This little Victorian cottage is surrounded by 30 acres of splendid gardens. Tours of the interior reveal numerous interesting historic family heirlooms.

Oakley House
Naturalist John James Audubon (see p111) tutored James Pirrie's daughter, Eliza, at this plantation. Many of Audubon's original prints are on display. Fascinating nature trails are also available.

KEY

▬▬ Major road

▬▬ Minor road

Exploring the Upper Mississippi Plantations

The French established Baton Rouge in 1719, when they built a fort to control access to the Mississippi River and the interior *(see pp146–7)*. After being controlled by the Spanish and the British, this city was finally incorporated into the United States in 1817, and became the state capital in 1849. North of Baton Rouge the plantations were established by British or Americans, who held on to their Anglo-Saxon heritage. A different architecture with Greek Revival influences is dominant in this area. Many of these plantations have been restored and are now charming B&Bs.

Old slave cabin at Cottage Plantation

Butler Greenwood, surrounded by beautiful gardens

🏛 Butler Greenwood

8345 Hwy 61, St. Francisville. *Tel* (225) 635-6312. 🕘 9am–5pm daily. 📷 🎫 www.butlergreenwood.com

Pennsylvania Quaker physician Samuel Flower founded this plantation in 1796. His daughter, Harriet, ran it for most of the 19th century as a cotton-producing plantation. Today it is still a working plantation operated by the eighth generation of the family. Family portraits hang throughout the house, which contains many of the original 19th-century furnishings, including a fine 12-piece parlor set made of rosewood and upholstered in the original scarlet-colored fabric. The plantation also offers lovely B&B-style accommodation.

Exhibit at Butler Greenwood

🏛 Catalpa

9508 Hwy 61, St. Francisville. *Tel* (225) 635-3372. 🕘 by appointment only. ⬤ Dec 15–Jan 31. 📷 🎫

The current building is a reconstruction of the original, which was destroyed in a fire in 1885. Carolinian William J. Fort established the plantation in the early 1800s. He was famous for his hospitality and for the many parties he gave in the gardens, which were landscaped with a pond complete with an island for picnics, a deer park, and several summer houses. He also maintained greenhouses filled with exotic tropical plants including banana, guava, and mandarin.

🏛 Cottage Plantation

10528 Cottage Lane, St. Francisville. *Tel* (225) 635-3674. 🕘 10am–4pm daily. ⬤ major holidays. 📷 🎫 www.cottageplantation.com

The land on which this house stands was granted to John Allen and Patrick Holland in 1795. Judge Thomas Butler purchased the original cottage and property in 1810. He was the son of Colonel Thomas Butler, one of the five fighting Butlers who served under General Washington during the American Revolution (1775–83). He extended the house to accommodate his family. The interiors are lavishly decorated with 14-karat gold-leaf wallpaper and plenty of *faux bois*.

The property includes several outbuildings, one of which has been converted into a restaurant. Overnight lodging is also offered.

🏚 Greenwood Plantation

6838 Highland Rd, St. Francisville. *Tel* (225) 655-4475. 🕘 Nov-Feb: 10am–4pm; Mar–Oct: 9am–5pm. ⬤ Jan 1, Jul 4, Thanksgiving, Dec 25. 📷 🎫 ♿ www.greenwoodplantation.com

In 1830, James Hammon Coulter designed this majestic Greek Revival home for William Ruffin Barrow, who had migrated from the Carolinas. It stood on 12,000 acres, which were worked by 750 slaves. Some 40 outbuildings housed workshops that made the plantation completely self-sufficient. The Barrows became one of the most prominent families in the area, but anticipating the Civil War they sold the plantation. It survived the war serving as a hospital, but afterward it deteriorated rapidly. In 1906 Mr. and Mrs. Frank Percy restored it,

Greenwood Plantation, furnished with impressive antebellum pieces

salvaging the marble mantels and silver hinges and doorknobs. Tragically, in 1960 lightning destroyed the entire structure, except for the 28 massive Doric columns. It has since been restored, and visitors can once again see the splendor of the 70-ft (21-m)-long central hall and the rest of the interior. Greenwood runs a B&B and is a popular venue for weddings.

Greenwood Plantation, one of the largest American-style plantations

🏛 The Myrtles

7747 Hwy 61, St. Francisville. **Tel** *(225) 635-6277.* 🚪 *9am–5pm daily.* ⬤ *major hols.* 📷 ☑ ♿ **www**.myrtlesplantation.com

A leader of the Whiskey Rebellion (1794) in Pennsylvania, Judge David Bradford fled south and established this plantation in 1796. He built the north wing of the house and in the early 1800s, his daughter and her husband, Judge Clark Woodruff, added the 107-ft (36-m)-long gallery. Ruffin Gray Stirling bought the house in 1834, and added the south wing. Local legend says that several murders were committed here and that the house is haunted. Special tours on Friday and Saturday nights highlight its haunted history. Bed-and-breakfast accommodation is also available.

The handsome cast-iron veranda surrounding The Myrtles

🏛 Rosedown Plantation

12501 Hwy 10, St Francisville. **Tel** *(225) 635-3332.* 🚪 *9am–5pm daily.* ⬤ *Thanksgiving, Dec 25, Jan 1.* 📷 ☑

Rosedown is one of the largest and most complete of the plantations along the river. The gabled central structure, built of cedar and cypress, has a double gallery supported by Doric columns. Other sections of the house feature Georgian details.

The Turnbull family owned and operated the plantation from 1835 to 1955. Practically all of the contents of the house are original, including rosewood furniture by Mallard and Seignoret, portraits by Thomas Sully, brocade draperies, and marble mantels. Daniel and Martha Turnbull, who established the plantation in 1835, purchased most of the furnishings on their initial Grand Tour of Europe in 1834 and on subsequent trips abroad. The grounds contain a kitchen building, the doctor's office, a barn, and a gardener's tool house. The 28 acres of French-style gardens are exquisite too. Martha Turnbull was a well-known horticulturist, who introduced the first azaleas and camellias to the region.

In 2000 the state of Louisiana purchased the plantation from a private owner, who had unfortunately sold some of the original furnishings. The estate has been renovated and now offers a fascinating 45-minute tour of the house and grounds.

🏛 Oakley House and Audubon State Historic Site

Hwy 965, St. Francisville. **Tel** *(225) 635-3739.* 🚪 *9am–5pm daily.* ⬤ *Thanksgiving, Dec 25, Jan 1.* 📷 ☑

Wealthy Scottish immigrant James Pirrie built this house between 1808 and 1810, and it is a splendid example of the way colonial architecture was adapted to the Louisiana climate. Since then, it has been surrounded by a bosky paradise inhabited by numerous species of birds.

In 1821, naturalist John James Audubon *(see p111)* and his assistant arrived to teach daughter Eliza Pirrie dancing, music, drawing, and math. He and his assistant received room and board and $60 a month. The arrangement did not last, and he left after only four months, having quarreled with his employer. Still, in that brief time he began at least 32 bird portraits, which later appeared in *The Birds of America.* Today, visitors can see the room Audubon stayed in and wander the trails around the property. Magnolias, beeches, and poplars still shelter abundant bird life in the state park surrounding the house.

Study used by John James Audubon in Oakley House

The Liberty Theater, home of the *Rendez-Vous des Cajuns* radio show

Eunice ❹

Cajun Country. 🏠 *11,000.*
🚊 *1238 W Landry St.* ℹ️ 200 South
CC Duson Dr, *(337) 457-2565.*
www.eunice-la.com

Every weekend there is a Cajun music celebration in this picturesque Louisiana town, where most of the main attractions are in the downtown area. The town was founded by C. C. Duson in 1893, who named it in honor of his wife. **The Liberty Theater** is the keeper of the flame of Cajun music – the Grand Ole Opry of Cajun music. It opened in the 1920s as a movie and vaudeville theater. Every Saturday from 6 to 8pm the theater hosts a live broadcast of the *Rendez-Vous des Cajuns* radio show. It is filled with Cajun and zydeco music and plenty of good Cajun humor. The master of ceremonies makes introductions in both English and French.

Visitors to **The Prairie Acadian Cultural Center**, located just behind the theater, can observe musical instruments and other items being made in the craft room. Other displays focus on aspects of Acadian culture, including the *Courir.* Literally "to run," this is the Cajun, and distinctly medieval, version of Mardi Gras. Participants wear a *capuchon* (a tall, cone-shaped hat, which covers the face as well as the head) and ride on horseback from farm to farm begging for the ingredients for a community

gumbo, which will be eaten at the end of the day. The key ingredient, a chicken, has to be chased down and caught live.

Located nearby are two other cultural centers. **The Cajun Music Hall of Fame & Museum**, which opened in 1997, honors the originators of Cajun music and the artists who have kept the tradition alive. It displays memorabilia, instruments such as accordions and violins, photographs, and biographies of the 40 inductees.

Cajun music is a blend of several traditions – German, Scottish, Irish, Spanish, Afro-Caribbean, and Native American – which have been laid over a base of French and French-Acadian folk

Cajun accordion in The Savoy Music Center

tradition. Zydeco developed from the same traditions but incorporates much more Afro-Caribbean rhythm and style.

The Hall of Fame features the great names in Cajun music, from such early musicians as Amédé Ardoin, Alphé Bergeron, Dennis McGee, Joe Falcon, Amédé Breaux, Iry Lejeune, and Lawrence Walker, to more recent interpreters, including Michael Doucet, Zachary Richard, and Wayne Toups.

Heading from Eunice to Opelousas along Highway 190, there is **The Savoy Music Center**, the informal headquarters for Cajun musicians in the area. The store is owned by accordion-maker-musician Marc Savoy and his wife, Ann. It sells musical instruments, CDs, and books on Cajun culture and music. On Saturday mornings local musicians assemble in the front of the store for a jam session around the upright piano. They bring accordions, triangles, and fiddles, and play together. People can bring beer, boudin, and other snacks. Visitors are welcome to listen and join in.

🏛 **The Prairie Acadian Cultural Center**
250 West Park Ave.
Tel (337) 457-8499.
⏰ 8am–5pm Tue–Fri, 8am–6pm
Sat. 🌑 25 Dec. ♿

Mardi Gras costume and memorabilia at The Prairie Acadian Cultural Center

For hotels and restaurants in this region see pp168–9 and pp184–5

Opelousas Museum and Interpretive Center

🏛 **The Cajun Music Hall of Fame & Museum**
240 South CC Duson Dr. *Tel (337) 457-6534.* ◯ *summer: 9am–5pm Tue–Sat; winter: 8:30am–4:30pm Tue–Sat.* ● *major hols.* 🔊

🎵 **The Liberty Theater**
200 Park Ave. *Tel (337) 457-7389.* ◯ *4pm Sat.* 🔊

🎵 **The Savoy Music Center**
Hwy 190 East, Savoy. *Tel (337) 457-9563.* ◯ *9am–5pm Tue–Fri, 9am–noon Sat.* ● *major hols.* 🔊

Opelousas ❺

Cajun Country. 🏘 *11,000.*
ℹ *828 E Landry St, (800) 424-5442.* **www.cityofopelousas.com**

This city, the capital of Confederate Louisiana briefly during the Civil War (*see pp18–19*), was named after the Native American tribe that lived in this area before the Europeans arrived. It was founded as a French trading post settlement during the 1700s, and today it is one of the liveliest towns in this district, thanks to its excellent cuisine and music.

The major collections of the **Opelousas Museum** focus on the local culture and history of the town. The museum's two main exhibit areas are devoted to the prehistory of the area, its agricultural and commercial development, and to the people of different races and religions who developed the region and contributed to its culture. One room is devoted to memorabilia from the Civil War, while another houses a fascinating collection of more than 400 dolls.

The **Opelousas Museum of Art** stands in the oldest part of the city, in a historic Federal-style brick building, built originally as a one-story tavern. The second story was added in 1828. Today, the museum mounts several shows each year featuring art on loan from major museums and private collections. Recent shows have focused on paintings by Louisiana's African American folk painter, Clementine Hunter, jazz photographs taken by William P. Gottlieb, and the wood engravings made by Winslow Homer for *Harper's Weekly*.

A slice of Opelousas life is on view at **Le Vieux Village**, a collection of buildings dating from the 1700s, including a church, schoolhouse and doctor's office, that offers visitors an opportunity to view the historic local architecture. A tourist information center is also located here, as well as a small museum devoted to native son Jim Bowie, who was the hero of the Alamo and the namesake of the well-known frontier knife.

Evangeline Downs Race-track & Casino is a state-of-the-art racing facility that opened in 2003. The track offers both quarter horse and thoroughbred racing (on separate dates). It is a "racino," that is, a racetrack with a full casino component, which is a growing institution among US racetracks. The casino consists primarily of slot machines.

🏛 **Opelousas Museum**
315 N Main St. *Tel (337) 948-2589.* ◯ *8am–4:30pm Mon–Fri, 10am–3pm Sat.* ● *major hols.* 🔊

🏛 **Opelousas Museum of Art**
106 North Union St. *Tel (337) 942-4991.* ◯ *1–5pm Tue–Fri, 9am–5pm Sat.* 🔊

🏚 **Le Vieux Village**
28 East Landry St. *Tel (337) 948-0561, toll-free 800-424-5442.* ◯ *10am–2pm Tue–Fri.* ● *major hols.* 🔊

Evangeline Downs Racetrack & Casino
2235 Creswell Lane Extension. *Tel (866) 472-2466, toll-free 800-424-5442.* ◯ *Feb–Sep (racetrack); 24 hrs daily (casino).* 🔊
www.evangelinedowns.com

Main façade of the Opelousas Museum of Art

Lafayette ●

When the first Acadians arrived in 1764, they settled along the bayous and in the prairie lands west of New Orleans. Being rural people, they worked as farmers and made a living from the swamps. Lafayette is Cajun country's largest city. It is at the heart of the Cajun culture, because of the strong Arcadian family traditions and cultural heritage. Community centers, restaurants, several detailed reconstructions of Cajun villages, and its own local architectural style have imprinted this city with a unique atmosphere and the distinctive feeling of being in the Cajun Country.

☆ Acadian Cultural Center

501 Fisher Rd, Lafayette. **Tel** *(337) 232-0789.* ◯ *8am–5pm daily.* ● *Dec 25.* ⚑
A 37-minute film dramatizes the British deportation of the Acadian population from Canada's Acadie, and charts their diaspora to France and to places along the east coast of North America, before their final arrival in Louisiana. In an adjacent display area, informative exhibits, featuring photographs and artifacts, focus on every aspect of Acadian culture, including language, music, architecture, religion, cuisine, the Cajun Mardi Gras, and all kinds of handcrafts.

Old-fashioned Cajun plough

☆ Vermilionville

300 Fisher Rd, Lafayette. **Tel** *(337) 233-4077.* ◯ *10am–4pm Tue–Sun (last admission 3pm).* ● *major hols.* ⚑ ⚑ www.vermilionville.org
This fascinating living-history museum features a collection of buildings dating from 1790 to 1890 assembled into a typical Cajun village on 23 acres. Its name, Vermilionville, was the original name for the city of Lafayette. Costumed artisans demonstrate the skills that were needed to survive in 18th- and 19th-century Louisiana; woodworking, blacksmithing, spinning, weaving, and cooking. It is pleasant to wander from building to building imagining what traditional Cajun life was like. A performance hall, where Cajun bands regularly entertain, is open in the afternoon.

⚏ Lafayette Museum/ Alexandre Mouton House

1122 Lafayette St, Lafayette. **Tel** *(337) 234-2208.* ◯ *9am–4:30pm Tue–Sat, 1–4pm Sun.* ● *major hols.* ⚑ ⚑
Jean Mouton, founder of Lafayette, built the original house around 1800. He and his wife Marie and their 12 children used it only on Sundays when they came from their plantation in Carencro to attend church and socialize. In 1825 the sixth son, Alexandre, moved his family and law practice into the house. He later became a United States senator and governor of

Harp on display at the Alexandre Mouton House

Louisiana – a notable example of Cajun success. The house contains furnishings, paintings, maps, and documents relating to the city's history, plus some glittering Mardi Gras costumes and regalia.

☆ University Art Museum

1710 East St. Mary Boulevard, Lafayette. **Tel** *(337) 482-2278.* ◯ *9am–5pm Tue–Thu, 9am–noon Fri, 10am–5pm Sat.* ● *major hols.* ⚑ ⚑ www.louisiana.edu/uam
This small art museum is located on the campus of the University of Louisiana at Lafayette, an institution with

Original Acadian chapel in Vermilionville

The University Art Museum, a 2001 design in steel, stone, and glass

17,000 students, which has an excellent Computer Science department and is also home to both the National Wetlands Research Center and the Center for Louisiana Studies. The University Art Museum was founded in 1968 and has a permanent collection of more than 1,500 works including paintings, sculpture, folk art, and textiles. The emphasis is on the cultural heritage of Louisiana. In 2001, the museum moved to a bold modern building of glass and steel with state-of-the-art exhibition spaces. It has many outstanding works of art, including European and American art from the 18th, 19th, and 20th centuries, and a wide assortment of 2nd century BC Egyptian artifacts. This permanent exhibition also includes an excellent collection of African American folk art. Diverse architectural drawings, as well as student works, are displayed along with temporary exhibits all year long.

🏛 The Acadian Village

200 Greenleaf Dr, Lafayette.
Tel *(337) 981-2364.* ⬭ *10am–4pm Tue–Sat.* ⬤ *Jan 1, Thanksgiving, Dec 25, Mardi Gras.* 📷 ♿
www.acadianvillage.org

At this version of a recreated 19th-century village, most of the buildings are original, although they have been moved here from other locations. The houses are furnished with typical Cajun furniture and tools, and are tended by costumed guides who demonstrate such skills as spinning, weaving, and blacksmithing. One of the residences was the birthplace of state senator Dudley LeBlanc, the creator of a cure-all tonic called Hadacol, which was still in use as recently as the 1950s.

Dentist's chair at the Acadian Village's infirmary

THE ACADIANS

Driven by the British from Acadia, in Nova Scotia, Canada, the Acadians (or "Cajuns") settled along the bayous of Louisiana in 1764, working as farmers. For generations they were disparaged, and in the 20th century their culture came under threat, first when compulsory education was introduced in 1916 and the French language was forbidden, and later in the 1930s when Huey Long *(see p146)* built roads across the swamps, opening their communities to a wider world. When oil was discovered, the transformation intensified; outsiders flooded in and the Francophone culture was endangered. The culture survived largely because Cajuns have a strong sense of family and attachment to place. Today Cajun Country is the largest French-speaking community in the United States. In the 1960s, Cajun pride was restored when the teaching of French returned to the classrooms. At the same time, Cajun and zydeco music started growing in popularity among a broader audience, and Cajun cuisine, promoted by chef Paul Prudhomme *(see p177)*, spread across the country.

Traditional Acadian dress

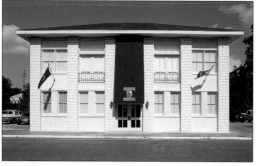

The Acadian Memorial in St. Martinville

St. Martinville ⓻

Cajun Country. 🏠 *8,000.* 🛈 *215 Evangeline Blvd, (337) 394-2233.* **www.**stmartinville.org

This small picturesque town on a natural levee of the Bayou Teche, was founded in 1765 as a military outpost. It became known as "Petit Paris" (little Paris) because many French noblemen settled there after fleeing the French Revolution.

Acadian Memorial

Located in the main square of this town is the **Acadian Memorial**, which houses the mural painted by Robert Dafford, *The Arrival of the Acadians in Louisiana,* which portrays some 40 people, who arrived in Louisiana between 1764 and 1788. The painter went so far as to model some of the portraits on contemporary descendants. Opposite the painting, the Wall of Names lists about 3,000 early Acadians. Behind the museum, an eternal flame burns in a small courtyard garden overlooking Bayou Teche.

Nearby stands the **Evangeline Oak**, marking the spot where the two famous Acadian lovers, Gabriel and Evangeline, supposedly encountered each other. Gabriel confessed that after three years in exile he had despaired of ever seeing her again and married another. She went mad and died soon after. Longfellow's poem changes the ending, placing

her as a nurse at his bedside as he lay dying.

St. Martin de Tours Church is the focal point of St. Martinville. Established in 1765 by French missionaries, it was the first church to serve the Acadian community. Fairly plain inside, it contains a baptismal font, which was a gift from Louis XVI, and a replica of the grotto at Lourdes. The grave of Evangeline Labiche (mythologized as Longfellow's Evangeline) and a bronze statue of her are located in the garden behind the church. The monument was donated by actress Dolores del Río, who played the role of Evangeline in the silent movie filmed here in 1929. Also on the church square there is the **Petit Paris Museum and Gift Shop**, which houses the historical records of the most important events in the town's life. The **Longfellow-Evangeline**

St. Martin de Tours church at the center of St. Martinville

State Commemorative Area is a 180-acre state park that stretches along Bayou Teche. It offers pleasant picnicking and walking trails among 300-year-old oaks. At the center of the park stands a reconstruction of a typical Acadian cabin representative of the 1790s. This can be contrasted with the Olivier House, a plantation home built in 1815. The cypress and brick structure has 14-inch (36-cm) thick walls. There is also a museum, which focuses on Acadian history and culture.

🏛 **Acadian Memorial**
121 South New Market St.
Tel *(337) 394-2258.* ⭕ *10am–4:30pm daily.* ⬤ *major hols.*
♿ 📷

🏛 **Petit Paris Museum and Gift Shop**
103 S Main St. ***Tel*** *(337) 394-7334.*
⭕ *9:30am–4:30pm daily.*
⬤ *Dec 25.* ♿ 📷

✝ **St. Martin de Tours Church**
133 S Main St. ***Tel*** *(337) 394-6021.*
⭕ *8am–6pm daily.*
⬤ *noon–6pm Fri.* ♿

🏛 **The Longfellow-Evangeline State Commemorative Area**
1200 N Main St. ***Tel*** *(337) 394-3754.*
⭕ *9am–5pm daily.* ⬤ *Thanksgiving, Dec 25, Jan 1.* ♿ 📷

New Iberia and Avery Island ⓼

Cajun Country. 🏠 *32,000.*
🚌 *1103 E Main St.* 🛈 *2513 Highway 14, (888) 942-3742.*
www.cityofnewiberia.com

New Iberia is notable for its many sugar cane plantations. The area also owes its wealth to oil drilling and salt mining. In fact, the so-called "islands" in the region, such as Avery and Jefferson, are not actually surrounded by water: rather they are domes located atop salt mines.

At the plantation home known as **Shadows on the Teche**, 40 trunks were found in the attic, filled with 17,000 letters, photographs, receipts, and papers relating to the family who lived here. This documentation is used as background for the fascinating tour of the house. A native of Maryland, David Weeks, built the plantation home in 1831. He died shortly thereafter, leaving his wife, Mary Clara, to run it. During the Civil War *(see pp18–19),* when Union General Nathaniel P. Banks seized it and made it his headquarters, Mary Clara retired to the attic where she died in 1863. The last owner, Weeks Hall, was a well-known artist and scholar, who restored the house and entertained many famous visitors in it, including director Cecil B. DeMille and writer Henry Miller. Their names are inscribed in the foyer.

On Avery Island the **McIlhenny Company Tabasco Factory and Jungle Gardens** is the source of the famous hot sauce, which is an essential ingredient in Bloody Marys and in local cuisine. Approximately 75 acres of pepper plants blaze their bright red color from August to November. A brief film explains the process in which the red chili peppers are crushed and combined with salt and vinegar to make the zesty sauce. Visitors can also tour the bottling factory.

The founder considered himself a botanist-naturalist and the Jungle Gardens that he assembled are spectacular. In addition to abundant camellias and azaleas, there are such exotica as Latin American papaya. The

Moss-draped oaks and spring-flowering plants in the Jungle Gardens

gardens also shelter a diverse population of egrets, herons, and peacocks, as well as the beaver-like nutria. In winter, wild fowl stop here too.

The **Rip Van Winkle House and Gardens** are located on the salt dome called Jefferson Island. It was built by the actor Joseph Jefferson in 1870 and named after the role he played 4,500 times. Architecturally, it is a hodgepodge of Moorish, Steamboat Gothic, and Victorian. The house is surrounded by 25 acres of beautiful gardens, which are on the banks of Lake Peigneur.

After Jefferson died in 1905, J. Lyle Bayless of the Salt Island Mining Company purchased the house. Shortly afterward, oil was discovered on the property. It was soon producing up to 250,000 barrels of oil a week from 30 wells. In

1972, the Texaco Oil Company mistakenly drilled through the salt dome, causing an explosion that set off a minor tidal wave on the lake. Miraculously, no one was killed.

🏠 Shadows on the Teche
317 E Main St, New Iberia.
Tel (337) 369-6446. ◻ 9am–4:30pm daily. ● major hols. 🖩
www.shadowsontheteche.org

🏛 McIlhenny Company Tabasco Factory and Jungle Gardens
Hwy 329, Avery Island. **Tel** (337) 365-8173. ◻ 9am–4pm daily. **Jungle Gardens Tel** (337) 369-6243. ◻ 9am–5pm daily. ● major hols. ♿ 🖩 📷 www.tabasco.com

🏠 Rip Van Winkle House and Gardens
5505 Rip Van Winkle Rd, Jefferson Island. **Tel** (337) 359-8525. ◻ 9am–4pm daily. ● public hols. ♿ 📷 www.ripvanwinklegardens.com

Shadows on the Teche in New Iberia

Food stalls in the French Market, New Orleans ▷

TRAVELERS' NEEDS

WHERE TO STAY

New Orleans is a big convention town, with many well-known hotel chains, including the Hyatt, Hilton, Marriott, and Sheraton. It also has some elegant hotels, like the Windsor Court, the Ritz Carlton, and Le Pavillon, and lovely boutique offerings, such as International House and Soniat House. Some of the best lodgings can be found in

Bellman

bed and breakfasts, like the House on Bayou Road, or in small inns such as the Maison de Ville and Audubon Cottages. The Fairmont, which closed after Hurricane Katrina due to damage, was reborn in 2009 as The Roosevelt, a return to its historic name and the name locals remember. It has undergone extensive renovation, and is now a Waldorf Astoria property.

Le Pavillon Hotel in the Business District (see p165)

WHERE TO LOOK

Most hotels are located in the French Quarter or in the Central Business District along Canal Street, the latter being within walking distance of both the Quarter and the Convention Center. Bed and breakfasts (B&Bs) are scattered throughout the city, uptown in the Garden District, and on the fringes of the Quarter in the Faubourgs Marigny and Treme.

HOTEL PRICES AND SERVICES

New Orleans has accommodations to fit any budget, from the least expensive motel to the fabulous French Quarter hotels and guest houses. Prices vary according to the location and the level of luxury; many boutique hotels are as expensive as the splendid high rises, and if the hotel or B&B is in the French Quarter, the price will reflect this sought-after location.

Prices can rise more than 50 percent during Mardi Gras and special events, and be prepared for a three- to five-day minimum stay.

All hotel accommodations, unless otherwise stated, include air-conditioning, elevators, non-smoking rooms, and full bathrooms.

During major holidays, such as Christmas, many hotels require a three- or four-night minimum stay. In the off-season, such as the summer, special rates and vacation packages offer amazing discounts.

BED AND BREAKFAST

Guest houses and boutique hotels are usually in renovated historic homes, and B&Bs are rooms in a private residence. All offer some meals, full breakfasts or just coffee and croissants, and often, afternoon tea or cocktails are provided. All have a limited number of rooms, so advance reservations

are necessary. Some of the budget-priced guest houses and B&Bs have shared bathrooms, and facilities for disabled guests can be limited.

HIDDEN EXTRAS

Taxes will add 13 percent to the bill plus an additional $1–$3 for "room night tax". Valet parking will cost from $12 to $25 a day. Some motels and B&Bs have free parking, so always ask ahead. Hotel telephone charges are often very high. It is always cheaper to use a pay phone in the lobby or use your cell phone, particularly when calling overseas. You will also pay a premium on products in your mini-bar. A tip of $1 to $2 per bag is usually paid to the bellman for carrying bags. Room-service waiters expect the standard 15 percent tip. If staying more than one night, you should leave $1 to $2 a day for the housekeeping staff.

Lobby of the Omni Royal Orleans hotel (see p162)

A perfect welcome at the Monteleone Hotel *(see p162)*

FACILITIES

Most establishments offer full facilities, such as well-appointed rooms, cable TV, phone, modems, mini-bars, and full bathrooms. Often the larger hotels have one or two fine restaurants, several bars, a fitness room, a swimming pool, and a business center. At virtually every hotel, you will find complimentary toiletries, a morning newspaper delivered to your door, room service, and wake-up and reservation services.

Because the weather in New Orleans is semi-tropical, all accommodations are air-conditioned. B&Bs generally do not offer all these amenities, but the ambience in these homes makes up for any lack.

HOW TO BOOK

If you want to visit the city during Mardi Gras or the Jazz and Heritage Festival, you will need to book six months to a year in advance. At other times, a few months' advance booking is recommended. You can make telephone or online reservations using a credit card. A deposit of one night is usually required, and there are specific cancellation policies that guests should clarify at the time of booking. If you anticipate arriving after 6pm, ask for guaranteed late arrival. Most hotels have toll-free reservation numbers, and many take reservations by fax or email.

SPECIAL RATES

When making reservations, it won't hurt to ask for special AAA, AARP, or senior citizen rates. Some chains offer discount rates, and look at hotel websites for special deals. You can reserve by using a major credit card. Package tours may also offer savings from hotel or B&B accommodations to airport/hotel transportation. Check the newspapers for specials.

A four-poster bed in one of the upscale bed and breakfasts

DISABLED TRAVELERS

Since 1992 all hotels in the United States have been required by law to provide wheelchair-accessible accommodations. However, older, listed, and historic properties are exempt from this provision, but most establishments have at least one room equipped for disabled guests. If you or any of your traveling companions have special needs, it is wise to call the hotel in advance to confirm suitability.

TRAVELING WITH CHILDREN

Most hotels welcome children, although New Orleans may not be an ideal destination for the young. Children aged up to 12, 16, or 18 (depending on the place) can usually stay free in their parents' room.

YOUTH AND BUDGET ACCOMMODATIONS

New Orleans has a few hostels, as well as some guest houses with rooms with shared bathrooms that are modestly priced. Many motels on the outskirts of the city are also fairly inexpensive.

DIRECTORY

RESERVATIONS

Bed And Breakfast Reservation Service
www.neworleansbandbs.com

New Orleans Bed & Breakfast and French Quarter Accommodations
Tel (504) 524-9918
or (888) 240-0070.
www.neworleansbandb.com

New Orleans Property Management Service
1000 Bourbon St,
Box 314, New Orleans,
LA 70116.
Tel (504) 343-2663.
www.neworleansreservations.com

ONLINE

Expedia
www.expedia.com

Hotels.com
www.hotels.com

Trip Advisor
www.tripadvisor.com

Choosing a Hotel

These hotels have been selected across a wide price range for their good value, excellent facilities, and location. This chart lists the hotels by area of the city in the same order as the rest of the guide. Within each area, entries are listed alphabetically within each price category, from the least expensive to the most expensive.

PRICE CATEGORIES
For a standard double room per night in the tourist season, including tax and service:

⑤ $50–$100
⑤⑤ $100–$150
⑤⑤⑤ $150–$200
⑤⑤⑤⑤ $200–$250
⑤⑤⑤⑤⑤ over $250

UPPER FRENCH QUARTER

Grenoble House   🅿 ▦   ⑤⑤
323 Dauphine St, 70112 **Tel** *(504) 522-1331* **Fax** *(504) 524-4968* **Rooms** *17*   **Map** *4 C2*

All the rooms are suites in this little-known French Quarter hotel. Kitchens and ample living space make this the perfect place for a family or a group (but no children under 12). Furnishings are utilitarian. The courtyard and small pool are lovely, and the staff are attentive and welcoming. **www.grenoblehouse.com**

Prince Conti Hotel   📶 🅿 ⑪   ⑤⑤
830 Conti St, 70112 **Tel** *(504) 529-4172* **Fax** *(504) 581-3802* **Rooms** *73*   **Map** *4 C2*

Generations of Southern families have stayed at the Prince Conti. Rooms vary in size and are handsomely furnished with antiques and art. The friendly, long-term staff make a point of getting to know guests. The hotel's bar, the Bombay Club, is renowned for its martinis. **www.princecontihotel.com**

Iberville Suites   📶 🅿 ⑪ ▦ 📺   ⑤⑤⑤
910 Iberville St, 70112 **Tel** *(504) 523-2400* **Fax** *(504) 524-1321* **Rooms** *230*   **Map** *4 C2*

This is the downscale segment of the Ritz-Carlton but it is still pretty luxe. All the rooms are junior suites with small fridges, coffeemakers, two TVs, and much more. Decor is chintz and mahogany. The famed Ritz service is good even for the not-so-rich guests who bunk here. **www.ibervillesuites.com**

Olivier House   📶 ▦   ⑤⑤⑤
828 Toulouse St, 70112 **Tel** *(504) 525-8456* **Fax** *(504) 529-2006* **Rooms** *58*   **Map** *4 C2*

Three townhouses and several other buildings compose this Quarter hotel. The entrance parlors are formal, but there is a free spirit about the Olivier House. Rooms range from no-frills options to shabby-chic suites. The courtyard is small but pretty. Pets are welcome. **www.olivierhousehotel.com**

Maison de Ville & Audubon Cottages   🅿 ⑪ ▦   ⑤⑤⑤⑤
727 Toulouse St, 70130 **Tel** *(504) 561-5858* **Fax** *(504) 528-9939* **Rooms** *24*   **Map** *4 C2*

The Maison de Ville is a beautiful Creole townhouse compound with richly decorated, if smallish, rooms. The even more expensive Audubon Cottages are a block away: idyllic private cottages in a tropical garden with a pool. This is how visitors dream their Quarter hotel will be. **www.hotelmaisondeville.com**

Monteleone Hotel   📶 🅿 ⑪ ▦ 📺   ⑤⑤⑤⑤
214 Royal St, 70130 **Tel** *(504) 523-3341* **Fax** *(504) 681-4491* **Rooms** *655*   **Map** *4 C3*

The Monteleone has been a French Quarter landmark since 1886. This family-owned hotel has undergone a major renovation, revamping its rooms with new fabrics, furniture, and amenities. Try booking one of the "literary rooms," named for writer guests such as Truman Capote and Ernest Hemingway. **www.hotelmonteleone.com**

Omni Royal Orleans   📶 🅿 ⑪ ▦ 📺   ⑤⑤⑤⑤
621 St. Louis St, 70130 **Tel** *(504) 529-5333* **Fax** *(504) 529-7089* **Rooms** *346*   **Map** *4 C2*

One of the largest hotels in the French Quarter, the Omni Royal is known for its attentive service. Rooms have an old New Orleans look but are fully equipped with dataports, Wi-Fi, and dual phones. Its restaurant, The Rib Room, is home to a popular local "power lunch" scene. **www.omniroyalorleans.com**

The Ritz-Carlton   📶 🅿 ⑪ ▦ 📺   ⑤⑤⑤⑤
921 Canal St, 70112 **Tel** *(504) 524-1331* **Fax** *(504) 524-7675* **Rooms** *527*   **Map** *4 B3*

This hotel actually comprises three hotels in one place (Iberville Suites and Maison Orleans are the other two). The largest segment is the Ritz-Carlton, which lives up to its reputation for luxury. Rooms are large with marble baths. The hotel spa, which is one of the best in the US, is pure bliss. **www.ritzcarlton.com**

Royal Sonesta Hotel   📶 🅿 ⑪ ▦ 📺   ⑤⑤⑤⑤
300 Bourbon St, 70130 **Tel** *(504) 586-0300* **Fax** *(504) 586-0335* **Rooms** *483*   **Map** *4 C2*

Covering almost a block in the Quarter, this hotel is like a little village with its own shops, cafés, courtyards, and personalities. Rooms range from basic to suites, all handsomely appointed. Ask to be as far away from Bourbon Street as possible to avoid street noise. **www.royalsonestano.com**

Key to Symbols *see back cover flap*

The Saint Hotel

931 Canal St, 70130 **Tel** *(504) 522-5400* **Rooms** *166*

Map *4 B3*

This majestic building dating to 1909 is decorated with Beaux Arts touches from top to bottom. The lobby and guest rooms are styled in a modern, hip fashion, with white walls, sky-blue ceilings, and crisp lines. The rooftop lounge offers a fantastic view above the French Quarter rooftops. **www.thesainthotelneworleans.com**

Maison Orleans

904 Iberville St, 70112 **Tel** *(504) 524-1331* **Fax** *(504) 524-7675* **Rooms** *75*

Map *4 C2*

The Ritz-Carlton goes over the top with the supremely luxurious Maison Orleans. It feels like a private club with your own staff rather than a hotel. Rooms have dreamy beds, gilt-encrusted furniture, and soaking tubs. Guests are served food and drink almost continually. **www.ritzcarlton.com**

W French Quarter

316 Chartres St, 70130 **Tel** *(504) 581-1200* **Fax** *(504) 522-3208* **Rooms** *98*

Map *4 C3*

W tries to find a middle ground between postmodern and French Quarter non-modern in this stylish hotel. Rooms have all the W signatures: most important, the lush bed. All the rooms are small, which is typical of the Quarter. The courtyard, often lit by candles, is stunning. **www.wfrenchquarter.com**

LOWER FRENCH QUARTER AND MARIGNY

Bon Maison Guesthouse

835 Bourbon St, 70116 **Tel** *(504) 561-8498* **Rooms** *3*

Map *5 D1*

On lower Bourbon Street, Bon Maison is an 1833 Creole townhouse with slave quarters. It is convenient to the gay bar scene, although non-gays also like the B&B for its historic ambience, well-appointed rooms, and great prices. Rooms have fridges and microwaves. The guest house doesn't accept children. **www.bonmaison.com**

Pierre Coulon Guesthouse

714 Spain St, 70117 **Tel** *(504) 943-6692* **Rooms** *1*

Map *5 F1*

Staying at this Marigny home is like living in New Orleans. Guests reside in the restored two-story slave quarters, equipped with a small kitchen. The rooms open out into a tranquil courtyard, shared with the main house. The hosts know the city intimately and cheerfully share tips. **www.pierrecoulonguesthouse.com**

Andrew Jackson Hotel

919 Royal St, 70116 **Tel** *(800) 654-0224* **Rooms** *22*

Map *5 D1*

This fine little hotel sits on a tranquil corner of Royal Street in a 19th-century villa. The best rooms are the balcony suites overlooking the street. It is worth the extra charge for the fine view. Rooms are traditional in style, with basic amenities. Most rooms open onto the courtyard. **www.frenchquarterinns.com**

Chateau Hotel

1001 Chartres St, 70116 **Tel** *(504) 524-9636* **Fax** *(504) 525-2989* **Rooms** *45*

Map *5 D2*

The Chateau is a hotchpotch of several historic and newer buildings cobbled together in the Lower (quieter) Quarter. Rooms come in a variety of sizes, some with antique pieces. The hotel has a long list of regulars who return year after year, giving it a clubhouse feel. **www.chateauhotel.com**

Cornstalk Hotel

915 Royal St, 70116 **Tel** *(504) 523-1515* **Fax** *(504) 522-5558* **Rooms** *14*

Map *5 D1*

Named for its charming cornstalk-shaped cast-iron fence, this hotel is a converted 19th-century home. Some of the rooms are tiny, but all are furnished with antiques. The second-story verandah is a favorite gathering place for sipping drinks while watching the Quarter pass by. **www.cornstalkhotel.com**

Frenchmen Hotel

417 Frenchmen St, 70116 **Tel** *(800) 831-1781* **Fax** *(504) 948-2258* **Rooms** *28*

Map *5 E1*

This hotel is just steps away from the French Quarter and the Frenchmen Street music scene. It's a compound of several 19th-century buildings. Rooms can be on the dark side, and the pool is tiny. Pluses include the friendly, helpful staff and the bohemian ambience. **www.frenchmenhotel.com**

Hotel Provincial

1024 Chartres St, 70116 **Tel** *(504) 581-4995* **Fax** *(504) 581-1018* **Rooms** *115*

Map *5 D2*

Popular with business travelers and families, the family-owned Provincial's rooms have a vintage look, with antiques and exposed brick. There are several courtyards, two pools, parking, and access to the motel's acclaimed eatery, Stella! **www.hotelprovincial.com**

Hotel Villa Convento

616 Ursulines St, 70116 **Tel** *(504) 522-1793* **Fax** *(504) 524-1902* **Rooms** *25*

Map *5 D1*

This is a family-owned inn of the old school: modest in amenities but rich in service and ambience. Rooms are basic and clean. The inn is on a quiet street in the Quarter and is a quick walk to clubs and attractions. Singer Jimmy Buffett lived here in the 1970s when it was a rooming house. **www.villaconvento.com**

Le Richelieu Hotel $$

1234 Chartres St, 70116 **Tel** *(504) 529-2492* **Fax** *(504) 524-8179* **Rooms** *86*　　　　**Map** *5 D1*

A Quarter favorite, this hotel is forever famous for Paul McCartney and his family staying here for months in the 1970s. Rooms have a vintage look, and suites are also available. The courtyard and pool are very pretty, and the large, park-it-yourself parking lot is a rarity in the Quarter. **www.lerichelieuhotel.com**

Lions Inn Bed & Breakfast $$

2517 Chartres St, 70117 **Tel** *(504) 945-2339* **Fax** *(504) 708-2688* **Rooms** *10*　　　　**Map** *5 F1*

The engaging house-party atmosphere makes this gay-friendly inn popular with straight people as well. The B&B's two adjoining houses open onto a large, jungle-like courtyard with a pool. Rooms vary in size from tiny to apartment with kitchenette. Two rooms have shared baths. **www.lionsinn.com**

Maison Dupuy Hotel $$

1001 Toulouse St, 70112 **Tel** *(504) 586-8000* **Fax** *(504) 525-5334* **Rooms** *200*　　　　**Map** *4 C2*

This hotel is at the "back of the Quarter" (opposite from the river). It is built around a courtyard, and some rooms have overlooking balconies. Rooms are decorated with local and soothing colors. Le Meritage, a wine-centric restaurant with abundant pairings, is part of the hotel. **www.maisondupuy.com**

Nine-O-Five Royal Hotel $$

905 Royal St, 70116 **Tel** *(504) 523-0219* **Fax** *(504) 525-3905* **Rooms** *13*　　　　**Map** *5 D2*

This small hotel in the French Quarter is a little-known jewel. Set in a large Victorian house on a quiet corner, it offers the best kind of basic stay – a good place to sleep and regroup in attractive surroundings with a helpful staff. Ask for one of the suites with a balcony. **www.905royalhotel.com**

Claiborne Mansion $$$

2111 Dauphine St, 70116 **Tel** *(504) 301-1027* **Rooms** *7*　　　　**Map** *3 E4*

This is one of New Orleans' best-kept secrets. The 1858 villa has been imaginatively restored using a subtle color palette and contemporary furniture. The rooms are airy and luxurious. The gardens feature a lap pool and a small cottage. A favorite of visiting celebrities. **www.claibornemansion.com**

Hotel de la Monnaie $$$

405 Esplanade Ave, 70116 **Tel** *(504) 947-0009* **Fax** *(504) 945-6841* **Rooms** *53*　　　　**Map** *5 E1*

Built in the 1980s, this Beaux-Arts style hotel is an ideal blend of the historic and the new. Rooms are clean, modern, and stylishly decorated. The Monnaie is across Esplanade Avenue from the French Market and Old Mint Museum. The hotel is a time-share but rents to non-owners. **www.hoteldelamonnaie.com**

Lafitte Guesthouse $$$

1003 Bourbon St, 70116 **Tel** *(504) 581-2678* **Fax** *(504) 581-2677* **Rooms** *14*　　　　**Map** *5 D1*

Ask for one of the two rooms with balconies overlooking Bourbon Street for a special experience. The 1840s Creole townhouse feels like the 19th century but with modern conveniences. On the minus side, the bathrooms are small, and there's no elevator for the house's four stories. **www.lafitteguesthouse.com**

Sunburst Inn $$$

819 Mandeville St, 70117 **Tel** *(504) 947-1799* **Rooms** *2*　　　　**Map** *3 F1*

Located six blocks from the French Quarter, in an area full of popular restaurants, live-music venues, and gay bars, this small inn is housed in a 1905 building that has been lovingly restored and painted in vibrant, cheerful hues. It offers high-end amenities and a welcoming atmosphere, with hosts who love to entertain. **www.sunburstinn.net**

Lanaux Mansion $$$$$

547 Esplanade Ave, 70119 **Tel** *(504) 330-2826* **Rooms** *4*　　　　**Map** *5 D1*

Esplanade Avenue, formerly known as "The Creole Promenade," has some of the grandest architecture you will see in the city. The mansion housing the Lanaux was built in 1879, and has been lovingly restored with stunning, wrought-iron balconies. Rooms feature antiques and Oriental rugs. The garden is also lovely. **www.lanauxmansion.com**

Soniat House $$$$$

1133 Chartres St, 70116 **Tel** *(504) 522-0570* **Fax** *(504) 524-0810* **Rooms** *33*　　　　**Map** *5 D1*

The Soniat House is a favorite with visiting celebrities and millionaires. The service is sublime and the rooms are beautifully appointed with Louisiana antiques, Oriental rugs, and big, enveloping beds. The hotel is located in restored Creole townhouses that face each other across Chartres Street. **www.soniathouse.com**

WAREHOUSE AND CENTRAL BUSINESS DISTRICTS

O'Keefe Plaza Hotel $

334 O'Keefe Ave, 70112 **Tel** *(504) 524-5400* **Fax** *(504) 524-5450* **Rooms** *129*　　　　**Map** *4 B3*

If you can get past the homely big-box look and dreary streetscape, this hotel has some lovely features. The prices are astoundingly low, and it's a clean, well-run facility. Rooms are plain but have all the basic necessities. The O'Keefe Plaza is close to the French Quarter and CBD offices. **www.okeefeplazahotel.com**

Key to Price Guide *see p162* **Key to Symbols** *see back cover flap*

Hampton Inn

$\circledS\circledS$

226 Carondelet St, 70130 **Tel** *(504) 529-9990* **Fax** *(504) 529-9996* **Rooms** *187*　　**Map** *4 B3*

This hotel is housed in a handsome historic office building in the Central Business District. Some rooms have four-poster beds. Business travelers will find everything they need here. The pool, courtyard, and breakfast buffet are especially good features. **www.neworleanshamptoninns.com**

La Quinta Inn & Suites

$\circledS\circledS$

301 Camp St, 70130 **Tel** *(504) 598-9977* **Fax** *(504) 598-9978* **Rooms** *182*　　**Map** *4 C3*

This handsome business hotel blends into the streetscape. While it may be short on charm, this branch of the La Quinta chain is big on efficiency, cleanliness, and good prices. A few blocks from the Quarter and close to the St. Charles Avenue streetcar, this hotel is also well placed. A large breakfast is included. **www.lq.com**

Royal St. Charles Hotel

$\circledS\circledS$

135 St. Charles Ave, 70130 **Tel** *(800) 455-3417* **Rooms** *143*　　**Map** *4 C3*

The slick exterior and boutique label make this hotel sound a little more exciting than it really is. The rooms are small but clean and comfortable. The hotel is suitably located on the St. Charles Avenue streetcar line and barely a block from the French Quarter. **www.royalsaintcharleshotel.com**

Staybridge Suites

$\circledS\circledS$

501 Tchoupitoulas St, 70130 **Tel** *(504) 571-1818* **Fax** *(504) 571-1811* **Rooms** *182*　　**Map** *4 C4*

Convenient to the Convention Center, the museum district, and the casino, this chain hotel delivers on all its promises. Rooms are bright and clean, and the breakfast is unusually fresh and abundant. The pool is a bit on the small side, but the fitness center covers the basics. **www.staybridgesuites.com**

Lafayette Hotel

$\circledS\circledS\circledS$

600 St. Charles Ave, 70130 **Tel** *(504) 524-4441* **Fax** *(504) 523-7327* **Rooms** *44*　　**Map** *4 B4*

Right on the St. Charles Avenue streetcar line, the Lafayette recalls the elegant residential hotels of an earlier era with its classic decor, friendly staff, and handsome Beaux-Arts building. Rooms are retreats with marble baths, soothing colors, and polished wood furniture. **www.thelafayettehotel.com**

Le Pavillon Hotel

$\circledS\circledS\circledS$

833 Poydras St, 70112 **Tel** *(504) 581-3111* **Fax** *(504) 620-4130* **Rooms** *219*　　**Map** *4 B3*

One of the city's grande dames, Le Pavillon wears its crown lightly. The courtly staff evoke the days of gracious hotel service. Rooms are decorated with fine art and period furniture. The rooftop pool, late-night lobby snacks, and cool bar add to the hotel's special allure. **www.lepavillon.com**

Loews Hotel

$\circledS\circledS\circledS$

300 Poydras St, 70130 **Tel** *(504) 594-3300* **Fax** *(504) 595-3310* **Rooms** *273*　　**Map** *4 C4*

This stylish hotel in the city's business and entertainment district is within a short walk of many galleries and restaurants. Rooms are luxurious, and some have views of the nearby Mississippi River; the hotel's Grand Luxury Suite is the largest in the city. There is also a popular bar and restaurant. Pets are welcome. **www.loewshotels.com**

Renaissance Arts Hotel

$\circledS\circledS\circledS$

700 Tchoupitoulas St, 70130 **Tel** *(504) 613-2330* **Fax** *(504) 613-2331* **Rooms** *217*　　**Map** *4 C4*

This hotel in the Warehouse District lives up to the "arts" in its name with a gallery and cutting-edge artworks everywhere. The large, airy rooms use bold colors and contemporary design. The hotel restaurant and bar, LaCote Brasserie, is on the local list of hot spots. **www.marriott.com**

Renaissance Pere Marquette Hotel

$\circledS\circledS\circledS$

817 Common St, 70130 **Tel** *(504) 525-1111* **Fax** *(504) 525-0688* **Rooms** *272*　　**Map** *4 B3*

The sophisticated Pere Marquette was built in 1925 as one of New Orleans' first "skyscrapers." There is a strong jazz theme throughout the hotel, and every room features luxurious amenities, whimsical decor, spacious baths, and Herman Miller Aeron chairs. The in-house restaurant MiLA is wonderful. **www.marriott.com**

International House

$\circledS\circledS\circledS\circledS$

221 Camp St, 70130 **Tel** *(504) 553-9550* **Fax** *(504) 553-9560* **Rooms** *119*　　**Map** *4 C3*

Staying here is an adventure – of the pleasant kind. Most months there's an elaborate voodoo altar in the lobby. Rooms are furnished with Louisiana-themed items. The marble bathrooms are extra large and have dual shower-heads, and big soaking tubs. The Loa bar is a local hot spot. **www.ihhotel.com**

W Hotel

$\circledS\circledS\circledS\circledS$

333 Poydras St, 70130 **Tel** *(504) 525-9444* **Fax** *(504) 581-7179* **Rooms** *423*　　**Map** *4 C4*

This seriously hip hotel has more going for it than just design. Rooms have super-luxurious beds and all the electronic amenities. The rooftop pool and cabanas are very trendy. The lobby is a popular meeting spot for beautiful 20-somethings who love the Whiskey Blue bar. **www.whotels.com**

The Hotel Modern New Orleans

$\circledS\circledS\circledS\circledS\circledS$

936 St. Charles Ave, 70130 **Tel** *(504) 962-0900* **Rooms** *135*　　**Map** *4 B5*

Opened by New York hotelier Klaus Ortlieb, the Modern is located on Lee Circle. The sleek, contemporary styling is offset by the eclectic, homey decor, with period furniture, books everywhere, and wine in each room. The lounge has a vaudevillian feel and hosts international music acts and the occasional burlesque dance troupe.

The Roosevelt

123 Baronne St, 70112 **Tel** *(504) 648-1200* **Fax** *(504) 585-1295* **Rooms** *504*   **Map** *4 B3*

This historic hotel, which was once the New Orleans headquarters of Louisiana political boss Huey Long, fully embraces its colorful past. After years as the Fairmont Hotel, it reopened in 2009 as the Roosevelt Hotel – its prior name. Today it is part of the esteemed Waldorf Astoria brand. **www.therooseveltneworleans.com**

Windsor Court Hotel

300 Gravier St, 70130 **Tel** *(504) 523-6000* **Fax** *(504) 596-4513* **Rooms** *324*   **Map** *4 C4*

Everything English is worshipped here. The hotel even does an authentic afternoon tea service. Luxury is the starting point for the Windsor Court, where rooms are magical retreats, and the lobby is truly palatial. The service is almost omniscient without being intrusive. **www.windsorcourthotel.com**

GARDEN DISTRICT AND UPTOWN

Avenue Inn B&B

4125 St. Charles Ave, 70115 **Tel** *(504) 269-2640* **Fax** *(504) 269-2641* **Rooms** *17*   **Map** *7 E4*

You see this 1891 mansion almost as its first occupants did; it has never been remodeled, only restored. Rooms are on all three floors, some with period pieces, all with private baths. The house is near Tulane and Loyola, right on the St. Charles Avenue streetcar line. **www.avenueinnbb.com**

Maison St. Charles Inn

1319 St. Charles Ave, 70130 **Tel** *(504) 522-0187* **Fax** *(504) 529-4379* **Rooms** *128*   **Map** *8 A2*

Although this inn is not located in the most elegant part of the Garden District, it is still on the St. Charles Avenue streetcar line. The rooms have a traditional decor and basic amenities. The central courtyard with pool, evening happy hour, and billiard table add to the conviviality. Special deals for cruise-ship travelers. **www.maisonstcharles.com**

Marquette House

2249 Carondelet St, 70130 **Tel** *(504) 523-3014* **Fax** *(504) 529-5933* **Rooms** *25*   **Map** *8 A3*

A loose-limbed hostel (not part of the international association), Marquette House has typical dormitory rooms for budget travelers. Apartments are also available in adjacent historic buildings and offer one of the best deals in town. The compound is a block from the St. Charles Avenue streetcar.

Prytania Park Hotel

1525 Prytania St, 70130 **Tel** *(504) 524-0427* **Fax** *(504) 522-2977* **Rooms** *74*   **Map** *8 A3*

One block from St. Charles Avenue, this compound of old and new buildings is a collection of suites and rooms. Furnishings are from the upscale furniture store across the street (owned by the same family). Kids will love the lofts in some suites, while everyone else will love the affordable rates. **www.prytaniaparkhotel.com**

St. Charles Guest House

1748 Prytania St, 70130 **Tel** *(504) 523-6556* **Fax** *(504) 522-6340* **Rooms** *35*   **Map** *8 A3*

Once a seamen's boarding house, the inn has grown to include several buildings near St. Charles. It's a friendly family-run place where guests get to know each other and return year after year. All rooms are different, ranging from no-frills to a few frills. No phones or TVs in the rooms. **www.stcharlesguesthouse.com**

Avenue Plaza

2111 St. Charles Ave, 70130 **Tel** *(504) 566-1212* **Fax** *(504) 525-6899* **Rooms** *258*   **Map** *8 A3*

This hotel is all suites (two sizes) with kitchens. The St. Charles Avenue streetcar stops at the front door. The hotel is a time-share and has undergone a refurbishing sequence. The main attraction is the courtyard pool, where guests can relax and enjoy a massage. **www.extraholidays.com**

Chimes Inn

1146 Constantinople St, 70115 **Tel** *(504) 899-2621* **Fax** *(504) 488-4639* **Rooms** *5*   **Map** *7 E4*

Guests stay in the four private rooms and one cottage in this Uptown home. Nicely decorated and perfectly maintained, the B&B is a good homebase for travelers. The hosts serve a deluxe continental breakfast and are enthusiastic guides to the city. **www.chimesneworleans.com**

Columns Hotel

3811 St. Charles Ave, 70115 **Tel** *(504) 899-9308* **Fax** *(504) 899-8170* **Rooms** *20*   **Map** *7 E4*

This small hotel is famous as the set for the Louis Malle film *Pretty Baby* and has plenty of fans for its laid-back ambience. The 1883 mansion's rooms are quirky and decorated with antiques and secondhand chic. The lounge, the Victorian Bar, is one of the city's best bars. **www.thecolumns.com**

Creole Gardens Guesthouse

1415 Prytania St, 70130 **Tel** *(504) 569-8700* **Fax** *(504) 895-2231* **Rooms** *25*   **Map** *8 B2*

Bright tropical blues and yellows signal a Caribbean mood for this lively guest house, popular with Europeans and younger travelers. Rooms are in various shapes and sizes. All three 19th-century buildings that constitute the hotel open onto the courtyard. Breakfast is included. **www.creolegardens.com**

Key to Price Guide *see p162* **Key to Symbols** *see back cover flap*

The Green House Inn

1212 Magazine St, 70130 **Tel** *(504) 525-1333* **Fax** *(504) 525-1383* **Rooms** *10*

Map 8 B2

This historic bed and breakfast in the Lower Garden District offers great access to downtown without the hustle and bustle. A tropical theme pervades the premises, and the surrounding neighborhood is bejeweled with architectural gems. The Green House is a pet-friendly establishment too. **www.thegreenhouseinn.com**

Hubbard Mansion

3535 St. Charles Ave, 70115 **Tel** *(504) 897-3535* **Fax** *(504) 899-8827* **Rooms** *5*

Map 7 E4

This Greek Revival house is actually a modern building, designed as a replica of a Natchez mansion. It's furnished with beautiful antiques, including rare Louisiana armoires. The host, Don Hubbard, is a New Orleans insider. Rooms are of different sizes, and all have marble baths. **www.hubbardmansion.com**

St. Charles Inn

3636 St. Charles Ave, 70115 **Tel** *(504) 899-8888* **Fax** *(504) 899-8892* **Rooms** *40*

Map 7 E4

The hotel is a wallflower on glamorous St. Charles but it is well worth seeking out, especially for the budget traveler. Rooms are motel-ordinary, and there's no lobby to speak of, but it's safe, comfortable, and on the streetcar line. Pluses are free parking, continental breakfast, and a fitness room. **www.bestwestern.com**

Terrell Guesthouse

1441 Magazine St, 70130 **Tel** *(504) 237-2076* **Fax** *(504) 247-0565* **Rooms** *8*

Map 8 B3

This charming inn is an 1858 villa in the Lower Garden District. Rooms are furnished with antiques and art, all with private baths, and there is a spacious courtyard. A full breakfast is served. The neighborhood is undergoing a renaissance of sorts. **www.terrellhouse.com**

Grand Victorian Inn

2727 St. Charles Ave, 70130 **Tel** *(504) 895-1104* **Fax** *(504) 896-8688* **Rooms** *8*

Map 7 F3

This meticulously restored Queen Anne-style mansion led the way for other B&Bs on St. Charles Avenue. The house is beautifully decorated with antiques and art. Bedrooms have four-poster and canopy beds along with private baths. Some rooms overlook the avenue, which is always a plus. **www.gvbb.com**

Hampton Inn

3626 St. Charles Ave, 70115 **Tel** *(504) 899-9990* **Fax** *(504) 899-9908* **Rooms** *100*

Map 7 4E

Well placed on St. Charles Avenue, this hotel has a cheery pastel exterior that sets the tone for the helpful staff and sunny lobby. Rooms are spacious and attractive. Big pluses are the free, non-valet parking and the ample breakfast buffet. The St. Charles Avenue streetcar stops almost in front of the hotel. **www.neworleanshamptoninns.com**

Laurel Street Bed & Breakfast

5127 Laurel St, 70115 **Tel** *(504) 269-5002* **Fax** *(504) 269-5309* **Rooms** *4*

Map 6 C5

Built in 1891 for the treasurer of the New Orleans Grand Opera House, this lovely B&B is housed in an old Eastlake cottage with a garden and a large porch with an attractive view. It is located in a quiet neighborhood, but close to the Mardi Gras parade routes and Audubon Park. Children are welcome.

Magnolia Mansion

2127 Prytania St, 70130 **Tel** *(504) 412-9500* **Fax** *(504) 412-9502* **Rooms** *9*

Map 8 A3

This is one of New Orleans' great antebellum houses. Now restored as a B&B, the grandeur remains. Guests must abide by a long list of rules (no children, no red wine, etc), and sometimes have to dodge weddings and camera crews. Rooms are lavishly decorated. **www.magnoliamansion.com**

McKendrick-Breaux House

1474 Magazine St, 70130 **Tel** *(504) 586-1700* **Fax** *(504) 522-7138* **Rooms** *9*

Map 8 B3

Situated on a reviving part of Magazine Street, this is one of the city's premier B&Bs. Two restored 1860s town-houses are joined by a tropical garden. Rooms have antique beds, contemporary art, and private phones, reflecting the inn's masterful blending of old and new. **www.mckendrick-breaux.com**

Sully Mansion

2631 Prytania St, 70130 **Tel** *(504) 891-0457* **Fax** *(504) 269-0793* **Rooms** *8*

Map 7 F3

This 1890 Queen Anne-style mansion is wonderfully intact with stunning stained-glass windows and interior moldings. Rooms are furnished with antiques and tasteful accessories. All rooms have modern baths. The B&B is in the Garden District, a block from the St. Charles Avenue streetcar. **www.sullymansion.com**

MID-CITY

Ashton's Bed & Breakfast

2023 Esplanade Ave, 70116 **Tel** *(504) 942-7048* **Rooms** *8*

Map 3 D3

Guests love sitting in the back garden under the ancient oak tree at this popular B&B. The 1861 mansion is situated near the Fair Grounds, making it ideal for the Jazz Fest. City Park is also nearby. Most rooms are furnished with period furniture and all have private baths. **www.ashtonsbb.com**

Degas House
 $$

2306 Esplanade Ave, 70119 **Tel** (504) 821-5009 **Fax** (504) 821-0870 **Rooms** 8 **Map** 2 C3

Painter Edgar Degas visited his American relatives here between 1872 and 1873. Guest rooms in the 1852 Italianate house include a garret, but it's not clear exactly which room Degas stayed in during his residency. The minimalist decor serves to show off the fine lines of the house itself. **www.degashouse.com**

O'Malley House
$$

120 S Pierce St, 70119 **Tel** (504) 488-5896 **Fax** (504) 483-3791 **Rooms** 8 **Map** 2 A3

One block off the Canal streetcar line, the O'Malley House is a marvel of elaborate Queen Anne-style architecture. Restored inside and out, the inn offers antique-filled rooms, an excellent breakfast, and hosts who go out of their way to make life interesting and easy for their guests. **www.1896Omalleyhouse.com**

Block-Keller House
P $$$

3620 Canal St, 70119 **Tel** (877) 588-3033 **Fax** (504) 483-3032 **Rooms** 5 **Map** 2 A3

This magnificently restored Neo-Classical villa is on the Canal streetcar line, just a short ride from the French Quarter. Built in 1912, it has beautiful gardens that have been restored since Hurricane Katrina. The innkeepers have two dogs, happy to be your "pets away from home." A generous breakfast is available. **www.blockkellerhouse.com**

House on Bayou Road
P ⑪ ▦ $$$

2275 Bayou Rd, 70119 **Tel** (504) 945-0992 **Fax** (504) 945-0993 **Rooms** 8 **Map** 2 C3

It's hard to believe you are in the city at this B&B. Called a "petite plantation," it is set on two acres of gardens. Guests stay in elegant rooms with fireplaces, four-poster beds, libraries, private verandahs, and other delights. A two-course gourmet plantation-style breakfast is offered each morning. **www.houseonbayouroad.com**

BEYOND NEW ORLEANS

BATON ROUGE Cook Hotel
 $$

3848 W Lakeshore Dr, Baton Rouge, 70808 **Tel** (866) 610-2665 **Fax** (225) 383-4200 **Rooms** 128

Nestled in the Louisiana State University campus, this hotel is primarily for students and conference attendees, but others can stay as well. All suites have kitchens. There is a laundry facility, and a super pool and fitness center. It is fun to stay on campus, and there is easy access to highways. **www.thecookhotel.com**

BATON ROUGE Stockade Bed & Breakfast Inn
P $$$

8860 Highland Rd, Baton Rouge, 70808 **Tel** (225) 769-7358 **Fax** (225) 769-7358 **Rooms** 5

Located on the grounds of a Civil War stockade, the grim name is belied by the expansive hospitality of the host. The modern Spanish-styled house is airy and light. All rooms have private baths. Breakfast can be continental or enormous. The house is near the LSU campus. **www.thestockade.com**

EUNICE L'Acadie Inn
 $

259 Tasso Loop, Eunice, 70535 **Tel** (337) 457-5211 **Rooms** 14

The Pitre family has revamped a 1950s roadside motel into a Cajun inn. The motel rooms are strictly no-frills, but they are clean and inexpensive. All the rooms have kitchenettes, which is very helpful in this country setting. The Pitres love sharing their vast knowledge of Cajun life. **www.hotboudin.com**

LAFAYETTE Bois des Chênes Inn
▩ P $

338 N Sterling St, Lafayette, 70501 **Tel** (337) 233-7816 **Fax** (337) 233-7816 **Rooms** 5

The town of Lafayette has grown around this 1820s French plantation house. There are two suites in the main house and three in the converted stables. All are furnished with period antiques. A full breakfast is served, and the helpful hosts are encyclopedias of knowledge about the area. **www.boisdechenes.com**

LAFAYETTE T'Frere's House
P $$

1905 Verot School Rd, Lafayette, 70508 **Tel** (337) 984-9347 **Rooms** 9

Innkeepers Maugie and Pat Pastor serve lavish breakfasts in the morning and bottomless drinks in the evening. Rooms in the main house and garden cottage are furnished with antiques. Ghost sightings are reported, but these are of the amusing rather than malicious type. **www.tfreres.com**

NAPOLEONVILLE Madewood Plantation
P $$$$$

4250 Hwy 308, Napoleonville, 70390 **Tel** (985) 369-7151 **Rooms** 8

Staying at Madewood is like being a houseguest during the plantation's plush years. The bedrooms are beautifully furnished with Louisiana antiques but are comfortable and welcoming. Dinner and breakfast are included, which is helpful since the house is deep in the country. **www.madewood.com**

NEW IBERIA Estorge-Norton House
P $

446 E Main St, New Iberia, 70560 **Tel** (337) 365-7603 **Rooms** 4

This lovingly maintained 1910 arts and crafts villa makes a nice change from plantation sites. It is in the New Iberia historic district, close to all the main sites. Rooms are furnished with American antiques. Three of the rooms have shared baths. A lavish breakfast is served in the dining room. **www.estorge-nortonhouse.com**

Key to Price Guide see p162 **Key to Symbols** see back cover flap

NEW IBERIA La Maison B&B
*8317 Weeks Island Rd, New Iberia, 70560 **Tel** (337) 364-2970 **Rooms** 2*

The house looks suburban, but the atmosphere is pure Cajun. Hostess Eleanor Naquin serves heroic breakfasts and loves to arrange for guests to have a full immersion into Acadian life. Pets are welcome, but children must be at least 12 and well-behaved.

NEW IBERIA Rip Van Winkle House & Gardens
*5505 Rip Van Winkle Road, New Iberia, 70560 **Tel** (337) 359-8525 **Fax** (337) 359-8526 **Rooms** 2*

Two small but roomy houses are available for overnight guests: Servants' Quarters and Cook's Cottage. Both date from the estate's early years. Furnished with four-poster beds, luxury linens, and kitchenettes, the cottages are surrounded by acres of manicured gardens. **www.ripvanwinklegardens.com**

ST. FRANCISVILLE 3-V Tourist Court
*5687 Commerce St, St. Francisville, 70775 **Tel** (225) 721-7003 **Rooms** 10*

This 1920s motor court has been restored with taste and whimsy. The cabins are small, even tiny, but have period furnishings and kitchenettes. The motor court is flanked by the excellent Magnolia Café and Birdman Coffeehouse & Books, all owned by the same family.

ST. FRANCISVILLE Butler Greenwood Plantation
*8345 Hwy 61, St. Francisville, 70775 **Tel** (225) 635-6312 **Fax** (225) 635-6370 **Rooms** 7*

The same family has owned this plantation since 1796. The 1810 main building is an unpretentious family house with centuries of history and is open for tours. Guests stay in one of seven cottages on the grounds, all with antiques, kitchens, and individual character. **www.butlergreenwood.com**

ST. FRANCISVILLE Cottage Plantation
*10528 Cottage Lane, St. Francisville, 70775 **Tel** (225) 635-3674 **Rooms** 7*

Unlike many plantation B&Bs, visitors stay in the big house at Cottage. Indeed, it is a huge house, built in stages between 1795 and 1859. There is also a cabin for guests. Rooms are furnished with antiques and have private baths. Shopping alert – an antique store is located on the grounds. **www.cottageplantation.com**

ST. FRANCISVILLE Greenwood Plantation
*6838 Highland Rd, St. Francisville, 70775 **Tel** (225) 655-4475 **Fax** (225) 655-3292 **Rooms** 12*

Staying in one of the modern cottages on the plantation grounds is an experience that anyone who loves solitude will enjoy. Greenwood is deep in the countryside. The cottages are comfortable and clean. A tour of the main house is occasionally included in the price. **www.greenwoodplantation.com**

ST. FRANCISVILLE Hemingbough Guesthouse
*10101 Hwy 965, St. Francisville, 70775 **Tel** (225) 635-6617 **Rooms** 8*

There's a slight tinge of Disneyland to this modern 240-acre (96-ha) Greek Revival retreat. Built in the 1990s, it hosts meetings, weddings, and cultural events. Overnight guests stay in a replica antebellum house with modern amenities and canopy beds. **www.hemingbough.com**

ST. FRANCISVILLE The Myrtles Plantation
*7747 Hwy 61, St. Francisville, 70775 **Tel** (225) 635-6277 **Fax** (225) 635-5837 **Rooms** 11*

The B&B at this historically and architecturally significant mansion is wildly popular because of its reputation of being haunted. Rooms in the main house and the caretaker's cottage are reputedly the ghost hangouts. Night-time tours of the house are given on weekends. **www.myrtlesplantation.com**

ST. FRANCISVILLE Shadetree Inn
*9704 Royal St, St. Francisville, 70775 **Tel** (225) 635-6116 **Fax** (225) 635-0072 **Rooms** 3*

The inn is on a small yet beautiful site, giving it a secret garden feel. The suites have a shabby-chic look that invites you to cuddle up in a canopied bed or overstuffed chair. Breakfast is delivered to the rooms, which have microwaves and fridges. Cocktails are served in the afternoons. **www.shadetreeinn.com**

ST. MARTINVILLE The Old Castillo Hotel B&B
*220 Evangeline Blvd, St. Martinville, 70582 **Tel** (337) 394-4010 **Rooms** 7*

A stay at the Old Castillo is an absolute bargain. Located in the heart of charming Cajun country and built in 1827, this restored building has been on the National Register of Historic Places since 1978. Each room is beautifully and luxuriously furnished with period antiques. Wi-Fi access available. **www.oldcastillo.com**

VACHERIE Oak Alley Plantation Bed & Breakfast
*3645 Hwy 18 (Great River Road), Vacherie, 70090 **Tel** (225) 265-2151 **Fax** (225) 265-7035 **Rooms** 7*

These charming cottages, adjacent to the Oak Alley Plantation, are offered in configurations of two, three, and four bedrooms, all with private baths and kitchens. (The price range shown is for a two-bedroom cottage.) A complimentary, if forgettable, breakfast is served in the plantation's restaurant. **www.oakalleyplantation.com**

WHITE CASTLE Nottoway
*30970 Hwy 405, White Castle, 70788 **Tel** (866) 527-6884 **Fax** (225) 545-8632 **Rooms** 13*

At Nottoway, guests may stay in the splendid 1859 home or a restored house on the grounds. Although you'll have to be up and out by tour time, staying in one of the plush rooms facing the river is the estate's peak experience. A full breakfast is served in an austere-looking basement room. **www.nottoway.com**

RESTAURANTS, CAFES, AND BARS

E ven when other major cities in the US were living in a culinary wasteland, New Orleans had a reputation for fine, flavorful Creole cuisine. Today the reputation is still intact, but it has been enhanced by the development of "modern" Creole cuisine, Cajun cuisine, and some delicious ethnic dining as well. In this city, food matters; locals

New Orleans waiter

argue about who sells the best oysters, where to secure the finest turtle soup or gumbo, who makes the best po'boy (sandwich), bread pudding, and so on. The same is true for drinks. A pharmacist in the city invented the cocktail, and bartenders here are adept at making Sazeracs, a range of mint juleps, and such hazardous concoctions as the Obituary Cocktail (see p174).

Diners at the Acme Oyster House (see p176)

PLACES TO EAT

Top-flight restaurants are found throughout the city, particularly in the French Quarter, the Warehouse District, and Uptown. Currently such chefs as Susan Spicer, Emeril Lagasse, Frank Brigtsen, John Besh, and others who are up-dating the traditional cuisine are generating the most excitement. There are plenty

Commander's Palace (see p182), one of the city's finest restaurants

of good-quality restaurants that are producing traditional Creole and Cajun dishes – gumbo, oysters Rockefeller, jambalaya, crawfish étouffée, barbecue shrimp, and other zesty specialties (see pp172–3).

In addition, there are Italian, Mediterranean, and other ethnic restaurants, plus plenty of places for cheap, good food, serving po'boys, New Orleans own *muffaletta* (a special local sandwich), pizza, and the ubiquitous dish of red beans and rice with sausage. New Orleans residents also care passionately about coffee, and the city has many good coffee and pastry shops.

OTHER PLACES TO EAT

New Orleans offers a broad range of venues other than restaurants in which to eat good

food. Many hotels have excellent dining rooms open to the public, and there are various Italian deli-catessens; these are mainly in the lower French Quarter, where you can buy a salad or a sandwich. Look out for the famous Lucky Dog hot dog carts in the Quarter.

HOURS AND PRICES

Breakfast is usually available between 7 and 11am and can be inexpensive or super-expensive – the price often depends on where it is served. Jazz brunches, a New Orleans tradition, are served between 10am and 3pm on weekends and can cost anywhere between $30 and $50.

At lunchtime, you can buy a light meal for about $7 or $10, usually between 11am and 2:30pm. In the better restaurants, prices are lower at lunchtime than at dinner. Dinner is generally served from 5 to 10pm, or until 11pm on Friday or Saturday nights. At a moderately priced place, main dishes might range from $14 to $24. In the very best restaurants, like Commander's Palace or Emeril's, be prepared to spend over $100 per person. A few places are open all night.

DINING ON A BUDGET

Do not eat breakfast at your hotel unless it is complimentary. Seek out a coffee shop or deli and feast on delicious croissants and strong coffee. At lunch, you can pop into a corner grocery and order a po'boy or *muffaletta*, and picnic somewhere. If you do sit down in a restaurant, you will find prices are lower than at dinner, as many establishments offer discounted menus early in the day. Otherwise, you can save money by ordering one course only (which is usually enough) and drinking less wine. Depending on the hour, some restaurants offer fixed-price menus that are usually cheaper.

TAXES AND TIPPING

A sales tax of 9 percent is added to meal and beverages checks in all restaurants. In general, you should tip 15 percent of the check for service; 20 percent if the service is superb. When the service is very bad you need not tip at all, but some restaurants automatically add a tip, especially for large groups, so check.

RESERVATIONS

At the very best restaurants you will need to make reservations considerably in advance. Some restaurants, however, do not take reservations, and you will have to stand in line or enjoy a cocktail in the bar while you wait.

DRESS CODE

New Orleans is a relaxed city and most places will allow

The Upperline restaurant, filled with art *(see p182)*

you to wear the standard attire of jeans and T-shirt. Several of the more upscale restaurants require a jacket, and can also lend you one; ties are rarely required. Just to be on the safe side, dress smart-casual.

CHILDREN

Children are welcome at any restaurant, and special facilities, such as booster seats or highchairs, are usually available. Some restaurants offer special menus for children. The legal drinking age is 21, and children are not allowed in bars.

WHEELCHAIR ACCESS

Although since 1992 all restaurants have been required by law to be wheelchair accessible, it is best to

call ahead to determine precisely how accessible a particular establishment is – whether there are steps outside or inside, for example, or whether the bathrooms are downstairs or upstairs.

The Grill Room at the Windsor Court Hotel *(see p180)*

SMOKING

Smoking is prohibited in most Louisiana restaurants. Some dining establishments that qualify as bars are exempt from the smoking ban, but always ask before lighting up.

VEGETARIAN FOOD

As in the rest of the United States, there is plenty of scope for vegetarians to eat well in New Orleans. Although much Creole and Cajun food is meat-based, most restaurants have vegetarian dishes such as salads or meat-free meals, if requested.

There are also exclusively vegetarian restaurants around town, plus Vietnamese and Thai restaurants, where vegetarian dishes are offered.

People enjoying coffee and *beignets* at Café du Monde *(see p176)*

The Flavors of New Orleans

New Orleans is one of America's culinary capitals, with a unique cuisine spawned by two distinct cultures: Creole and Cajun. Creole is the legacy of refined, city-dwelling descendants of the early French settlers. From the application of classic French techniques to local produce, a rich, sophisticated new cuisine was created. The Cajuns settled in Louisiana after being ousted from both France and Acadia (Nova Scotia), living in the bayous, hunting and fishing for indigenous foods. Their traditional dishes are spicier, the fiery seasonings tempered by long-simmering. A glossary of typical dishes and ingredients can be found on page 175.

Hot chili peppers

A plate of luscious Louisiana crawfish on a bed of rice

ONLY IN NEW ORLEANS

Several dishes are unique to New Orleans. A breakfast of *beignets* (deep-fried, sugary-sweet donuts) and chicory coffee shows the French influence. The city's contributions to sandwich culture include the *muffaletta*, a large, round roll containing cold cuts of meat, Provolone cheese and a dressing of chopped olives, olive oil, onions, cauliflower, and garlic. It owes its origins to Italian dock workers. Another is the po'boy, a submarine roll piled high with roast beef, ham, shrimp, or oysters, along with mustard, onions, herbs, and spices. You may be asked if you want your sandwich "dressed," which will include the addition of tomatoes, lettuce, pickles, and mayonnaise.

LOUISIANA PRODUCE

One of the best-known Louisiana products is crawfish (called crayfish elsewhere), which are grown locally. They breed in the muddy bayous and ponds of Cajun country, and are harvested in little boats from December to May. Meanwhile, oyster aficionados will tell you there's nothing as good as plump, salty Louisiana oysters on the half shell.

Shrimp   **Oysters**   **Crab**   **Crawfish**

Selection of the finest Louisiana shellfish

LOCAL DISHES AND SPECIALTIES

Both Cajun and Creole cooking often begin with a roux, the base of many dishes including gumbos, *etouffées* and sauces. A roux is simply flour and oil, stirred constantly over a flame until the right shade of brown for each dish is achieved. The darker the roux, the more intense the flavor. It is the deep, dark roux that gives a distinctive smoky, nutty flavor to gumbo. Every cook has his or her own gumbo recipe, but it always

Okra pods

begins with the roux used to thicken and flavor homemade stock, and includes sausage, a "trinity" of onion, celery, and bell pepper, scallions, cayenne pepper and a sprinkling of *filé* power (ground sassafras leaves) on the top. *Filé* is used to thicken as well as to season; another thickening is okra, which lends a silky texture to dishes.

Jambalaya *Similar to Spanish paella, this spicy rice dish may feature seafood, ham, chicken,* andouille, *and more besides.*

Some key ingredients of New Orleans cuisine at the French Market

Sassafras is a Native American ingredient that features strongly in New Orleans cuisine, while okra was introduced by African slaves. Two local pork products show their French origins in their names. Almost every Cajun chef has a personal recipe for *boudin* sausage, a highly seasoned pork and rice sausage. *Andouille* is another classic which, unlike its French namesake, is a hard, spicy smoked Cajun pork sausage.

OLD VERSUS NEW

The current culinary battle in New Orleans pits the old school of traditional cooking versus the new wave of chefs who want to innovate. One of the first to gain renown was Paul Prudhomme, the creator of "blackened fish," a dish that was never a part of Cajun fare but is now widely associated with it.

Emeril Lagasse is the best known of those bringing "nouveau" touches, including Asian influences, to classic dishes. Other culinary stars in the city are Susan Spicer of Bayona *(see p176)*; John Besh of Restaurant August *(see p180)*, and Donald Link at Herbsaint *(see p179)*.

Display of traditional Louisiana hot pepper sauces

HOT STUFF!

Peppery sauces are a staple of Cajun cooking and a favorite New Orleans souvenir. Food shops offer as many as 40 varieties, from mild to blazing hot, and some have "tasting bars" where you can sample before you buy. Tabasco, made on a Louisiana plantation since the 1800s, is now a favorite worldwide.

CLASSIC DINING

Antoine's Founded in 1840 and filled with memorabilia. Oysters Rockefeller was invented here *(see p176)*.

Arnaud's A maze of dining rooms decorated with theatrical panache. The jazz brunch is recommended *(see p176)*.

Brennan's Famous for turtle soup, Bananas Foster and the decadently rich "Breakfast at Brennan's" *(see p176)*.

Commander's Palace A classic – don't miss the bread pudding soufflé *(see p182)*.

Galatoire's A 1905 landmark that still draws some of the city's best old families *(see p177)*.

The French Market This outdoor and covered market features superb fresh local produce *(see p70)*.

Bon Ton Café A downtown old-timer that sticks to tradition with seafood specialties and all the Creole favorites *(see p179)*.

Crawfish Etouffée *The name means "smothered," with sautéed crawfish being served in a thick, piquant sauce.*

Gumbo *Made with rice and okra, as well as chicken, seafood or* andouille, *this Creole soup is as thick as a stew.*

Bananas Foster Bananas *are sautéed in butter, sugar, and cinnamon, flamed in rum and served over ice.*

What to Drink in New Orleans

A long tradition of good drinking is one of New Orleans' trademarks. There are a wide variety of cocktails served throughout the city, some of which were invented here. Delicious and easy to drink, many are extremely potent concoctions. The local beers are also worthy: New Orleans has a top-class microbrewery. The city is a coffee-drinker's delight and has its own distinctive chicory-flavored dark roast coffee – a favorite of residents and visitors alike.

Pat O'Brien's (see p47), where the popular Hurricane was created

The Sazerac   The Hurricane   Mint Julep

Vieux Carré Cocktail   Obituary Cocktail   Ramos Gin Fizz

BEER AND WINE

New Orleans is a beer town. Look for such local brews as Abita and Dixie, plus those made by the microbrewery Crescent City Brewhouse. A variety of wines are also available in the city's restaurants, particularly fine French and California vintages.

Dixie and Abita Amber, local beers

Red and white California wines

COCKTAILS

New Orleans was the birthplace of many cocktails. Local pharmacist Antoine Peychaud's store was located near the corner of Royal and St. Louis streets, and he is said to have invented the cocktail around 1830 when he combined cognac "Sazerac" mixed with his own bitters recipe, a drop of water, and a pinch of sugar. Peychaud mixed this in an egg cup "*coquetier*," which his English-speaking customers mispronounced as "cocktail." Today, the Sazerac is one of New Orleans' most famous drinks: rye whiskey (or bourbon) is combined with bitters and sugar, and flavored with Pernod and lemon peel.

The Hurricane, served in a special glass, is very sweet and combines dark rum with passion fruit and other juices. The Mint Julep is made with bourbon, sugar, fresh mint, and crushed ice. The Vieux Carré mixes rye, cognac, vermouth, bitters, and a dash of Benedictine. For the Obituary Cocktail, a lethal drink created at Lafitte's (see p78), add half a jigger of Pernod to a gin Martini. Bartender Henry Ramos shook the first Ramos Gin Fizz in 1888, combining sugar, orange flower water, citrus juice, gin, egg white, cream, and seltzer into a refreshing drink. Pousse Café is a mix of six cordials – raspberry and maraschino syrups, crème de menthe, curaçao, chartreuse, and cognac.

COFFEE

New Orleanians love coffee, and it comes in all roasts and styles. Community Coffee, French Market, and CDM are the three most famous Louisiana brands. The Café du Monde (see p76) serves "café au lait," the traditional dark roast chicory-flavored coffee with hot milk.

If you don't like the somewhat bitter taste of chicory, just ask for "pure" coffee; you'll get a tasty cup of dark or medium roast coffee. Espresso, extra-strong coffee, is also available.

"Pure" coffee

Café espresso

Glossary of New Orleans Food

The distinctive cuisine of New Orleans has its own vocabulary. Some styles and ingredients are particular to Creole and Cajun cooking; others are more common but take on that special Louisiana touch. Creole dishes often have as their base peppers, onions, and tomatoes, and can be more refined than the flavorful Cajun one-pot dishes.

Vegetables and fruit for sale in the French Market

Andouille
A hard, smoked, spicy Cajun sausage made with pork.

Bananas Foster
Bananas sprinkled with brown sugar and flambéed in rum and banana liqueur (see p173).

Barbecued Shrimp
Jumbo shrimp in their shells sautéed in oil and butter, garlic, peppers, and spices.

Beignet
Deep-fried square donut (no hole), covered in powdered sugar.

Biscuits
Flour and baking powder rolled and baked, often served with eggs at breakfast.

Boudin
Highly seasoned Cajun pork sausage combined with rice.

Bouillabaisse New Orleans-style
A spicier version of the French seafood dish.

Cajun
A style of cooking that combines French methods with local Southern ingredients.

Calas
Fried sweet rice cakes.

Chow Chow
A relish usually made with green pickles, green tomatoes, and green cayenne peppers.

Courtbouillon of Redfish
A seafood stew, prepared with local fish, spices, and white wine.

Oranges and other fruits, used as ingredients in Creole food

Crawfish
Known elsewhere as crayfish, these deliciously sweet, small crustaceans are prepared in various ways like stews, étouffée, or boiled (see p173).

Crawfish Boil
Crawfish boiled in water seasoned with mustard, coriander, dill, cloves, allspice, bay leaves, and the main ingredient, dried chilies.

Ripe bananas, used for desserts

Dirty Rice
Rice cooked with chicken livers and gizzards, and other seasonings.

Eggs Sardou
Eggs poached on artichoke bottoms, cradled on a bed of creamed spinach, and covered with hollandaise.

Etouffée
Literally "smothered," a method of cooking slowly with little liquid, in a covered pan.

Filé
Filé refers to the dried ground sassafras leaves used to thicken and flavor gumbos.

Grits
Ground, cooked corn grains served at breakfast with butter, salt, pepper, and eggs.

Gumbo
A spicy, thick soup containing shrimp, crawfish, oysters, okra, and served over rice (see p173).

Shrimp cocktail

Gumbo z'Herbes
A meatless version of gumbo, made during Lent.

Jambalaya
A mixture of rice, seafood, Tasso (ham), vegetables, and seasoned with onion, green peppers, and celery (see p172).

King Cake
A round cake made during Mardi Gras. It is sprinkled with granulated and colored sugars. A tiny doll, representing the baby Jesus, is hidden inside.

Maque Choux
A Cajun dish made with a mixture of corn, tomatoes, onions, and cayenne pepper.

Mirliton
A pear-shaped squash with prickly ribbed skin.

Muffaletta
A sandwich combining Italian deli meats, and one or two kinds of cheese on an Italian round loaf slathered with olive salad – pickled olives, celery, olive oil, carrots, cauliflower, and garlic.

Okra
A pod vegetable, originally from Africa, served as a side dish or used in Cajun gumbos and stews.

Pain Perdu
The local version of French toast (bread fried with eggs).

Po'Boy
A big French bread sandwich, with shrimp, oysters, ham, roast beef, or a combination.

Pompano en Papillotte
A sweet fish common in Gulf waters, baked in an oiled paper bag to retain its full flavor.

Pralines
A candy patty made with brown sugar and pecans.

Shrimp Remoulade
Shrimp with a mayonnaise-based sauce seasoned with mustard, anchovies, gherkins, scallions, lemon, spices, and herbs.

Sweet Potato Pie
Made with sweet potatoes flavored with cinnamon, nutmeg, and ginger.

Tasso
Highly spiced smoked ham seasoned with red pepper.

Choosing a Restaurant

The restaurants in this guide have been selected across a wide range of price categories for their exceptional food, good value, interesting location, and attractive ambience. Within each area, entries are listed alphabetically within each price category, from the least to the most expensive.

PRICE CATEGORIES
For a three-course meal for one, half a bottle of house wine, and all unavoidable extra charges including tax:
$ under $25
$$ $25–$40
$$$ $40–$55
$$$$ $55–$70
$$$$$ over $70

UPPER FRENCH QUARTER

Café du Monde $
*800 Decatur St, 70116 **Tel** (504) 525-4544*   **Map** 5 D2

You cannot visit New Orleans without sampling *beignets*, and this is their home. The charming green- and white-striped awnings beckon from blocks away, as does the smell of the chicory coffee and powdered sugar. Fried dough dunked into milky coffee never tasted so good. They are open 24 hours.

Johnny's Po-Boy $
*511 St. Louis St, 70116 **Tel** (504) 524-8129*   **Map** 4 C2

This is your standard po'boy shop and really one of the only decent ones in the French Quarter. They offer all the standard stuffings such as fried seafood and cold cuts. The roast beef is especially good in a very messy way. Locals like to order takeout as there is not much ambience, and the Moonwalk provides a nearby picnic spot.

Acme Oyster House $$
*724 Iberville St, 70130 **Tel** (504) 522-5973*   **Map** 4 C3

The line usually snakes out the door for this popular seafood joint, and with good reason as the raw oysters are big and fresh. A variety of dependably good fried seafood is on offer as well. However, the scene might seem a bit touristy for those wanting a more authentic New Orleans experience.

Bourbon House Seafood & Oyster Bar $$$
*144 Bourbon St, 70130 **Tel** (504) 522-0111*   **Map** 4 C3

This handsome brasserie, run by the Brennan family, is firmly focused on local seafood. Oysters are served raw, topped with caviar, or broiled. The menu also includes classic renditions of New Orleans finfish and shrimp dishes, seasonal seafood salads, and a few beef dishes. The bar specializes in fine bourbons.

Iris $$$
*321 North Peters St, 70130 **Tel** (504) 299-3944*   **Map** 5 D3

When you can't face another platter of fried shrimp or the umpteenth rich sauce, head to Iris, inside the Bienville House Hotel. Here the kitchen blends Italian, French, and Oriental flavors with a deft and refreshingly light hand. There's a young, hip vibe to the dining room. Reservations recommended. Open dinner Mon & Wed–Sat; also lunch Thu & Fri.

Antoine's $$$$
*713 St. Louis St, 70130 **Tel** (504) 581-4422*   **Map** 4 C2

This old guard restaurant is the famed birthplace of Oysters Rockefeller and recalls days gone by with its beautiful tiled floors and ceiling fans. The menu offers classic French Creole fare that fits the setting. Ask for a tour of the splendid private dining rooms on the other floors.

Arnaud's $$$$
*813 Bienville St, 70112 **Tel** (504) 533-5433*   **Map** 4 C2

The Mardi Gras museum at this palatial dining institution really rivals the cuisine. Upstairs, you will find all the grand costumes of the former owner set amidst the finery of the many ornate dining rooms. The signature dish here is the famed shrimp remoulade. There's an excellent, unobtrusive jazz band.

Bayona $$$$
*430 Dauphine St, 70112 **Tel** (504) 525-4455*   **Map** 4 C2

Renowned chef Susan Spicer lives up to all expectations here at her flagship restaurant. The service, setting, and menu embody elegance. It would be difficult to order badly, but signature dishes such as her quail salad and legendary sweetbreads are sure to please. The wine list is also excellent, so take your time going through it.

Brennan's $$$$
*417 Royal St, 70130 **Tel** (504) 525-9711*   **Map** 4 C2

This is the original restaurant of the Brennan's dining empire, and its brunch continues to romance visitors and locals alike. You should expect a wait (even with reservations), and service can be a bit unreliable. But everyone loves the Bananas Foster cooking demonstration, which is a Brennan's creation.

Key to Symbols *see back cover flap*

Galatoire's

$$$$$

209 Bourbon St, 70130 **Tel** *(504) 525-2021*

Map 4 C3

The pomp and circumstance of this blue blood favorite are what make it so wonderful, and of all the old restaurants, this one is the most reliable. The menu is made up of Creole classics such as trout *Amandine*, which never fail to please the palate. Expect a wait to sit in the esteemed dining room downstairs.

K-Paul's Louisiana Kitchen
$$$$$

416 Chartres St, 70130 **Tel** *(504) 596-2530*

Map 4 C2

Chef Paul Prudhomme introduced the world to the cuisine of South Louisiana back in the 1980s when he reigned supreme over the New Orleans restaurant scene. This place still draws crowds, but the prices seem a bit inflated. However, this is a landmark restaurant and should be given due respect.

Nola
$$$$$

534 St. Louis St, 70130 **Tel** *(504) 522-6652*

Map 4 C2

This is the most downscale of chef Emeril Lagasse's restaurants, but still expect *haute cuisine* and high prices. Things are a bit funkier here with more fusion dishes and less formal service. Reservations are also easier to come by as the huge space seats hundreds. An especially enjoyable table is located near the open kitchen.

LOWER FRENCH QUARTER AND MARIGNY

Central Grocery
$

923 Decatur St, 70116 **Tel** *(504) 523-1620*

Map 5 D2

This classic New Orleans grocery and deli offers just one prepared food item – the famed *muffaletta*, an Italian sandwich loaded with meat, cheese, and olive salad. You can enjoy this beauty in the store or take it to the nearby riverfront for a picnic. The walls are lined with jars filled with Italian delicacies such as roasted peppers and anchovies.

Clover Grill
$

900 Bourbon St, 70116 **Tel** *(504) 598-1010*

Map 5 D1

The fun never stops at this quirky diner where the flamboyant staff turns on the charm constantly. Plus, the burgers are cooked under hubcaps to juicy perfection, and they actually serve malt milkshakes, taking you back to the golden days – just set to a different tune. Expect a cabaret atmosphere.

Croissant d'Or Patisserie
$

617 Ursulines Ave, 70116 **Tel** *(504) 524-4663*

Map 5 D1

You will imagine that you have stepped into Paris when you enter this little bakery. Their buttery pastries are outstanding. They also serve some sandwiches and salads, but the sweets are really the way to go. The eclairs and tarts warm the heart, and the early morning sunshine casts a spell that is sure to charm. Great for an early breakfast.

The Joint

$

801 Poland Ave, 70117 **Tel** *(504) 949-3232*

The quirky charm of the Bywater neighborhood comes across strong at this little barbecue joint. The bright decor, hip jukebox, and the smokey meats all work together. Ask about specials that might not be on the menu, such as the smoked bowl of tangy coleslaw topped with shredded pork. Also sip on a Rattler for good measure.

Verti Marte

$

1201 Royal St, 70116 **Tel** *(504) 525-4767*

Map 5 D1

If you need some good ol' greasy grub after an exhausting day in the Quarter, head to this corner store where takeout rules. Whether you prefer a traditional po'boy or an original creation such as the shrimp cheesesteak, you will be satisfied. The prepared salads can vary in quality, but the mac and cheese is a solid choice.

Adolfo's
$$

611 Frenchmen St, 70116 **Tel** *(504) 948-3800*

Map 5 E1

Perched above a bar and overlooking the lively nightlife of Frenchmen Street, Adolfo's is a funky neighborhood café where value and flavor take precedence over creature comforts. The tiny open kitchen produces a mix of classic, casual Italian fare and local seafood, with a large selection of fish.

Bennachin
$$

1212 Royal St, 70116 **Tel** *(504) 522-1230*

Map 5 D1

A sweet family runs this African restaurant, and they are definitely part of the charm. There is also the quaint storefront and heartwarming dishes that are sure to win you over. The menu provides plenty of vegetarian options such as the addictive plantains and sautéed spinach. Carnivores should try a meaty stew or the grilled chicken.

Coop's Place
$$

1109 Decatur St, 70116 **Tel** *(504) 525-9053*

Map 5 D1

This is the hidden gem of the Quarter. Here, the loaded jambalaya, enormous sandwiches, and superbly greasy cheese fries always hit the spot. The local clientele adds to the ambience with plenty of eccentric characters who have stories to tell. It is also a good watering hole.

Eat New Orleans

900 Dumaine St, 70116 **Tel** *(504) 522-7222*

$$\text{Map 4 C1}$$

For a quick sandwich or a hearty meal of New Orleans staples like jambalaya and barbecue shrimp, this bright, stylish, and relaxed café is a solid bet and the prices are very reasonable. Eat New Orleans is also a good place for a casual Sunday brunch. A bring-your-own-bottle policy is encouraged.

El Gato Negro

81 French Market Pl, 70116 **Tel** *(504) 525-9752*

Map 5 E1

Built in a former French Market icehouse, El Gato Negro is the spot for authentic Mexican fare. Tacos, *burritos*, and *enchiladas* are made according to traditional Mexican recipes, and fish, steak, and chicken entrées have elaborate preparations. The carrot juice margaritas are uncommonly refreshing. Mexican breakfasts are served on weekends.

Elizabeth's Restaurant

601 Gallier St, 70117 **Tel** *(504) 944-9272*

This homely diner has seen a few ownership changes, but all remains the same with their hearty breakfast and lunch fare. In the morning, try the praline, bacon, and stuffed French toast; at midday the po'boys or plate lunches are the way to go. Saturday means an all-day brunch with over-the-top egg dishes and huge lines. No reservations.

Fiorella's

1136 Decatur St, 70116 **Tel** *(504) 553-2155*

Map 5 D1

If you are craving fried chicken in the Quarter, you should seek out this friendly, no-frills eatery. Everything on the menu is a safe bet, but highlights are the fried pickles, mac and cheese, and the stupendous chicken. Their Italian fare is tasty as well, and they offer great deals on buckets of beer.

Mimi's

2601 Royal St, 70117 **Tel** *(504) 872-9868*

Map 5 F1

This tapas bar serves authentic Spanish treats such as marinated olives, sharp cheeses, and plenty of affordable wine. There are also hot dishes, but the cold fare seems of better quality. Enjoy these nibbles while gazing down onto quiet neighborhood streets. On weekends, they also have great dance parties that take place late at night.

Monaghan's 13

517 Frenchmen St, 70116 **Tel** *(504) 942-1345*

Map 5 E1

Monaghan's offers quick and easy bar food that will fuel you for a night of dancing in the neighboring music clubs. The menu leans toward greasy vegetarian, such as a roasted vegetable sandwich or a pita pizza. The loaded Tater Tots are especially satisfying, and their Bloody Mary could well be a cure for whatever ails you.

Napoleon House

500 Chartres St, 70130 **Tel** *(504) 524-9752*

Map 4 C2

The charming courtyard in this historic building sets the mood for sipping the café's signature drink of a Pimm's cup. While some might doubt the ability of a New Orleans bar to pull off such a decidedly British drink, here they succeed. The refreshing Pimm's perfectly complements the *muffaletta*. Other menu items pale in comparison.

Port of Call

838 Esplanade Ave, 70116 **Tel** *(504) 523-0120*

Map 5 D1

The line usually streams out of the door at this famed burger joint. Both locals and visitors love the strong rum drinks and super thick burgers. Serious eaters also go for the loaded baked potato that rivals the burger in size. The beach bar feel seems to encourage copious eating and drinking, and there are always interesting scenes as the night progresses.

Sukho Thai

1913 Royal St, 70116 **Tel** *(504) 948-9309*

Map 5 E1

Good Thai is hard to come by in New Orleans, and this quality Marigny place is a gem. The ingredients are always fresh, and the spice is just right. Their BYOB policy makes for a fun time with friends, especially at one of the side-walk tables. Best bets are the soups, curries, and desserts. The coconut black rice pudding really tickles the palate.

Café Amelie

912 Royal St, 70116 **Tel** *(504) 412-8965*

Map 5 D1

A picture-perfect courtyard serves as the main dining room at this gorgeous, secluded café. Surrounded by flowers and paving stones, diners choose from a menu of familiar contemporary American fare, including salmon or steaks, or local dishes such as gumbo and *muffalettas*. Reservations recommended. Closed Sun dinner; Mon & Tue; Aug.

Feelings Café

2600 Chartres St, 70117 **Tel** *(504) 945-2222*

Map 5 F1

The courtyard at this neighborhood fine-dining eatery positively seduces, especially on picturesque spring and fall evenings. The menu offers traditional New Orleans dishes such as fried oysters and barbecue shrimp. There are no surprises to blow your mind, but that's what makes this spot a classic. Try the peanut butter pie for dessert.

Marigny Brasserie

640 Frenchmen St, 70116 **Tel** *(504) 945-4472*

Map 5 E1

Here, you will find seasonal dishes prepared in a hearty fashion. The large windows that look out on the ever-happening Frenchmen Street provide plenty of entertainment as you enjoy a quiet meal. The wine list is ample, and the waitstaff are quick to answer any questions. The inviting bar is an ideal spot for drinks and music.

Meauxbar Bistro

$$$

942 N Rampart St, 70116 **Tel** *(504) 569-9979*

Map 4 C1

With a flourish of bright Caribbean yellow on the outside and stylish Art Deco touches on the inside, Meauxbar can be either an upscale spin on the neighborhood joint serving burgers, pasta dishes, and fish and chips, or a fine dining destination for traditional French bistro cuisine, fusion-style dishes, and great homemade ice cream.

Irene's Cuisine

$$$$

539 St. Phillip St, 70116 **Tel** *(504) 529-8811*

Map 5 D2

You will smell the aroma of garlic long before you see the doors, and that's a good sign. The mostly Italian fare of this romantic Quarter hideout boasts strong flavors that really satisfy the appetite. Locals and visitors alike line up early as reservations are not taken. Try to go on a weeknight as weekends mean a long wait, but it is worth it.

Muriel's

$$$$

801 Chartres St, 70116 **Tel** *(504) 568-1885*

Map 5 D2

The appearance of this upscale Jackson Square eatery might seem a bit much for a new guard restaurant as there is an abundance of lavish decorations. Still, devotees swear that the cuisine lives up to the look. Popular dishes include an appetizer of crawfish and goat's cheese crêpe and an entrée of pecan-crusted puppy drum.

Stella!

$$$$$

1032 Chartres St, 70116 **Tel** *(504) 587-0091*

Map 5 D1

This cutting-edge Quarter restaurant offers some of the most inventive cooking in town. The menu changes with the seasons, but expect lots of local seafood that is often prepared with an Asian twist. The risotto is a standout. The wine list might not be as extensive as some of the other major fine-dining establishments, but it is good quality.

WAREHOUSE AND CENTRAL BUSINESS DISTRICTS

Commerce Restaurant

$

300 Camp St, 70130 **Tel** *(504) 561-9239*

Map 4 C3

There is nothing like a hearty breakfast of a tasty po'boy from a bonafide lunch counter. The long narrow room with plenty of gleaming metal harks back to days of old, and many regulars could probably tell you a tale or two from that era. They could also fill you in on the best dishes such as red beans on Mondays. Closed on weekends.

Horinoya

$$

920 Poydras St, 70112 **Tel** *(504) 561-8914*

Map 4 B4

The seafood is impeccable at this hidden sushi bar. The business crowd knows the secret for lunch, but in the evening you will have the Zen environs to yourself. The rolls are excellent, and the cooked fare impresses as well. Be daring and try an exotic item as you can count on freshness. Go with a group and dine in the traditional back dining rooms.

Mother's Restaurant

$$

401 Poydras St, 70130 **Tel** *(504) 523-9656*

Map 4 C4

People stand in line for hours at this 60-something-year-old restaurant to dine on traditional po'boys such as the signature roast beef that locals call "debris." Devotees swear by the gravy on this sandwich, but detractors claim that it is not worth the wait. Just be sure to go as early as possible.

Bon Ton Café

$$$

401 Magazine St, 70130 **Tel** *(504) 524-3386*

Map 4 C4

This historic downtown restaurant is a favorite among the old-school business lunch crowd with its traditional New Orleans fare. Dishes such as shrimp Creole and crawfish *étouffée* give you a taste from the past. You can always count on fresh Louisiana seafood and courteous servers. The dated atmosphere fits the golden age sentiment perfectly.

Cochon

$$$

930 Tchoupitoulas St, 70130 **Tel** *(504) 588-2123*

Map 4 C5

Chefs Donald Link and Stephen Stryjewski bring a refined hand to the hearty flavors of the South (particularly Cajun Country) at this unique and popular restaurant. Whole pigs are turned into an array of traditional and creative dishes, though seafood and lighter items are on offer too. Reservations recommended. Closed Sat lunch; Sun.

Grand Isle Restaurant

$$$

575 Convention Center Blvd, 70130 **Tel** *(504) 520-8530*

Map 4 C4

Grand Isle focuses on local staples, such as fried seafood, grilled fish, boiled shrimp, raw oysters, and po'boys, all prepared with a higher degree of polish than other neighborhood restaurants – and with higher prices to match. A dining room decorated with cypress trees and a gleaming marble bar top gives the place a vintage feel.

Herbsaint

$$$

701 St. Charles Ave, 70130 **Tel** *(504) 524-4114*

Map 4 B4

There is simply nothing better than a menu that showcases quality ingredients paired thoughtfully, and that is the case with every dish at this elegant bistro. The "small plates" give you the opportunity to try a variety, and that's really the best plan of action as everything impresses. Their signature shrimp bisque and perfect *frites* are not to be missed.

Palace Café

 $$$

605 Canal St, 70130 **Tel** *(504) 523-1661* **Map** 4 C3

This Brennan's establishment is in an historic storefront that has been renovated beautifully. Appetizers include a crabmeat cheesecake and an oyster pan roast. Popular entrées are the *andouille* crusted fish and catfish pecan *meunière*. Their white chocolate bread pudding has become legendary in a short time. Brunch is always lively.

Restaurant August

$$$$

301 Tchoupitoulas St, 70130 **Tel** *(504) 299-9777* **Map** 4 C3

Chef John Besh deserves the accolades he receives for his flagship restaurant. He approaches all dishes with an artist's touch and demands the same attention to detail from his well-versed staff. Recommendations are difficult as the menu changes with the seasons, but there is really no chance of misordering given the level of excellence.

RioMar

$$$$

800 S. Peters St, 70130 **Tel** *(504) 525-3474* **Map** 4 C5

Dedicated to serving delicious, fresh seafood, chef Adolfo Garcia succeeds admirably here. His Spanish heritage shines throughout the menu, but especially on dishes such as the ceviche sampler and lunch tapas. The somewhat bare interior can increase the noise level, but the food makes up for any such shortcomings. Try a traditional Spanish dessert.

Tommy's Cuisine

$$$$

746 Tchoupitoulas St, 70130 **Tel** *(504) 581-1103* **Map** 4 C4

There is a long story behind the connection between this Warehouse District restaurant and Irene's in the Quarter, but suffice it to say that the menus are similar. Here, you can count on Italian cuisine with a New Orleans flair (just like Irene's). The tiled floors and dark wood set the mood for a real feast.

Emeril's

$$$$$

800 Tchoupitoulas St, 70130 **Tel** *(504) 528-9393* **Map** 4 C5

This is the original location where the now celebrity chef made his name, and, consequently, utmost care is taken with every detail. Chef Emeril innovatively and deliciously blends different styles of cooking such as Southwestern and New England. The staff is efficient, and the menu should impress most.

The Grill Room

$$$$$

300 Gravier St, 70130 **Tel** *(504) 522-1994* **Map** 4 C3

The flagship restaurant of the elegant Windsor Court Hotel *(see p166)* maintains a high standard of opulence in its formal dining rooms, with elaborate floral arrangements and white-glove service. The menu is a mix of contemporary Creole cuisine and some tamer fare for less adventurous diners.

GARDEN DISTRICT AND UPTOWN

Café Reconcile

$

1631 Oretha Castle Haley Blvd, 70113 **Tel** *(504) 568-1157* **Map** 8 A2

There is nothing like combining a good cause with good food, and that is just the case at this Central City eatery. Local kids learn about the restaurant industry while providing you with food such as fried chicken, and mac and cheese. On Thursdays, their white beans and shrimp draw diners from all over the city. Do not skip the cornbread.

Camellia Grill

$

626 S Carrollton Ave, 70118 **Tel** *(504) 309-2679* **Map** 6 A1

This landmark New Orleans diner was resurrected after Hurricane Katrina by new owners who made a few sensible behind-the-scenes upgrades but left the classic ambience and menu of omelettes and burgers unchanged. Seating is at the counter only, and the line to get in can be long, but the high-spirited servers make the wait worthwhile.

Chez Nous

$

5701 Magazine St, 70115 **Tel** *(504) 899-7303* **Map** 6 C4

The prepared food at this gourmet-to-go shop is as close to New Orleans home cooking as you can come by without knocking on someone's door. Everyday means a different special such as seafood gumbo, grillades and grits, or shrimp Creole. There are also many prepared salads and a variety of cakes and pies. Limited dining space.

Domilise's

$

5240 Annunciation St, 70115 **Tel** *(504) 899-9126* **Map** 6 C5

Most Uptown locals swear that these are the best po'boys in town, and it is a good argument considering the fresh local seafood is fried to perfection. Plus, the family atmosphere makes you feel right at home crowded around small tables bumping elbows with regular customers. If seafood isn't your thing, try the roast beef.

The Grocery

 $

2854 St. Charles Ave, 70115 **Tel** *(504) 895-9524* **Map** 7 F3

The pressed sandwiches provide a welcome reprieve from po'boys. The Cuban is a classic, but the veggie melt is also good. Their gumbo also impresses, especially when eaten with a scoop of potato salad in lieu of rice. The salads are topped with homemade dressings, and the cookies and brownies are tempting. Lunch only and closed on Sundays.

Joey K's

$

3001 Magazine St, 70115 **Tel** (504) 891-0997

Map 7 F4

Although located on the edge of the elegant Garden District, this casual corner joint offers food from the humble but delicious traditions of Creole pot cooking. The daily blackboard specials feature comfort food classics at bargain prices. Wash them down with a beer or margarita served in a huge, frozen-schooner glass.

St. James Cheese Co.

$

5004 Prytania St, 70115 **Tel** (504) 899-4737

Map 7 D4

An astounding array of imported and domestic artisanal cheeses has earned St. James a reputation as one of the most ambitious cheese shops in the South. Take a courtyard seat for a pressed sandwich or cheese board at lunch, or sample the imported and locally made *charcuterie* items. Beer and wine are served.

Casamento's

$$

4330 Magazine St, 70115 **Tel** (504) 895-9761

Map 7 E4

This is the quintessential oyster bar to the point that it closes when the salty bivalves are out of season in June, July, and August. The raw oysters are undoubtedly a must, but the sandwiches and stew also prove quite tasty. The atmosphere plays a major role as the spotless white tiles covering the floors and walls really set the perfect tone.

Franky & Johnny's

$$

321 Arabella St, 70118 **Tel** (504) 899-9146

Map 6 C4

Uptown families pile into this friendly neighborhood joint that specializes in fried and boiled seasonal seafood. There is also an element of New Orleans-Italian cuisine, but that pales in comparison to the Gulf fare. Po'boys and fried platters are the best, and you must start with some fried bell pepper rings.

Saltwater Grill

$$

710 S Carrollton Ave, 70118 **Tel** (504) 324-6640

Map 6 A1

Veterans of the Brennan's empire opened this seafood restaurant and oyster bar not far from Tulane and Loyola universities. They renovated an old building into a family eatery. The oyster bar always pleases, and the po'boys are some of the best in the area thanks to fresh local seafood. An excellent choice for those traveling with children.

Surrey's Juice Bar

$$

1418 Magazine St, 70130 **Tel** (504) 524-3828

Map 8 B3

Healthy eating is not a top priority in New Orleans, but this hip little café makes it fun. Their fresh fruit juices will set you straight after a late night, and the Latin-influenced brunch fare always hits the spot. There are many vegetarian options, including a stellar eggplant *muffaletta*. Open for breakfast and lunch only. Go early on the weekends.

Theo's

$$

4218 Magazine St, 70115 **Tel** (504) 894-8554

Map 7 E4

The pizza here is supposedly St. Louis style, meaning that the crust is somewhere between Chicago and New York. Whatever the definition, the pizza rocks, especially specialties such as the Jammer. Their wings prove an excellent starter, and root beer floats or chocolate cake make for a perfect ending. The young owners are always very friendly.

Whole Foods Market

$$

5600 Magazine St, 70115 **Tel** (504) 899-9119

Map 6 C4

If you are ever in a hunger emergency, Whole Foods Market can surely bail you out. Their variety of prepared foods runs the gamut from sushi to pizza, and their bakery is exceptional. Of course, you can also stock up on some gourmet groceries and fine wine. Just beware of the parking lot at this location as the small confines can be quite tight.

Ye Olde College Inn

$$

3000 S Carrollton Ave, 70118 **Tel** (504) 866-3683

Map 1 B4

This 1930s stalwart has seen enormous change since a new owner took over and Hurricane Katrina forced a move to an adjacent address. Yet the down-home New Orleans feel remains intact, with the same regulars lining the bar and families still filling the dining room for foot-long oyster loaves and hamburger steaks.

Dick & Jenny's

$$$

4501 Tchoupitoulas St, 70115 **Tel** (504) 894-9880

Map 7 E5

There is a no reservations policy at this Uptown eatery, but the excellent, upscale, and funky food is well worth the wait. The kitchen offers creative local cuisine that changes with the seasons, and the staff always knows the ins-and-outs of the menu. The cheerful surroundings add to the good time evoked by the standout food.

La Crêpe Nanou

$$$

1410 Robert St, 70115 **Tel** (504) 899-2670

Map 7 D4

The authentic European café feel of this Uptown charmer keeps it packed. The menu is classic French bistro with excellent mussels and frites, and, in fact, the whole selection is good. They are only open for dinner, and the crowds come early. Save room for a dessert crêpe. Closed Sundays.

Brigtsen's

$$$$

723 Dante St, 70118 **Tel** (504) 861-7610

Map 6 A1

Earning his stripes under the tutelage of none other than Paul Prudhomme, chef Frank Brigtsen's credentials propelled his namesake restaurant into the spotlight, where it has stayed. He is an avid Louisiana sportsman and always offers an array of local seafood and game. A charming Uptown house provides the perfect setting.

Clancy's
6100 Annunciation St, 70118 **Tel** *(504) 895-1111*

♻ $$$$

Map 6 B5

This neighborhood fine-dining restaurant is a favorite among blue blood New Orleanians who love the dependable food and service. The menu rarely changes, which these diners love. Popular items include the oysters with brie, smoked soft shell crab, and peppermint ice cream. The highly experienced staff will be happy to assist you.

Dante's Kitchen
736 Dante St, 70118 **Tel** *(504) 861-3121*

$$$$

Map 6 A1

A Commander's Palace veteran opened this Riverbend eatery to showcase local ingredients prepared in a refined yet approachable fashion. The historic home setting provides the perfect backdrop for starters such as shrimp and grits with redeye gravy. Popular entrées include the *trois mignons* (three beef filets) and the grilled redfish.

Eleven79
1179 Annunciation St, 70130 **Tel** *(504) 299-1179*

♻ $$$$

Map 8 B2

This tucked away, swanky Italian restaurant feels a bit like a gangster movie set, and the cuisine lives up to those high standards. Regulars recommend the Oysters Panaré as an appetizer (*panéed* oysters topped with caviar) and the Veal Eleven79 (topped with peppers, mozzarella, and asparagus) wins as an entrée. Finish with tiramisu.

Gautreau's
1728 Soniat St, 70115 **Tel** *(504) 899-7397*

$$$$

Map 7 D3

This upscale neighborhood eatery always keeps a professional staff. Chefs seem to earn accolades here and then move on – making way for more young talent. The menu changes with the seasons, but your server's opinion should be trusted concerning all food and wine recommendations. Great for a date.

Jacques-Imo's Café
8324 Oak St, 70118 **Tel** *(504) 861-0886*

$$$$

Map 6 B1

This popular restaurant serves Creole and Cajun specialties at reasonable prices. The chef/owner, Jack Leonardi, is a local character who is often part of the entertainment, and you can dine in the bed of a pickup truck out front. Reservations aren't taken for groups smaller than five, so it's first come first served. Closed Sundays.

Lilette
3637 Magazine St, 70115 **Tel** *(504) 895-1636*

$$$$

Map 7 E4

Chef John Harris received immediate and deserved recognition when he opened this stylish, *haute* eatery. The marrow toast sends shivers up the spine, and the pork belly happily overwhelms. The menu rarely changes, and faulty ordering is simply not possible as all is cooked to perfection. The cocktail menu is just as impressive.

Martinique Bistro
5908 Magazine St, 70115 **Tel** *(504) 891-8495*

$$$$

Map 6 B4

The courtyard alone is enough to keep Uptowners coming back to Martinique again and again. The pleasant tropical setting complements the menu of approachable, eclectic French fare perfectly. Seafood dishes such as *bouillabaisse* are standouts. This is a perfect location for a romantic dinner away from the downtown bustle. Linger over dessert.

Pascal's Manale
1838 Napoleon Ave, 70115 **Tel** *(504) 895-4877*

$$$$

Map 7 D3

This is supposedly the birthplace of the legendary barbecue shrimp and worth a visit. The beautiful old oyster bar is also notable, but don't expect too much from other parts of the menu. This would be a nice spot to tickle your appetite before enjoying entrées elsewhere. It is just a few blocks from the St. Charles Avenue streetcar.

Patois
6078 Laurel St, 70115 **Tel** *(504) 895-9441*

$$$$

Map 6 B5

This former bar room has been beautifully transformed into an artfully designed Uptown gourmet destination. Louisiana regional dishes take center stage, but there are plenty of influences from French, Italian, and Spanish cuisines as well. The restaurant can get very loud at dinner, though Sunday brunch is a more laid-back affair.

Upperline
1413 Upperline St, 70115 **Tel** *(504) 891-9822*

$$$$

Map 7 D4

Everyone loves the classic Creole fare at this quirky, yet upscale restaurant. They claim to have invented the fried green tomato topped with shrimp remoulade that you see all over the city, and it is entirely possible considering how long owner JoAnn Clevenger and her chefs have been perfecting the art. Go hungry and order every course.

Commander's Palace
1403 Washington Ave, 70130 **Tel** *(504) 899-8221*

$$$$$

Map 7 F3

The Brennan family set the standard for New Orleans fine dining when they opened this culinary palace in the 1970s. An extensive renovation after Hurricane Katrina has left the restaurant looking fresher and brighter, while the cuisine remains a blend of Creole classics with innovative twists. The jazz brunch is an especially celebratory meal here.

Emeril's Delmonico
1300 St. Charles Ave, 70130 **Tel** *(504) 525-4937*

$$$$$

Map 8 A2

This historic New Orleans restaurant came under Emeril's wing at the turn of the millennium, and he has made great strides in renovating the grand old place. Both the atmosphere and the menu offer some of the old while enlivening things with just enough new. The menu changes with the current *chef de cuisine*, but the aged steaks are a definite win.

Key to Price Guide *see p176* **Key to Symbols** *see back cover flap*

MID-CITY

Angelo Brocato's Ice Cream & Confectionary

214 N Carrollton Ave, 70119 **Tel** *(504) 486-1465*   **Map** *2 A3*

This traditional Sicilian ice-cream parlor has been a New Orleans institution for more than a century. The wide assortment of flavors includes specialties like tiramisu, pistachio, and the best-selling lemon flavor, while fresh, local fruit is made into Italian ices (a type of sorbet). An old, brass espresso-maker produces great coffee drinks.

Juan's Flying Burrito

4724 S Carrollton Ave, 70119 **Tel** *(504) 486-9950*   **Map** *2 A3*

A rock 'n' roll vibe and family-friendly atmosphere mix at this neighborhood cantina just off the Canal streetcar route. Fat California-style *burritos* are the specialty of the house, although local shrimp and fish, Caribbean jerk chicken, and plenty of vegetarian choices add variety to the tortilla-based menu.

K-Jean's Seafood

224 N Carrollton Ave, 70119 **Tel** *(504) 488-7503*   **Map** *2 A2*

Amenities may be slim to nil at this takeout-only seafood market, but the heady aroma of boiling shrimp, crabs, or crawfish is enough to ensure a constant flow of customers. Get a po'boy or a few pounds of spicy, boiled, seasonal seafood, and make a picnic of it at nearby City Park.

Willie Mae's Scotch House

2401 St. Ann St, 70119 **Tel** *(504) 822-9503*   **Map** *2 C3*

Located in a rather unsavoury part of town (take a taxi), this eatery is famous for its Southern soul food. The Scotch House suffered extensive damage as a result of Hurricane Katrina, but the local community rallied together for a clean-up operation, and the restaurant reopened to great fanfare in 2007. Open lunchtimes only, Mon–Sat.

Dooky Chase

2301 Orleans Ave, 70119 **Tel** *(504) 821-0600*   **Map** *2 C3*

Chef Leah Chase deserves utmost recognition for her famed restaurant that was considered by many as the headquarters of the New Orleans Civil Rights movement. Her food is classic Creole cuisine and Creole soul in a welcoming, classy atmosphere. Non-natives might want to take a cab as the neighborhood can intimidate.

Liuzza's by the Track

1518 N Lopez St, 70119 **Tel** *(504) 218-7888*   **Map** *2 C2*

This is the consummate neighborhood restaurant. The staff are friendly, and the menu offers an array of very original po'boys and salads. Their gumbo is reminiscent of a home kitchen, and the french fries simply must be ordered. Add gigantic frozen beers and loaded Bloody Marys to the mix, and you have got a recipe for a great time.

Liuzza's Restaurant and Bar

3636 Bienville Ave, 70119 **Tel** *(504) 482-9120*   **Map** *2 A3*

This is no relation to the restaurant of the same name, but they do resemble in quality of food and service. Here, you find perfectly fried seafood and hearty New Orleans-Italian fare. The fried pickles or onion rings are good starters, and you should order the stuffed artichoke. They also serve giant frozen beers, and the peanut butter pie is a must.

Parkway Bakery & Tavern

538 N Hagan Ave, 70119 **Tel** *(504) 482-3047*   **Map** *2 B3*

Founded in 1911, this resurrected po'boy icon resides by the picturesque Bayou St. John, which is nice to walk along before or after chewing on some fried seafood. You could even order takeout and picnic beside the waterway. Especially try the messy roast beef po'boy. Closed Tue.

Café Degas

3127 Esplanade Ave, 70119 **Tel** *(504) 945-5635*   **Map** *2 B2*

The white twinkle lights will catch your eye immediately, and that is just the beginning of the charm. Trees actually grow through the dining room of this little bistro where classic French café food abounds. There is French onion soup, quiche, and pâté. More substantial dishes include veal cheeks and duck. Close to the New Orleans Museum of Art.

Café Minh

4139 Canal St, 70119 **Tel** *(504) 482-6266*   **Map** *2 A3*

Chef/owner Minh Bui moved from Vietnam to New Orleans at a young age and spent many years working behind the scenes at the city's top Creole restaurants. His own restaurant features a deft fusion of Vietnamese and Creole cuisines, prepared with all the trappings of the city's best upscale bistros.

Crescent City Steakhouse

1001 N Broad Ave, 70119 **Tel** *(504) 821-3271*   **Map** *2 C3*

It doesn't get any more classic than this 1930s-era steakhouse, home to the New Orleans-style steak, served sizzling with butter. The sturdy dining room, with its tile floors and discreet dining booths with privacy curtains, has not changed for generations. The steaks are prime, the service is friendly, and the prices are reasonable.

Lola's
    $$$

3312 Esplanade Ave, 70119 **Tel** *(504) 488-6946*   **Map** *2 B2*

This charming and colorful Spanish café does not take reservations, and there is usually a wait, meaning plenty of time to sip wine before dinner. They serve authentic gazpacho that goes well with crusty French bread smeared with the super garlic butter. Paellas are the entrées to order, if in a group. Not open for lunch.

Mandina's
$$$

3800 Canal St, 70119 **Tel** *(504) 482-9179*   **Map** *2 A3*

Every detail harks back to another era. Here, large families still dine together, and regulars wait at the stand-only bar, sipping on stiff cocktails. All the Creole classics are on the menu such as turtle soup, trout *amandine*, and bread pudding, and they all live up to the priceless atmosphere. No reservations – so, embrace the wait.

Ralph's on the Park
$$$$

900 City Park Ave, 70119 **Tel** *(504) 488-1000*   **Map** *2 A2*

Yet another specimen of the Brennan's restaurant chain that turns fine dining into an art. At Ralph's, the beautiful location overlooking City Park makes for an ideal experience. The salads are well considered, and the local seafood dishes are a must.

BEYOND NEW ORLEANS

ABITA SPRINGS Abita Brew Pub
$$

72011 Holly St, Abita Springs, 70420 **Tel** *(985) 892-5837*

You can sample limited runs of Abita beer that are not found elsewhere, while enjoying their own version of bar food such as Chicken Abitafeller – grilled chicken with fried oysters and spinach-artichoke dip. The quaint town of Abita Springs is nice to walk around, and there is even a bike trail right beside the restaurant.

AVONDALE Mosca's
    $$$$

4137 Hwy 90 W, Avondale, 70094 **Tel** *(504) 436-8950*

There are all sorts of Mafia-related rumors surrounding this little Italian spot, and the rural, isolated setting certainly adds to that mystique. But the real draw is the family-style fare. Highlights are the Italian salads featuring tangy olives and sweet lumps of crabmeat and tasty chicken. Be sure to check out the jukebox that will take you back in time.

BREAUX BRIDGE Poche's
$$

3015A Main Hwy, Breaux Bridge, 70517 **Tel** *(337) 332-2108*

This is where to go for all those specialty Cajun meats such as *andouille* and *boudin*. They also serve plate lunches such as smothered rabbit, fried catfish, and crawfish *étouffée*. The Poche family has been in the meat business since the 1960s and should be able to answer any questions about the *charcuterie* tradition.

BREAUX BRIDGE Café des Amis
    $$$$

140 E Bridge St, Breaux Bridge, 70517 **Tel** *(337) 332-5273*

This famed dancehall and restaurant really gives you a peek into Cajun culture with plenty of two-stepping and culinary delights such as crawfish pies and cornbread and eggplant wheels. Expect a crowd, especially on weekends in the fall and spring when plenty of tour buses bring in the masses. Still, the more the merrier.

CHALMETTE Rocky & Carlo's
    $

613 W St. Bernard Hwy, Chalmette, 70043 **Tel** *(504) 279-8323*

A family restaurant, bar, and de facto community clubhouse, Rocky & Carlo's is a scruffy but beloved institution in St. Bernard Parish and the place to enjoy Creole-Italian comfort food. Impossibly gooey macaroni and cheese with brown gravy, the Italian meatloaf *bracciolini*, and hulking fried oyster po'boys are among the culinary charms.

COVINGTON The Dakota
$$$

629 N Hwy 190, Covington, 70433 **Tel** *(985) 892-3712*

Long a favorite on the North Shore, this fine-dining place offers excellent food and service. They are known for their fresh, seasonal ingredients and, consequently, the menu changes often. The soft shell crabs are a must if in season, and the pork tenderloin is another popular entrée. Also, explore their extensive wine selection.

DARROW Latil's Landing
$$$$$

40136 Hwy 942, River Road, Darrow, 70725 **Tel** *(225) 473-9380*

A visit to Houmas House Plantation and Gardens *(see p137)* is meant to evoke Louisiana's prosperous past, but a meal at its fine-dining restaurant, Latil's Landing, is all about contemporary, cosmopolitan renditions of Creole cuisine. No expense is spared in decor or amenities, and elaborate tasting menus are available nightly.

DES ALLEMANDS Spahr's
    $

3682 Hwy 90, Des Allemands, 70030 **Tel** *(985) 758-1602*

If you are looking for some road food as you drive west from New Orleans then you should definitely stop here. They are famous for their Bloody Marys and fried seafood, and with good reason. The Bloody Mary is basically a meal in itself, and their fried oysters, shrimp, and catfish are all exemplary. Be on the lookout – it is hidden in a gas station.

Key to Price Guide *see p176* **Key to Symbols** *see back cover flap*

GRETNA Kim Son

349 Whitney Ave, Gretna, 70056 **Tel** *(504) 366-2489*

The west bank of the Mississippi River offers great ethnic cuisine, especially from Vietnam. Kim Son serves Chinese and Vietnamese dishes, and the latter are the standout. Claypot specialties are sure to please, as are the salt-baked shrimp, lobster, and crab. There is basic Cantonese fare for the less adventurous but if you are daring, talk to the staff.

LACOMBE La Provence

25020 Hwy 190, Lacombe, 70445 **Tel** *(985) 626-7662*

The French country home feel sets the stage for classic French fare such as leg of lamb and roasted duck. There are also some local dishes including chicken and *andouille* gumbo. Their "market menu" special is a good deal featuring a reasonably priced three-course dinner. The 30-something-year history of the restaurant makes it special.

LAFAYETTE Poupart Bakery

1902 West Pinhook Rd, Lafayette, 70508 **Tel** *(337) 232-7921*

On the outskirts of Lafayette, in an unassuming suburban area, is this family-run bakery, a local institution since the 1960s. The baguettes and rustic loaves are fantastic, and they are used to create a short list of lunch sandwiches. Get a King Cake during Mardi Gras or a crawfish pie at any time. Open 7am–6:30pm Tue–Sat, 7am–4pm Sun.

LAFAYETTE Don's Seafood and Steakhouse

301 E Vermillion St, Lafayette, 70501 **Tel** *(337) 235-3551*

This family-owned local favorite is always bustling and has been for about 70 years. They offer terrific fresh local seafood (mostly fried), and big juicy steaks. They are known for their hushpuppies, and bread pudding is the signature dessert. A great place to eat if you are traveling with kids, thanks to the welcoming atmosphere and friendly staff.

LAFAYETTE Alesi Pizza House

4110 Johnston St, Lafayette, 70503 **Tel** *(337) 984-1823*

This mom-and-pop restaurant has been hooking locals with their pizza and pasta for years. It is a sure charmer with red- and white-checked tablecloths and a friendly staff. Their steaks, sandwiches, and salads are popular alternatives to traditional Italian fare. A great place to go if you are traveling with children, thanks to the family atmosphere.

LAFAYETTE Prejean's

3480 I-49 N, Lafayette, 70507 **Tel** *(337) 896-3247*

The focal point in this authentic Cajun dancehall is a 14-ft (4.2-m) long stuffed alligator named "Big Al." He watches over the nightly dancing and eating. The extensive menu offers many options, mostly of the Cajun variety, such as crawfish *boudin* balls, and seafood stuffed mushrooms as starters. Entrées include crawfish pasta and fried alligator.

LAFAYETTE Randol's

2320 Kaliste Saloom Rd, Lafayette, 70508 **Tel** *(337) 981-7080*

This dancehall/restaurant places a strong emphasis on fresh ingredients. They raise their own crabs and crawfish and grow herbs for seasoning. Highlights of the menu are crab fingers, fried oyster Caesar salad, shrimp *au gratin*, and boiled crawfish and crabs when in season. They also sell their fresh seafood, which they will ship home for you.

MANCHAC Middendorf's Seafood

30160 Hwy 51 S, Manchac, 70421 **Tel** *(985) 386-6666*

There are actually two side-by-side locations of this fried seafood haven. Their specialty is catfish, and you can enjoy its crispy goodness as you relax surrounded by the waters of Lake Manchac. It is fun to go here on a Saturday or Sunday afternoon when the weather is nice and local families turn out in droves, giving you a feel for true Louisiana living.

MANDEVILLE Trey Yuen Cuisine of China

600 N Causeway Blvd, Mandeville, 70448 **Tel** *(985) 626-4476*

There is no lack of flair at this landmark Northshore restaurant, which was modeled after a Chinese palace, complete with courtyard gardens and ponds. The menu offers most of the familiar Chinese-American standards, but the kitchen also works in local ingredients like crawfish and oysters for some original dishes.

METAIRIE Andrea's

3100 19th St, Metairie, 70002 **Tel** *(504) 834-8583*

This Metairie mainstay does not look much from the outside, but locals have revered it for years because of its delicious Italian fare. Popular starters are the antipasti and Caprese salad, and favorite entrées are the risotto New Orleans and veal chops. All seafood dishes are fresh, and the chef's tasting menu ensures a nice sampling.

METAIRIE Drago's

3232 N Arnoult Rd, Metairie, 70002 **Tel** *(504) 888-9254*

This unassuming Croatian restaurant became famous for the perfection of its grilled oysters. Topped with garlic and butter and cooked until just done, they are worth a trip to Metairie. They also offer a variety of other local seafood dishes, but the oysters are the standout.

NEW IBERIA Clementine Dining & Spirits

113 E Main St, New Iberia, 70560 **Tel** *(337) 560-1007*

The focal point in this historic building is an antique bar made of tiger oak and mahogany; a perfect place for a pre-dinner cocktail. Dine in the courtyard and enjoy some of their signature dishes such as roasted red pepper bisque with wild mushrooms and crabmeat, and their addictive fried green tomatoes. Locals swear by their steaks.

SHOPPING IN NEW ORLEANS

As the gateway to the Mississippi, New Orleans has long been a place for buying and selling goods, and it still maintains a talent for filling its stores with irresistible treasures. Antiques are among the city's finest buys, and it is possible to find anything from 18th-century French furniture to 1950s vintage dresses. Other specialties include imaginative masks, handmade crafts, rare books, and the best jazz records. Shopping in New Orleans is an initiation into local culture. Each of the city's many shopping areas has a unique character, with the French Quarter, Magazine Street, Carrollton, and Julia Street all offering vibrant, rich experiences. These pages highlight the best stops in the city.

Antique porcelain jar

The exterior of the upscale Canal Place shopping mall

WHEN TO SHOP

Stores in the Central Business District, along Magazine Street, and in the French Quarter tend to operate from 9am to 5pm or 10am to 6pm. Many open on Sundays, but always call in advance to avoid disappointment. Some shops in the Quarter don't open until noon, but they close late, too.

HOW TO PAY

Major credit cards are accepted everywhere, and there are plenty of Automated Teller Machines (ATMs) from which to get cash for a small fee. Traveler's checks are almost universally accepted. Some shops will also take personal checks with sufficient identification.

SALES TAX REIMBURSEMENT

If you are a foreign visitor, you can get back the 10 percent sales tax on tangible goods, but you must show the vendor your passport and ask for a refund voucher.

At the airport, go to the **Louisiana Tax Free Shopping Refund Center** and show your passport, sales receipts, refund vouchers, and air ticket (which may be up to a maximum of a 90-day trip). If you do not manage to get reimbursed at the airport, send copies of everything, along with an explanation, to the Refund Center.

SHIPPING

If you would prefer to send your purchases home rather than take them with you, ask the store to handle the task for you – New Orleans merchants are accustomed to shipping goods anywhere. For large buys such as furniture and art objects, professional packing and/or shipping is a necessity. A good source is **The Wooden Box** on South Peters Street. For smaller items, a reliable company is the **Royal Mail Service**.

MALLS AND SHOPPING CENTERS

New Orleans currently has only two traditional in-town malls. **Canal Place** *(see p94)*, on the edge of the French Quarter, has upscale shops such as Ann Taylor, Williams-Sonoma, Saks Fifth Avenue, and Coach. The unique **Riverwalk Marketplace**, which stretches alongside the Mississippi River from Canal Street up to the Convention Center, has dozens of small shops and a liberal share of chains such as Chico's, Nine West, and others. Outside there is a concrete deck above the river, which has lovely views, and useful information plaques pointing out places of interest.

Jax Brewery, in the French Quarter, is a former beer factory that has been transformed into a sprawling, three-story retail space.

Visitors who want a more traditional mall experience can venture into the suburbs. **Lakeside Shopping Center** in Metairie is the biggest mall in

A band outside Riverwalk Marketplace

the metropolitan area. It has three anchor stores, Dillard's, J. C. Penney, and Macy's, and more than 100 other shops, including 15 shoe stores.

ART AND ANTIQUES

Since its earliest days, New Orleans has been a treasure trove of artistic and vintage luxuries. The locals' knack for dealing in rare and remarkable objects continues to this very day. Another big advantage of shopping for antiques in New Orleans is relative affordability. While prices may still be steep for rare and highly sought-after pieces, they are usually lower than in other US cities. Even when shipping costs are taken into consideration, buyers do very well for themselves. Vintage art can be found in abundance here, though it leans toward the pretty and comfortable; visit Julia Street for more cutting-edge works.

There are antiques shops all over the city, but the biggest concentrations can be found on Royal Street in the French Quarter and along Magazine Street in Uptown. The former is a fabulous showcase of high-end antiques, while the latter leans more toward the fun and funky. Many of the shops in the Quarter are family-run enterprises, often several generations in. This history has contributed to their developing a comfortable, easy atmosphere for all customers, especially novices.

Established in 1912, **M. S. Rau** is internationally known for its range of American, English, and French antique furniture. **Keil's Antiques** is a family-run business dating from 1899. It stocks superb antique jewelry, as well as chandeliers, furniture, and mirrors. On Chartres Street, **Lucullus** focuses on kitchen antiques, ranging from china and linens to 200-year-old French farm tables, while on Decatur Street, **Greg's Antiques** is a must for treasure hunters. Their motto is "This ain't your

Grandma's antique shop," and the tattoo-covered employees confirm this. Jammed with all manner of things from the region, the store is best known for unbelievably affordable prices on bedroom suites,

Linke cabinet crafted with kingwood and doré bronze, at M. S. Rau

armoires, and chandeliers. Sometimes the prices seem so cheap you think there must be a mistake.

The antiques shops on Magazine Street tend to be heavier on 20th-century wares than those in the French Quarter. **Bush Antiques** has a large range of eye-popping vintage beds, many of which come from France. Celebrities who happen to be in town can often be spotted here. **Simon of New Orleans** has a changing stock of offbeat tables, chairs, and metalwork. However, the shop is best known for proprietor and chef-turned-artist Simon Hardeveld's charming faux folk-art signs.

New Orleans also offers a wide selection of art galleries, the most famous of which is probably the **Rodrigue Studio**, in the French Quarter.

It is home to Cajun artist George Rodrigue and his distinctive *Blue Dog* paintings. Make sure you look at his other works too, such as the scenes from Cajun community life. Also in the Quarter is the **Stone & Press Gallery**, with dazzlingly detailed works on paper, etchings, lithographs, wood carvings, and mezzotints.

The artist James Michalopoulos, who owns the eponymous gallery **Michalopoulos**, has become popular for his idiosyncratic depictions of New Orleans architecture. The exaggerated silhouettes are true-to-life representations of the city.

When you are in the French Quarter, don't forget to check out the artists who hang their works on the fence around Jackson Square. While some of the pieces on display are amateur at best, there are also some very talented artists who choose this one-on-one interaction with the public rather than taking the more formal gallery route.

Julia Street, in the Warehouse District, is New Orleans' genuine gallery neighborhood. Most of the galleries here concentrate on local and regional artists, which means that you'll have a chance to see exceptional work by painters, sculptors, and photographers not well known outside of Louisiana. **LeMieux Galleries** shows both emerging and established artists from Louisiana and the

Bush Antiques interior displaying a vintage sleigh bed

An array of Louisiana hot sauces to recreate the magic of Creole cuisine

Gulf Coast, often with strong New Orleans themes in their work.

Quite a few non-Louisiana artists are represented by **Arthur Roger**, including big names such as Dale Chihuly, with his art glass, and film-maker John Waters, with his quirky photographs. The **Steve Martin Studio** is an all-white space above a 19th-century storefront. The starkness shows off owner Steve Martin's wire sculptures to great advantage, and acts as an ideal backdrop for the large canvases that his emerging artists seem to favor. For avant-garde work that explores exciting installation and conceptual art, the **Jonathan Ferrara Gallery** is the place to go.

The **Stella Jones Gallery** in the CBD is the city's premier African and African-American showplace. Modern masters such as Elizabeth Catlett are on the gallery's list of artists. The **New Orleans School of Glassworks** has an exhibition space for the art glass created by its members. If possible, time your visit to observe one of the daily demos of the highly skilled artists blowing glass.

If you happen to be in New Orleans on the third Saturday of any month, a visit to the outdoors **Bywater Art Market** is a must. Join the locals as they wander among the 50-plus painters, jewelry-makers, photographers, textile artists, and woodworkers who set up for the special one-day event, come rain or shine.

JEWELRY

The oldest jewelry store in New Orleans is **Adler's**, which dates back to 1898. This is the best place for traditional rings, necklaces, and other precious items. **Mignon Faget** has become the standard for contemporary jewelry, producing handcrafted pieces in gold and silver. There are three Faget shops in the metropolitan area. **Katy Beh Contemporary Jewelry** is a stylish store that represents more than 30 modern jewelry-makers. The line of "commitment rings" is a romantic's dream come true.

Many of the antiques shops also carry an extensive stock of vintage earrings, bracelets, necklaces, and decorative pieces. **New Orleans Silversmiths** is a big favorite with many collectors.

FOOD

If you fall in love with Cajun and Creole cuisine during your stay in New Orleans,

A gifts and souvenirs stand at the popular French Quarter Flea Market

it is possible to take those unique flavors home with you. The distinctive spices, sauces, and mixes used in local dishes are readily available in jars and bottles. You'll see them all over the French Quarter in souvenir shops, but these are often wildly overpriced, so try a regular grocery store instead for *beignet* mix, coffee with chicory, crab boil, and other products – the quality is the same, but the prices are far lower. Try **Rouse's Market**, which is almost a full-service grocery store in the French Quarter, or the historic **Central Grocery** *(see p76)*, another Quarter outlet that, besides its famous *muffaletta (see p172)*, also stocks sauces, mustards, and all kinds of Italian delicacies. Pralines are a must-try for many visitors. The greatest fun is to sample the different outlets before hitting upon a favorite. The tastiest bets are **Laura's Candies** and **Aunt Sally's Praline Shop**.

If you want to take home crawfish, crab, or *andouille* sausage, head for the **Big Fisherman** on Magazine Street, where the locals go for their fare. An advantage is that the staff is expert at packing these meaty perishables for travel.

CRAFTS

For a wide selection of items made out of ceramics, wood, paper, metal, and glass, try the third floor of Canal Place, where **Rhino Contemporary Craft Co.** features crafts from a range of regional artists. The **Idea Factory** is filled with handmade woodcrafted toys, games, vases, sculptures, boxes, and all sorts of other collectibles. The Idea Factory manages to be both primitive and sophisticated.

The fun **French Quarter Flea Market** *(see p70)* is host to a number of vendors selling all sorts of strange and alluring crafts. These include wood carvings that, in spite of their questionable African origins, make delightful gifts. Quirky handmade toys and jewelry are also available here.

GIFTS AND SPECIALTY STORES

Located in a handsome old-fashioned store, **Hové Parfumeur** has been sweetly scenting New Orleanians since 1931. At **Santa's Quarters**, it is Christmas all year round. You will find lovely holiday ornaments and decorative objects at this store, which is a real boon for those who prefer to finish their Christmas shopping before winter.

If you wish to buy one of the gas lamps that flicker in the Quarter for your own front door, stop by **Bevolo Gas and Electric Lights**, while **Scriptura** is the place to go for beautiful paper products, from journals and sketch books to handmade paper and calligraphy sets.

New Orleans has strong links with the Caribbean, and there are several cigar-making stores in the city. At the **Cigar Factory**, visitors can watch the cigars being rolled and cut, then proceed to select their stogie of choice from the humidor.

Mardi Gras souvenirs such as masks and other regalia are available at several stores. The best place to find a flattering art mask is at the fair before Mardi Gras, but if you're not in town at that time of year, then stop by **Maskarade**. They also sell

A flamboyant Mardi Gras mask from Maskarade, sold all year round

quaint voodoo dolls that have purportedly been inspired by the Louisiana swampland. There are quite a few tarot readers in Jackson Square, but for a private session in rather unusual surroundings, opt for the **Bottom of the Cup Tea Room**.

Located within the same eclectic block of Magazine Street, **Branch Out**, **Green Serene**, and **Aidan Gill for Men** all offer specialty items.

Colorful fashion feathers at Funky Monkey

Branch Out and Green Serene both feature clothing, accessories, and gifts made with recycled materials or eco-friendly fabrics, while Aidan Gill is an old-fashioned gentlemen's parlor with a fine range of wristwatches, lapel pins, and grooming items.

FASHION

For mainstream apparel for men, women, and children, you can rely on department stores such as Dillard's, Macy's, and J. C. Penney, in the shopping malls. However, it is the depth and variety of formal clothing that makes New Orleans different from most other cities in the US. Everyone here attends Mardi Gras balls, from street cleaners to bank presidents, so numerous shops also carry frilly ball gowns, dancing slippers, evening purses, and other accessories.

New Orleans is the perfect place to pick out a tuxedo, since there's a wide selection and the salespeople know all about fittings. **Perlis** is almost a New Orleans tradition in formal clothing for men. The shop's signature fashion is a polo shirt with a crawfish logo (note that Perlis does also have departments dedicated to women's clothing). Another old-line store that caters to men is **Rubenstein's**. **Style Lab**, featuring fashionable casual clothing, is also an oft-frequented place for menswear.

Mimi, on Magazine Street, is the top designer-fashion shop for women, carrying Michael Kors and Vera Wang among others. It also has a popular cosmetics counter. While Mimi's sleek and stylish look represents reigning fashion trends, New Orleans continues its love affair with overstated apparel that is characterized by ruffles, flounces, and other such flourishes. Despite the similarity in name and style, **Fleur de Paris** and **Yvonne LaFleur** are unrelated shops. The former is a lush temple to femininity in the French Quarter. Hats are the store's signature items, and they feature frothy decorations of feathers, fruits, flowers, and ribbons. Back in the Riverbend area of Uptown, Yvonne LaFleur offers lavish evening gowns and romantic hats that Scarlett O'Hara would have loved. The shop even has its own tiara department. Designer Harold Clarke's French Quarter outlet, **Harold Clarke Couturier**, is much loved by debutantes and Mardi Gras royalty. His dreamy ball gowns are always on display thanks to the full-length windows in his shop.

Magazine Street is home to a number of happening shops that specialize in funky outfits for club nights and bohemian days. **Trashy Diva** and **Funky Monkey** both stock wild and outrageous clothes that you might see on teenage pop stars. For vintage fashions, a good choice is **On the Other Hand**, a boutique that offers a fine and wide selection of secondhand clothes.

Meyer the Hatter is one of the city's most beloved shops. The family-owned store has been supplying New Orleanians of both sexes with hats for more than 100 years. Every conceivable type of hat can be found here, including Stetsons, derbies, fedoras, and berets, all of which are not only elegant and well crafted, but reasonably priced.

BOOKS

Independent bookstores are still going strong in New Orleans. At **Octavia Books**, located in the Uptown area, volumes are carefully chosen and sold by the book-loving staffers. The **Garden District Bookshop** has an admirable selection of non-fiction and regional titles, and it also has strong ties to writer Anne Rice, who has done several

signings here. **Maple Street Bookshop**, near the Tulane University campus, is devoted to showcasing Southern literature and is a favorite of locals as well as visiting writers. In the French Quarter, **Faulkner House Books** is a charming little shop with a surprising number of books in stock. It also has many rare first editions, especially by William Faulkner, who once lived in the building. For used books, the French Quarter has **Librairie Book Shop**, a treasure trove of both intellectual and offbeat volumes. **Beckham's Bookshop** includes comfy reading chairs and friendly cats.

MUSIC

Music is the lifeblood of New Orleans. The greatest place to explore local music, from jazz to zydeco, is the famous **Louisiana Music**

Factory, which stocks a well-cataloged range of artists. Be sure to check for free in-store performances by artists promoting their new albums. The staff members are very helpful too.

For collectors, the city has several outstanding hunting grounds. One of the best is **Jim Russell's Rare Records**, which has a great stock of rock 'n' roll 78s among its thousands of records.

A record by Oscar "Papa" Celestin, founder of the Tuxedo Brass Band

DIRECTORY

DIRECTORY

JEWELRY

Adler's
722 Canal St. **Map** 4 B3.
Tel 523-5292.
www.adlersjewelry.com

Katy Beh Contemporary Jewelry
3701 Magazine St.
Map 7 F4. Tel *896-9600.*
www.katybeh.com

Mignon Faget
3801 Magazine St.
Map 7 F4.
Tel 891-2005.
www.mignonfaget.com

New Orleans Silversmiths
600 Chartres St.
Map 4 C2. **Tel** *522-8333.*
www.neworleans
silversmiths.com

FOOD

Aunt Sally's Praline Shop
810 Decatur St.
Map 5 D2. **Tel** *524-3373.*
www.auntsallys.com

Big Fisherman
3301 Magazine St.
Map 7 F4. **Tel** *897-9907.*
www.bigfisherman
seafood.com

Central Grocery
923 Decatur St.
Map 5 D2. **Tel** *523-1620.*

Laura's Candies
331 Chartres St.
Map 4 C3. **Tel** *525-3880.*
www.laurascandies.com

Rouse's Market
701 Royal St.
Map 5 D2. **Tel** *523-1353.*
www.rouses.com

CRAFTS

French Quarter Flea Market
Decatur & St. Philip Sts.
Map 5 D2.
Tel 522-2621.
www.frenchmarket.org

Idea Factory
838 Chartres St.
Map 5 D1.
Tel 524-5195.
www.ideafactory
neworleans.com

Rhino Contemporary Craft Co.
Canal Place, 3rd floor.
Map 4 C3.
Tel 523-7945.
www.rhinocrafts.com

GIFTS AND SPECIALTY STORES

Aidan Gill for Men
2026 Magazine St.
Map 8 A3.
Tel 587-9090. www.
aidangillformen.com

Bevolo Gas and Electric Lights
521 Conti St.
Map 4 C2.
Tel 522-9485.
www.bevolo.com

Bottom of the Cup Tea Room
327 Chartres St.
Map 4 C3.
Tel 524-1997.
www.bottomof
thecup.com

Branch Out
2022 Magazine St.
Map 8 A3.
Tel 371-5913.
www.branchoutshop.
com

Cigar Factory
415 Decatur St.
Map 5 D3. **Tel** *568-1003.*
www.cigarfactory
neworleans.com

Green Serene
2041 Magazine St.
Map 8 A3.
Tel 252-9861.
www.greenserene.biz

Hové Parfumeur
824 Royal St.
Map 5 D1.
Tel 525-7827. www.
Hoveparfumeur.com

Maskarade
630 St. Ann St.
Map 4 D2.
Tel 568-1018.
www.frenchquarter
maskstore.com

Santa's Quarters
1025 Decatur St.
Map 5 D2. **Tel** *581-5820.*
www.santas
quartersno.com

Scriptura
5423 Magazine St.
Map 6 C4.
Tel 897-1555.
www.scriptura.com

FASHION

Fleur de Paris
523 Royal St.
Map 4 C2.
Tel 525-1899.
www.fleurdeparis.net

Funky Monkey
3127 Magazine St.
Map 7 F4. **Tel** *899-5587.*

Harold Clarke Couturier
901 Iberville St.
Map 4 C2. **Tel** *568-0440.*
www.haroldclarke.com

Meyer the Hatter
120 St. Charles Ave.
Map 4 C3.
Tel 525-1048.
www.meyerthehatter.com

Mimi
5500 Magazine St.
Map 6 C4. **Tel** *269-6464.*
www.miminola.com

On the Other Hand
8204 Oak St. **Map** 6 A1.
Tel 861-0159.
www.ontheotherhand
consignment.com

Perlis
6070 Magazine St.
Map 6 B4. **Tel** *895-8661.*
www.perlis.com
One of four locations.

Rubenstein's
102 St. Charles Ave.
Map 4 C3. **Tel** *581-6666.*
www.rubensteins
neworleans.com

Style Lab
3641 Magazine St.
Map 7 E4. **Tel** *304-5072.*
www.stylelabformen.com

Trashy Diva
829 Chartres St.
Map 5 D2. **Tel** *581-4555.*
www.trashydiva
One of two locations.

Yvonne LaFleur
8131 Hampson St.
Map 6 A1. **Tel** *866-9666.*
www.yvonnelafleur.com

BOOKS

Beckham's Bookshop
228 Decatur St.
Map 4 C3. **Tel** *522-9875.*

Faulkner House Books
624 Pirate's Alley.
Map 5 D2. **Tel** *524-2940.*
www.faulknerhouse
books.net

Garden District Bookshop
2727 Prytania St.
Map 7 F4. **Tel** *895-2266.*
www.gardendistrict
bookshop.com

Librairie Book Shop
823 Chartres St.
Map 5 D2. **Tel** *525-4837.*

Maple Street Bookshop
7523 Maple St.
Map 6 A2. **Tel** *866-4916.*
www.maplestreet
bookshop.com

Octavia Books
513 Octavia St.
Map 6 C5. **Tel** *899-7323.*
www.octaviabooks.com

MUSIC

Jim Russell's Rare Records
1837 Magazine St.
Map 8 B3. **Tel** *522-2602.*
www.jimrussellrecords.
com

Louisiana Music Factory
210 Decatur St.
Map 4 C3. **Tel** *586-1094.*
www.louisiana
musicfactory.com

What to Buy in New Orleans

Mardi Gras mask

New Orleans is the best place to discover original small boutiques that are owned by artists and designers of all sorts – jewelers, painters, potters, milliners, clothes designers, and many more – rather than large department stores. In addition to these, there are various tourist memorabilia and trinket stores, which sell T-shirts, rubber alligators, Mardi Gras beads, and other typical kitsch souvenirs. However, to experience the quintessential New Orleans, look out for the things that New Orleans does best – cuisine, cocktails, and music.

Mardi Gras poster

MARDI GRAS MEMORABILIA

Mardi Gras is New Orleans' biggest and longest party, and there are plenty of souvenirs that visitors can take home. Masks are the most alluring, and they can be found in shops and stalls throughout the city. Prices can range from as little as $20 to hundreds of dollars. Masks are often handmade by individual artists including theater costume designers. Less authentic trinkets include beads, mugs, T-shirts, and other typical souvenirs.

Flea market stands with Mardi Gras souvenirs

African Art and Crafts

The heritage of New Orleans' African cultures can be found in a number of shops. Here you can buy African art and crafts, including masks, drums, sculptures, pipes, tables, and items of personal jewelry.

African wood drum

Wood–carved African sculptures

Music

Music is the lifeblood of the city, and a musical souvenir is essential. Record stores sell recordings of great artists playing traditional and modern jazz, gospel, blues, R&B, Cajun, and zydeco.

Hand-Rolled Cigars

New Orleans is close to the Caribbean, both physically and culturally, and has a strong tradition of importing Caribbean cigars. There are several stores where cigars are still hand-rolled. Even a single cigar or a rather expensive box make a perfect gift for any cigar aficionado.

Voodoo Accoutrements

New Orleans is the one place in the United States where the voodoo religion was once openly practiced and celebrated (see p83). Supplies of the materials needed to perform voodoo healings and other rituals – candles, gris-gris to control the boss, ensure safe travel, or promote love, voodoo dolls, and more – can still be purchased at several shops in the French Quarter. These always make colorful and unusual gifts.

Voodoo candle

Gris-gris bags

Antiques

New Orleans is famous for its tradition of dealing in fine antiques. You can find 19th-century furniture and jewelry, as well as other decorative objects, for all tastes and prices.

Antique shop on Royal Street

THE FLAVORS OF LOUISIANA

Louisiana is famous the world over for spicy, flavorsome cuisine *(see pp172–5)*. Most visitors want to take some of it home and duplicate those flavors in their own kitchens. In many stores, shelves are lined with hot sauces such as Tabasco, Crystal, Panola, and Cajun Chef. Strands of peppers and garlic and bottles of Cajun and Creole seasoning can be found at the French Market and numerous stores in the area. Here are some of the city's quintessential food gifts.

Roux mix for gumbos

Hats

Southerners and New Orleanians in particular love hats. There are several stores selling terrific ones for both men and women (see pp189–90). They stock every available kind, from classic fedoras, derbies, and Stetsons to berets, French legion caps, and squashy barman hats.

Olive salad dressing

Beignet flour mix

An instant traditional dish

ENTERTAINMENT IN NEW ORLEANS

In 1817, a visitor to New Orleans wrote, "There are few places where human life can be enjoyed with more pleasure." Little has changed since then, and New Orleans remains a party town to this day. Even when it is not Mardi Gras, the mood is festive, and there is always a party somewhere. Music underpins the atmosphere, from tiny neighborhood bars to late-night

Marching-band tuba player

brass band joints and the annual Jazz Fest. The rallying cry of *Laissez les bons temps rouler!* ("Let the good times roll!") is taken quite literally here. You'll also find good times in sports, including football, basketball, and horseracing, as well as casinos, stage productions, and bars, which approach an art form in the Big Easy. For New Orleans' best music venues, see pp200–1.

Street musicians playing jazz on Jackson Square

ENTERTAINMENT GUIDES

It's easy to find out what's on in New Orleans. The best guides are the monthly magazine **Offbeat**, found free in cafés, hotels, and other public places; the **Times-Picayune**'s Friday tabloid *Lagniappe*; and the weekly alternative paper **Gambit**. For gay events and entertainments, check the bi-monthly newspaper **Ambush**, distributed to gay bars and clubs in the French Quarter and the Marigny. Other sources of information are the roots music radio station **WWOZ** (90.7 FM) and classical and jazz music station **WWNO** (89.9 FM).

Alcohol plays a big role in the *bon temps* in New Orleans. Although the city has a fairly relaxed attitude toward drinking, there are still a few unbreakable rules. As in the rest of the US, the drinking age is 21, but anyone under 30 should expect to be "carded"

(asked to show a picture ID certifying one's age). Unlike most American cities, it is legal to walk around with drinks in New Orleans, but they must be in plastic cups, or "go cups." It is illegal, however, to have open alcoholic beverages in automobiles, even for passengers. Police keep a careful eye on popular gathering spots and are easy-going about tipsy folks except if there is fighting or public urination, both of which will land miscreants in jail immediately.

TICKETS

The easiest way to buy tickets for concerts, football games, theatrical productions, and other events is to call the relevant box office or **Ticketmaster** (www.ticketmaster.com). The major hotels and B&Bs usually have a concierge who can facilitate booking tickets. Student and senior-citizen discounts are available for many events.

ROCK, BLUES, AND OTHER MUSIC VENUES

Music clubs in New Orleans are almost celebrities in themselves, with their own fans, personalities, and idiosyncrasies. The **House of Blues** *(see p201)* and **Tipitina's** are the two leading ones by virtue of the big names they book and their unerring instinct for New Orleans authenticity. House of Blues is the largest and most expensive of the clubs; as well as enjoying top lineups, visitors here can dine at the excellent on-site restaurant.

Frenchmen Street, in the Marigny, is where the locals go for the full music experience, drifting among the various bars and clubs. The **Blue Nile** is another club with a big dance floor where Latin, alternative rock, and brass bands play. Hipsters hang out at **Dragon's Den**, where the music often goes

Jazz parade and band on the streets of the French Quarter

Live music at The Famous Door, Bourbon Street

on until daylight. Also on Frenchmen is **d.b.a.** featuring interesting musicians (often acoustic), and the crown jewel of local jazz clubs, the **Snug Harbor Jazz Bistro**.

Bars in Bourbon Street are mostly frequented by tourists, and the music played here tends to be mainstream Top 40 rock covers. There are a couple of genuine pearls on Bourbon – **The Famous Door** has live music daily, while at **Fritzel's** you can hear the best of local jazz talents – but generally speaking, to find the real New Orleans, you need to look a little farther.

The **Balcony Music Club**, on Esplanade Avenue, hosts everything from brass bands to jazz singers. Although not a club, the **Louisiana Music Factory** record store *(see p190)*, on Decatur, has an impressive lineup of free concerts. The shop is a great place for close encounters with blues, jazz, zydeco, and Cajun musicians who have daytime "in-stores" – live performances and autographing sessions – to promote new albums and concerts.

On Toulouse Street, **One-Eyed Jack's** is the latest incarnation of a longtime Quarter joint. The club is a bubbly mixture of alternative rock and hip-hop and Sunday night burlesque shows. A Las Vegas-style show can be enjoyed at the **Chris Owens Club**. The iconic Owens has been performing in the Quarter for at least three decades. For clubs offering topless dancers, head to Bourbon Street.

In the Warehouse District, the **Howlin' Wolf** club is renowned for booking breaking new bands and hosting original events such as the annual Thanksgiving Turkey Bowl. The **Circle Bar** on Lee Circle is a tiny space that rocks, while **Le Bon Temps Roule**, located Uptown on Magazine Street, is a favorite spot to catch live local bands. There are several pool tables, an extensive on-tap beer selection, and better-than-average bar food.

Dance clubs are not a big New Orleans thing, but the **& Club** (say "Ampersand") in the CBD draws large crowds of young singles, who dance into the small hours with DJs who know how to keep the party going.

For refined nightclubs that recall the elegance of earlier eras, there is **The Davenport Lounge**, in the Ritz-Carlton Hotel. The room itself is

lovely, with numerous romantic nooks and crannies. On weekends dapper young jazz star Jeremy Davenport and his band play to sophisticated crowds. The **Bombay Club** in the Prince Conti Hotel is another oasis of retro sophistication, with plush decor, perfect martinis, and light jazz.

Republic, a cabaret-style music lounge that harkens back to the 1940s, should appeal to those who favor hip and beautiful crowds. The venue offers everything from indie-rock concerts to fashion shows and branded theme parties with celebrity sightings. The city's major music venues will allow you to buy tickets at the door or order them by phone or online. At clubs there's usually a cover charge on weekends and for name acts. Most clubs with live music have a one- or two-drink minimum policy.

BARS

Street musician

It is possible to drink around the clock in New Orleans, which is reported to have more bars per capita than any other American city, all catering to the local passion for a good beer or a nice cocktail. As an added bonus, many bars offer free Wi-Fi access to their patrons.

There are several famous bars in the French Quarter that deserve a visit. **Pat O'Brien's** is a classic bar with its own trademark drink, the lethal rum-and-fruit Hurricane

Fritzel's, Bourbon Street's traditional European jazz club

(see p174). It also has a lush courtyard with a flaming fountain and lighthearted piano music. The attractively shabby **Napoleon House** *(see p59)* is the kind of place where you could see aspiring novelists write their story as they nurse a drink in one of the dim corners. **Lafitte's Blacksmith Shop** *(see p78),* in a crumbling 18th-century building, sends waiters out to passing horse-drawn carriages to take drink orders.

New Orleans can do sleek and upscale, too, as you'll find at the **Polo Lounge** at the Windsor Court Hotel, **Whiskey Blue** at the W Hotel, and the **Swizzle Stick Bar** in Loews Hotel. In a class of its own, however, is the Hotel Monteleone's **Carousel Bar**, where the bar slowly revolves while the bartenders at the center dispense brandy Alexanders and other cocktails. The sleek **Loft 523** and **Loa at International House** are both distinctive and full of personality – and personalities!

Irish bars are a reliable source of good fun. On Decatur Street, **Kerry Irish Pub** has Guinness on tap and live music. **Molly's at the Market** is more New Orleans Irish than authentic Irish, but it is a center of Celticism, holding its own St. Patrick's Day parade every year. Uptown is **Parasol's Bar**, perhaps the most famous Irish bar of them all. It is a neighborhood hangout that turns green on St. Patrick's Day, with a huge street party that extends several blocks around the bar.

Serious drinkers will find

Gathering around Pat O'Brien's famous fire fountain

Cooter Brown's Tavern an impressive site, with its selection of more than 400 beers. **The Bulldog**, also in the Uptown area, has a huge beer selection as well, but is better known as a college pick-up bar than for its drinks. **Bacchanal Fine Wines** in Bywater is a laid-back wine shop that holds more-or-less continual wine tastings.

Neighborhood bars are mostly friendly, welcoming places, even if you accidentally sit on a stool that is "owned" by a regular punter. **Vaughan's Lounge**, in Bywater, is a gritty spot that has live music on Thursdays and a bohemian working-class *esprit de corps* every night. Finally, the **F & M Patio Bar** is known for attracting big crowds after Mardi Gras balls and debutante parties, when people flock here to drink on the patio, dance, and play pool.

GAY AND LESBIAN BARS AND CLUBS

The gay community in New Orleans is large and visible. During Mardi Gras *(see p40)* and Southern Decadence ("the gay Mardi Gras") *(see p41),* the streets of the Lower French Quarter are full of wild humor and outrageous cos-tumes. The two most

popular dance clubs are the **Bourbon Pub & Parade Disco** and **Oz**, both on Bourbon Street. Nearby is **Café Lafitte in Exile**, the town's oldest gay bar, with a balcony for watching the street scene. **Good Friends** is a relaxed spot where conversation is easy.

The **Golden Lantern** is a historic landmark, the place where Southern Decadence first began more than 30 years ago, while **The Friendly Bar** has the feel of a neigh-borhood joint, with pool tables, cook-outs, and regulars who truly embody the bar's name.

Flamboyant parade costume

THEATER, DANCE, AND CLASSICAL MUSIC

Jazz and contemporary music may dominate the arts scene in New Orleans, but there are also many gems to be found among the classical performing arts. The city has a long and affectionate history with opera. The **New Orleans Opera Association** is a small but valiant outfit bringing in recognized stars to headline its four annual productions. The company, which has staged such beloved classics as *La Traviata, Faust,* and *Carmen,* usually performs at the Mahalia Jackson Theater of the Performing Arts *(see p80).*

The Mahalia Jackson Theater of the Performing Arts underwent a massive

The brightly lit and slowly revolving Carousel Bar in the Hotel Monteleone

renovation to reverse the damage done by the levee breaks of 2005. As a result, the building has recaptured all of the glimmer and glamor of its youth. Four more of the city's premier downtown venues were damaged by the disaster: the Municipal Auditorium, the Saenger Theatre, the State Palace Theatre, and the Orpheum (the longtime home of the local orchestra). Along with the old Joy moviehouse on Canal Street, these venues are in various stages of planning for redevelopment

The musicians of the Louisiana Philharmonic Orchestra

as part of a grand vision for a new theater district.

The **Louisiana Philharmonic Orchestra** (LPO) also has a strong traditional slant and produces highly acclaimed performances. The orchestra currently performs in the Mahalia Jackson Theater and other venues around town. The symphony also holds several outdoor concerts each year, in either Audubon or City Park.

Theater in New Orleans has become exciting with the rise of new playwrights, adventurous productions, and an experimental stage. The **Southern Repertory Theater** is the city's leading theater company. It presents strong new works from around the country, while actively seeking out Louisiana playwrights.

There are also several nomad theater groups that perform in bars, coffeehouses, and other unconventional spaces, producing original works with New Orleans

themes and reinterpreting the classics – *La Bohème* in drag, for instance.

In the Marigny, **The AllWays Lounge** is a bar and theater presenting more edgy material in an intimate, colorful performance space.

The **New Orleans Contemporary Arts Center** *(see p97)* doesn't have a resident company but hosts numerous productions every year, many of them multimedia, avant-garde works. **Le Petit Théâtre du Vieux Carré** *(see p55)* is the city's oldest theater troupe, dating from 1916. The company leans toward musicals and comedies, usually with elaborate sets and costumes.

Professional dance companies visit New Orleans several times a year under the aegis of the **New Orleans Ballet Association**. There hasn't been a New Orleans Ballet since 1991, but the organization presents important companies such as the Alvin Ailey American Dance Theater, the Miami Ballet, and the Joffrey Ballet. Several times a year, dance performances are also held at Newcomb College of Tulane University *(see pp110–11)*, a former women's college with a long history of dance innovation and study.

CASINOS

Legal gambling came to New Orleans in the 1990s, but the law allows only one full-fledged casino to exist

at any one site. **Harrah's Casino** *(see p89)* is a full-service casino that is dazzling inside, with interiors that suggest a frozen Mardi Gras theme. Slot machines predominate, but there are also tables for blackjack, craps, baccarat, and poker. Harrah's has slowly ventured into live entertainment as well, with comedy and a Las Vegas-type revue. The area has two riverboat casinos – **Treasure Chest** in Kenner and **Boomtown Casino** on the West Bank.

SPORTS AND MAJOR ARENAS

New Orleans loves its sports. The vast **Louisiana Superdome** *(see p95)* is a national venue for sports, home of the annual Sugar Bowl *(see p43)*, and host to high-profile events such as the Super Bowl. The hometown teams are the **New Orleans Saints** for football and the **New Orleans Hornets** for basketball. After Katrina, the venue was closed but reopened in 2006 after a multimillion-dollar restoration.

For baseball, the city has the Triple-A minor-league Zephyrs, a farm team of the New York Mets. They play at **Zephyr Stadium**, in suburban Jefferson Parish, a state-of-the-art facility that even has a hot tub for use if you rent the private picnic area. College baseball is a big draw, especially the Tulane, University of New Orleans, and Louisiana State University teams.

Horseracing has a long history here. The **Fair Grounds** race course *(see p126)* is one of the oldest continuously

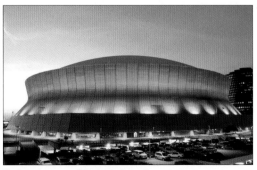

The Superdome, one of the country's premier sports venues

operated tracks in the country. The season runs from November to March.

A major golf tournament is held at the **TPC Golf Course** on the West Bank, usually in the last week of April. The name of the event changes every few years depending on the corporate sponsorship.

TOURS

Tours, especially walking tours, are a great way to experience New Orleans. They are also the best option if you intend to visit the local cemeteries, some of which are not safe for lone visitors.

The **Historic New Orleans Walking Tours** offers the best regularly scheduled tours of the French Quarter (with a cemetery component) and of the Garden District.

In the French Quarter, the volunteer **Friends of the Cabildo** also runs a good tour; the **Jean Lafitte National Historical Park** gives an excellent free daily tour of the Quarter, but there are limited spaces. Contact the **Visitors' Bureau (NOCVB)** for information on sign-up times.

Specialty tours can be good fun. For cemetery-only tours, contact the non-profit **Save Our Cemeteries** group. The **New Orleans Jazz National Historical Park** hosts free walking tours that trace the growth of jazz. These don't have regular schedules, so check with the NOMCVB. The **New Orleans Original Cocktail Tour** explains that the cocktail was invented in New Orleans and delves into the history of French Quarter bars. The **Culinary History Tour** visits restaurants and

provides information about New Orleans food and culture.

The adventurous might enjoy a trip aboard an all-terrain airboat or a swamp tour. The **Airboat Swamp Tours** are fast and exciting; for a slower and more ecological look at swamps, try the **Pearl River Eco-Tours** or **Dr. Wagner's Honey Island Swamp Tours**. **Cajun Pride Tours** also visits swamps and plantations.

Some outfits offer combination tours with a hotel pick-up and drop-off. Be aware that bus tours around the city have limited access to the French Quarter, which bans large buses from its fragile interior streets. **Tours by Isabelle** does both city and plantation tours in small buses and vans. **New Orleans Tours Inc.** offers a wide range of tours around the city, as well as to plantations and swamps.

DIRECTORY

DIRECTORY

Lafitte's Blacksmith Shop
941 Bourbon St.
Map 4 D1. **Tel** 593-9761.

Loa at International House
221 Camp St. **Map** 4 C3.
Tel 553-9550.
www.ihhotel.com/loa

Loft 523
523 Gravier St. **Map** 4 C3.
Tel 200-6523.
www.loft523.com

Molly's at the Market
1107 Decatur St. **Map** 5 D2. **Tel** 525-5169. www.mollysatthemarket.net

Napoleon House
500 Chartres St.
Map 4 C2. **Tel** 524-9752.
www.napoleonhouse.com

Parasol's Bar
2533 Constance St.
Map 8 A4. **Tel** 897-5413.
www.parasols.com

Pat O'Brien's
718 St. Peter St.
Map 4 C2. **Tel** 525-4823.
www.patobriens.com

Polo Lounge
Windson Court Hotel, 300 Gravier St. **Map** 4 C4.
Tel 523-6000. www.windsorcourthotel.com

Swizzle Stick Bar
Loews Hotel, 300 Poydras St. **Map** 4 C4.
Tel 595-3305.
www.cafeadelaide.com

Vaughan's Lounge
800 Lesseps St.
Tel 947-5562.

Whiskey Blue
W Hotel, 333 Poydras St.
Map 4 C4. **Tel** 525-9444.
www.mocbars.com

GAY AND LESBIAN BARS AND CLUBS

Bourbon Pub & Parade Disco
801 Bourbon St.
Map 4 C2. **Tel** 529-2107.
www.bourbonpub.com

Café Lafitte in Exile
901 Bourbon St.
Map 4 C1. **Tel** 522-8397.
www.lafittes.com

The Friendly Bar
2301 Chartres St.
Map 5 E1.
Tel 943-8929.

Golden Lantern
1239 Royal St. **Map** 5 D1.
Tel 529-2860.

Good Friends
740 Dauphine St.
Map 4 C2. **Tel** 566-7191.
www.goodfriendsbar.com

Oz
800 Bourbon St.
Map 4 C2. **Tel** 593-9491.
www.oznewⁿorleans.com

THEATER, DANCE, AND CLASSICAL MUSIC

The AllWays Lounge
2240 St. Claude Ave.
Map 3 F3.
Tel 218-5778. www.theallwayslounge.net

Dixon Hall
Tulane University,
6823 St. Charles Ave.
Map 8 B1.

Louisiana Philharmonic Orchestra
Tel 523-6530.
www.lpomusic.org

New Orleans Ballet Association
Tel 522-0996.
www.nobadance.com

New Orleans Opera Association
Tel 529-2278. www.neworleansopera.org

Southern Repertory Theater
Canal Place Mall, 3rd floor.
Map 4 C3. **Tel** 522-6545.
www.southernrep.

CASINOS

Boomtown Casino
4132 Peters Road, Harvey.
Tel 366-7711.
www.boomtownneworleans.com

Harrah's Casino
8 Canal St. **Map** 4 C4.
Tel 533-6000. www.harrahsneworleans.com

Treasure Chest
5050 Williams Blvd,
Kenner. **Tel** 443-8000.
www.treasurechestcasino.com

SPORTS AND MAJOR ARENAS

New Orleans Hornets
Tel 525-4667.
www.hornets.com

New Orleans Saints
Tel 731-1700. www.neworleanssaints.com

TPC Golf Course
Zurich Classic Golf
Tournament, 11001
Lapalco Blvd, Avondale.
Tel 436-8721.
www.tpc.com
www.pga.com

Zephyr Stadium
6000 Airline Hwy.
Tel 734-5155. www.zephyrsbaseball.com

TOURS

Airboat Swamp Tours
4262 Hwy 90.
Tel (985) 758-5531.
www.airboattours.com

Cajun Pride Tours
Tel 467-0758. www.cajunprideswamptours.com

Culinary History Tour
Tel 427-9595. www.noculinarytours.com

Dr. Wagner's Honey Island Swamp Tours
Tel 242-5877. www.honeyislandswamp.com

Friends of the Cabildo
523 St. Ann St.
Map 5 D2.
Tel 523-3939. www.friendsofthecabildo.org

Historic New Orleans Walking Tours
Tel 947-2120. www.tourneworleans.com

Jean Lafitte National Historical Park
419 Decatur St.
Map 4 C3.
Tel 589-2636.
www.nps.gov/jela

New Orleans Jazz National Historical Park
916 N Peters St.
Map 5 D2. **Tel** 589-4841.
www.nps.gov/jazz

New Orleans Original Cocktail Tour
Tel 569-1401. www.graylineneworleans.com

New Orleans Tours Inc.
Tel 592-1991.
www.notours.com

NOCVB (New Orleans Convention and Visitors' Bureau)
2020 St. Charles Ave.
Tel (504) 566-5011.
www.neworleanscvb

Pearl River Eco-Tours
55050 US 90, Slidell.
Tel (866) 597-9267.
www.laecotour.com

Save Our Cemeteries
Tel 525-3377. www.saveourcemeteries.org

Tours by Isabelle
Tel (877) 665-8687.
www.toursbyisabelle.com

New Orleans' Best: Music Venues

In New Orleans, where every night is Saturday
night and every Saturday night is New Year's Eve,
there's always live music playing. Look beyond
Bourbon Street and the French Quarter for the
real scene. You'll find world-class jazz, rock 'n'
roll, blues, Latin, funk, Cajun, zydeco, and that
New Orleans hybrid, brass-band funk, every night
(and some days) of the week. These clubs are
the cream of the city's club culture.

Chickie Wah Wah
*Popular in part because
it's one of the few non-
smoking venues in town,
this bar features rocka-
billy and Cajun bands,
among others.*

Maison Bourbon Jazz Club
*A favorite with visitors to the city, this
club is one of the few places on Bourbon
Street where you can hear a live Dixieland band. Good cocktails and a refined
atmosphere complete the picture.*

| 0 meters | 500 |
| 0 yards | 500 |

MID-CITY   TREME

WAREHOUSE AND
CENTRAL BUSINESS
DISTRICTS

GARDEN
DISTRICT AND
UPTOWN

Maple Leaf Bar
*The quintessential off-the-
beaten-path club, hidden
in the Carrollton district.
The music starts late and
goes on for hours, with
an energized crowd that
loves to dance. The Maple
Leaf Bar is also famed
for Sunday afternoon
poetry readings.*

One-Eyed Jack's
*Once called the
Shim Sham Club,
this vintage theater
showcases everything
from Cajun bands
and alternative rock-
ers to burlesque acts.*

Palm Court Jazz Café
The place for a classic jazz evening led by great bands; the hostess-owner loves to lead a second line.

Snug Harbor Bistro
Not just New Orleans' premier jazz club but one of the best in the US, hosting little-known local virtuosos and big names on tour.

MARIGNY

LOWER FRENCH QUARTER

UPPER FRENCH QUARTER

Fritzel's European Jazz Pub
Fritzel's blends reverence for traditional jazz with a lively atmosphere. A favorite drop-in for visiting musicians.

Preservation Hall
The place that kept traditional jazz alive and vital. The atmosphere is musty, dusty, and old school, but the music is worth it. No food or drinks are allowed or served.

House of Blues
Technically part of a chain, but HOB is a dream rock club with several stages, bars, and hangout spots. Big names play here.

Children's Entertainment and Outdoor Activities

Storyland at City Park

New Orleans is renowned as an adult playground, but there are many places in the area designed especially for the younger generation. There is an enormous variety of attractions and entertainment, from the thrill rides in City Park to a ride across the mighty Mississippi on the Canal Street ferry. The city also offers numerous outdoor activities for all ages, from deep-sea fishing, tennis, and golf, to swamp tours, birdwatching, biking, watersports, and horseback riding.

Roller coaster ride at Storyland in City Park

Supermarket for children at the Louisiana Children's Museum

MUSEUMS FOR CHILDREN

Many museums in and around New Orleans have arts and educational programs designed specifically for young audiences. **The New Orleans Museum of Art** (NOMA) *(see p120–23)* has a museum-on-wheels program for kids, and also offers guided tours focused on children's interests. The **Louisiana Children's Museum** *(see p97)* caters to kids and parents, and is specifically designed to inspire questions through hands-on exhibits, including role-playing games.

Three museums in Kenner are the **Toy Train Museum**, the **Mardi Gras Museum**, and the adjacent **Kenner Planetarium** and they are well worth the short trip outside the city. Kenner is located to the west of the city, between New Orleans and Baton Rouge on the I-10.

ZOOS, AQUARIUMS, AND AMUSEMENT PARKS

Two major attractions for children and grown-ups alike are the **Audubon Zoo** *(see pp112–13)* and the **Audubon Aquarium of the Americas** *(see pp90–91)*. The zoo is home to more than 1,500 animals, many of which roam about in natural habitats. The Louisiana Swamp exhibit, the Jaguar Jungle, and the touchy-feely Embraceable Zoo are all geared toward education and understanding animals. The spectacular Audubon Aquarium of the Americas houses thousands of fish, marine mammals, and water birds. An IMAX Theater shows documentaries on ocean life, and the Caribbean Reef exhibit gives kids the opportunity to explore an underwater habitat.

Storyland *(see p118)* in City Park has 26 "storybook" exhibits by the master Mardi

Gras float creator Blaine Kern *(see p88)*. A working antique carousel with 54 beautifully carved animals, bumper cars, a miniature train, and the ubiquitous Tilt-a-Whirl complete the carnival atmosphere.

FISHING

New Orleans is a famous port. Farther south toward the Gulf, shrimp boats and the larger deep-sea boats offer a glimpse of the industries that keep Louisiana rich. Anglers can fish in Lake Pontchartrain or in City Park's lagoons, or charter a boat and try your luck at the big fish: tarpon, snapper, and marlin. **Angelle's Atchafalaya Basin Swamp Tours**, **Griffin Fishing Charters**, and **Capt. Phil Robichaux's Saltwater Guide Service** all offer fishing tours and/or charters into the swamp, coastal waterways, and marshes. Hotel shuttles, licenses, camera and film, and all equipment are provided by these companies.

Visitors at the Audubon Zoo

RIVER CRUISES

A peaceful boat ride is an alternative to the party atmosphere and noise of the city. Paddlewheelers offer short excursions up and down the Mississippi River from the French Quarter wharves. Swamp tours by flat-boat or seaplane also abound, charter boats and houseboats are readily available, and you can splash out and book a week-long cruise on the famous Delta Queen, which runs from Pittsburgh all the way to New Orleans and is operated by the **Majestic America Line**.

GOLF AND TENNIS

City Park's **Bayou Oaks** is the South's largest public golf course, offering four 18-hole courses. The golf courses sustained heavy damage from flooding after Hurricane Katrina and are being rebuilt and reopened in stages, one course at a time. The driving range reopened in 2007, and the North course in 2008. Other courses are under redevelopment. The 18-hole course in **Audubon Park** (*see p111*) has undergone a $6-million redesign. It is a

Lake Pontchartrain fishing area

flat, fast course and the surroundings are beautiful. A bonus is the park's Golf Club, which serves as a bar and restaurant. The wrap-around porch is the perfect place to enjoy lunch before or after your game.

There are many country golf clubs that allow guests, and some of the best and most accessible of these are **Belle Terre**, **Lakewood**, **Oak Harbor**, and the **Chateau Country Golf Club**. Golf is a year-round sport, but winter is the busiest season. If you play in summer, start early to avoid the heat and the late

afternoon thunderstorms. Greens fees vary from under $20 to over $75 per person, and are highest in winter.

The **City Park Tennis Center** (*see p119*) has 16 hard courts and 10 clay courts. All are well-lit at night.

FITNESS CENTERS

Many hotels have on-site fitness centers where you can use the weights room, swim laps, relax in the sauna, or burn those extra calories on the treadmill. The **Downtown Fitness Center** welcomes guests.

DIRECTORY

MUSEUMS FOR CHILDREN

Kenner Planetarium
2020 4th St,
Rivertown, Kenner.
Tel 468-7231.
www.rivertown
kenner.com

Mardi Gras Museum
415 Williams Blvd,
Rivertown, Kenner.
Tel 468-7231.
www.rivertown
kenner.com

Toy Train Museum
519 Williams Blvd,
Rivertown, Kenner.
Tel 468-7231.
www.rivertown
kenner.com

FISHING/SWAMP TOURS

Angelle's Atchafalaya Basin Swamp Tours
Tel (337) 228-8567.

Capt. Phil Robichaux's Saltwater Guide Service
1842 Jean Lafitte Blvd,
Jean Lafitte.
Tel 689-2006.

Griffin Fishing Charters
Tel (800) 741-1340.

RIVER CRUISES

Majestic America Line/Delta Queen
Robin St Wharf,
1380 Port of New Orleans Place. **Map** 8 C3.
Tel (800) 434-1332.
www.majestic
americaline.com

GOLF AND TENNIS

Bayou Oaks
City Park, Filmore Ave.
Map 2 A1.
Tel 483-9397.
www.neworleans
citypark.com

Belle Terre
111 Fairway Dr, LaPlace.
Tel (985) 652-5000.

Chateau Country Club Golf
3600 Chateau Blvd,
Metairie. *Tel 467-1351.*
www.chateaugc.com

Lakewood
4801 Gen. DeGaulle Dr.
Tel 235-5638.

Oak Harbor
201 Oak Harbor Blvd,
Slidell. *Tel (985) 646-0110.* www.oak
harborgolf.com

FITNESS CENTERS

Downtown Fitness Center
333 Canal St, Suite 380.
Map 4 C3. *Tel 525-1404.*
www.downtown
fitnesscenter.com

St. Charles Avenue streetcar ▷

SURVIVAL
GUIDE

PRACTICAL INFORMATION

New Orleans is renowned all over the world for its lively social life and friendly atmosphere. As long as visitors take a few sensible measures, they should enjoy a trouble-free stay. The Survival Guide that follows contains information that will help you plan your

Historical street sign

visit. Personal Security and Health *(pp208–9)* outlines a number of recommended precautions. Banking and Currency *(pp210–11)* answers essential financial questions, while Communications and Media *(pp212–13)* has information on the phone and postal services.

VISAS AND PASSPORTS

Visitors traveling from outside the United States should always check current entry requirements with a US embassy or consulate before departure. All foreigners must have a valid passport, and visitors from most countries must also have a non-immigrant visitor's visa. Citizens of Australia, New Zealand, South Africa, Japan, the UK, and EU countries can visit the US without a visa if they plan to stay for fewer than 90 days. Those traveling under the Visa Waiver Program must pre-register with the Department of Homeland Security's **Electronic System for Travel Authorization (ESTA)** well in advance of their departure.

CUSTOMS INFORMATION

Visitors over the age of 21 traveling from abroad have the right to carry up to 200 cigarettes, 1 liter of alcohol, and 4.4 lb (2 kg) of any kind of pipe tobacco. Plants, fresh foods such as cheese, and all kinds of meat are prohibited, as, of course, are weapons and non-prescription drugs.

TOURIST INFORMATION

The **New Orleans Convention and Visitors' Bureau (NOCVB)** and the **New Orleans Tourism Marketing Corporation** are useful sources of information. The NOCVB offers free maps and tourist guides, as well as discount coupons for certain establishments. It also helps in cases of loss or theft of personal items, and accidents, supplying relevant information such as telephone numbers.

ADMISSION PRICES

Museum admission charges range from $5 to $10, with up to 50 percent off for students (with ID cards) and senior citizens. Some museums allow free admission for children under the age of 12. Many do not charge entrance fees but welcome a donation, while in others it is possible to buy membership on the spot. Most museums have guided tours, souvenir stores, publications, independent exhibitions, and other events.

Exterior of the Ogden Museum of Southern Art, New Orleans

OPENING HOURS

Museums tend to open from 10am–5pm. Most stores are open from 10am–6pm, but souvenir stores in the French Quarter close later. Restaurants usually start evening service at 5pm and continue until 10pm (11pm Friday and Saturday), or until the last diner leaves. Live music usually starts at 10pm, and it is a tradition not to close until the last guest has left. Banks operate from 9am–4pm.

ETIQUETTE AND SMOKING

Smoking is prohibited in all public buildings, including stores and restaurants. The legal age for drinking alcohol is 21; however, anybody may be asked for photo ID to get into bars. If you wish to consume an alcoholic drink on the street, it must be in a plastic container, or "go cup."

Public restrooms can be found at most city parks; additional facilities are made available during large events such as Mardi Gras. Public urination is an offense and will result in arrest and fines.

TAXES AND TIPPING

Tax-free shopping is available at participating merchants to foreign visitors who are staying in the US for fewer than 90 days. For more information on getting a refund on sales taxes, visit the **Tax-Free Counter** in the main ticket lobby at the International Airport or the **Downtown Refund Center**.

Tipping is expected for most services. Tip restaurant staff 15 to 20 percent of the bill, bartenders 50 cents to $1 per drink, porters $1 per bag, and valet parking attendants $1.

TRAVELERS WITH SPECIAL NEEDS

Ramps, elevators, and special parking spaces can be found all around the city. However, not many historic buildings have these facilities, nor do most restaurants and bars. Always enquire about mobility restrictions in advance.

Outside of the French Quarter and Downtown areas, sidewalks may be in a state of disrepair and not suitable for wheelchairs. The Canal and Riverfront streetcar routes and all RTA buses have wheelchair ramps. For more information, contact the **Advocacy Center**.

SENIOR TRAVELERS

Anyone over the age of 65 is eligible for various discounts with proof of age, including up to 50 percent off the entry fee for museums and galleries. The **American Association of Retired Persons** can provide more details. The international senior travel organization **Road Scholar** is another great source of information.

GAY AND LESBIAN TRAVELERS

New Orleans is a welcoming destination for lesbian, gay, bisexual, and transgender (LGBT) travelers, with many bars, nightclubs, and hotels that cater specifically to the needs of this community, not to mention LGBT-friendly events and entertainment. Among the many annual LGBT festivals, the largest is Southern Decadence, which takes place in the first week of September.

NEW ORLEANS TIME

New Orleans and Louisiana are in the Central Standard Time Zone (CST), which is 6 hours behind Greenwich Mean Time (GMT). If making an international call from the city, add 6 hours for the UK, 17 hours for Australia, and 19 hours for New Zealand. Time differences for Australia and New Zealand may vary due to Daylight Saving Time.

ELECTRICITY

Electrical current flows at 110 volts AC (alternating current), and appliances require two-prong plugs. Some non-US appliances will require both a plug converter and a 110–120-volt adaptor, compatible with the US electricity system.

CONVERSION CHART

US Standard to Metric

Bear in mind that 1 US pint (0.5 liter) is a smaller measure than 1 UK pint (0.6 liter).
1 inch = 2.54 centimeters
1 foot = 30 centimeters
1 mile = 1.6 kilometers
1 ounce = 28 grams
1 pound = 454 grams
1 US quart = 0.947 liter
1 US gallon = 3.8 liters

Metric to US Standard

1 centimeter = 0.4 inch
1 meter = 3 feet 3 inches
1 kilometer = 0.6 miles
1 gram = 0.04 ounce
1 kilogram = 2.2 pounds
1 liter = 1.1 US quarts

RESPONSIBLE TOURISM

Although destructive industrial practices have previously done great harm to the local environment, there is now a drive in the city to be more eco-friendly. New Orleans' recycling pick-up program is limited to residents, but visitors may be able to access their hotels' recycling services. Many hotels and B&Bs claim to use green practices, but check for independent certification before booking. Visitors can support the local community by buying meat and dairy produce at farmers' markets.

Crescent City Farmers Market organizes three sales per week: on Tuesdays (9am–1pm, 200 Broadway St), Thursdays (3–7pm, 3700 Orleans Ave), and Saturdays (8am–noon, 700 Magazine St).

DIRECTORY

VISAS AND PASSPORTS

Electronic System for Travel Authorization (ESTA)
https://esta.cbp.dhs.gov

TOURIST INFORMATION

New Orleans Convention and Visitors' Bureau (NOCVB)
2020 St. Charles Ave. **Map** 8 A3.
Tel (800) 672-6124.
www.neworleanscvb.com

New Orleans Tourism Marketing Corporation
365 Canal St. **Map** 4 C3.
Tel (504) 524-4784.
www.neworleansonline.com

TAXES

Downtown Refund Center
Riverwalk Marketplace,
1 Poydras St. **Map** 5 D4.
Tel (504) 568-3605.

Tax-Free Counter
New Orleans International Airport.
Tel (504) 467-0723.
www.louisianataxfree.com

TRAVELERS WITH SPECIAL NEEDS

Advocacy Center
8325 Oak Street. **Map** 6 A1.
Tel (800) 960-7705.
www.advocacyla.org

SENIOR TRAVELERS

American Association of Retired Persons
Tel (800) 687-2277.
www.aarp.org

Road Scholar
Tel (877) 454-5768.
www.roadscholar.org

RESPONSIBLE TOURISM

Crescent City Farmers Market
www.crescentcityfarmers
market.org

A customer being served at a local market in New Orleans

Personal Security and Health

New Orleans is a very friendly city, and visitors can expect people to help should anything go wrong. However, as in any large city, you must take some simple precautions for safety. Learn how to recognize and locate law enforcement officers, and also how to identify the less safe areas of the city. Always check with friends and hotel staff before going out in the evening. It is also important to know how to find medical help if necessary. Although the weather is generally good, New Orleans experiences some extreme weather, with high heat and humidity in the summer and occasional damaging hurricanes.

Two policemen riding horses on Bourbon Street, French Quarter

POLICE

The New Orleans Police Department patrols the city streets on foot, on bicycles, on motorcycles, on horseback, and in cars. Patrols focus on popular areas such as the French Quarter, the Garden District, and the Central Business District (CBD). There are also private security companies that patrol the CBD, the Garden District, and a few other Uptown neighborhoods. As New Orleans has a lively nightlife, there is a strong police presence 24 hours a day.

WHAT TO BE AWARE OF

New Orleans has made great strides in reducing crime rates, but visitors still need to be alert. If possible, stay in a large group when sightseeing outside, and do not challenge a thief – no camera or amount of money is worth the risk. Even though there is a considerable police presence

in the tourist areas, it is still wise to use common sense. Do not advertise the fact that you are a visitor, but prepare the day's itinerary in advance, and study your map before setting off. Avoid wearing flashy jewelry, and carry your camera securely. Only carry small amounts of cash; credit cards and traveler's checks are more secure options. Keep these close to your body in a money belt or an inside pocket.

Before leaving home, take photocopies of all important documents, including your passport and visa, and keep them with you, separate from the originals. Make a note of your credit card numbers, in the event of their being stolen. Keep an eye on your belongings at all times, whether checking into or out of a hotel, standing at the airport, or sitting in a bar or restaurant. Keep any valuables in the hotel safe, as most hotels will not guarantee their security if they are left in the room. Also be careful not to tell strangers where you are staying, and do not let anyone you do not know into your room.

When parking your car, avoid dark and quiet streets, and whenever possible use well-lit public parking lots or the valet parking services of hotels and restaurants.

It is important to realize that most crime

is largely contained within blighted and economically depressed neighborhoods. It is unlikely that a visitor to the city would wander into one of these areas since they are largely devoid of tourist attractions. The streets of New Orleans are generally safe just as long as you are aware of your surroundings and exercise good judgment.

IN AN EMERGENCY

To contact the authorities for fire, medical, or police emergencies, dial 911. This call is free of charge from any phone. If urgent medical care is needed, you can also proceed to the emergency room at the **Medical Center of Louisiana** or the one at **Touro Infirmary**. For dental emergencies, call either the **New Orleans Dental Association** or the Medical Center of Louisiana; both are open 24 hours a day.

The police patrol have a wealth of experience dealing with property crime, violent crime, and crowd control during large events such as Mardi Gras (*see pp28–9*). If you are arrested for

Police car

Ambulance

Fire engine

any reason, you have the right to remain silent and are permitted to make one telephone call. Non-US citizens should contact their embassy or consulate for legal assistance.

LOST AND STOLEN PROPERTY

Even though the chances of retrieving stolen or lost property are slim, it is important to report any such losses to the police. Keep a copy of the police report if you are planning to make an insurance claim. Most credit card companies have toll-free numbers for reporting a loss, as do Thomas Cook and American Express for lost traveler's checks (see p211). If you lose your passport, contact your embassy or consulate immediately.

Airport Operations retains items that have been lost in public areas of the terminal. The office is open 24 hours a day. If they remain unclaimed after 30 days, items turned in to this Lost and Found office are donated to charity. If you lose something in an airline's exclusive areas (ticket counters, gate areas, or airplanes), check with the relevant airline's baggage office on the lower level.

HOSPITALS AND PHARMACIES

Even if your insurance offers medical coverage, you may still have to pay for any services you use, and then claim reimbursement from your insurance company. If you take medication, it is wise to bring a back-up prescription with you. There are many **RiteAid** and **Walgreens** pharmacies in the city. Those close to the French Quarter are open daily from 9am to 7pm. At any other time, there are several 24-hour pharmacies; ask your hotel for assistance.

In the event of a non-emergency health issue, there are a number of care facilities throughout the city.

Walgreens, one of New Orleans' 24-hour pharmacies

NATURAL HAZARDS

Hurricanes are infrequent but devastating when they do strike. There are tried and tested emergency procedures, and if the worst should happen, follow the announcements on local television and radio. If an evacuation order is issued, leave the region immediately. Ignoring this order, or waiting until the last possible minute, could prove disastrous. In case of emergency, a hotline may be set up before a storm strikes. You may also check the National Hurricane Center's forecasts online (www.nhc.noaa.gov).

Despite Louisiana's hurricanes being notorious, the most frequent climatic hazard to affect visitors is the sun. Use high-factor sunscreen lotions and wear a hat. Be aware that heat can be as big a problem as sunlight; drink plenty of fluids to stay hydrated.

Hospital sign

There are several venomous snakes native to Louisiana, but unless you are in dense swamp or forest you are unlikely to encounter any. Alligators are plentiful in most swamps and bodies of water just outside the city, so use caution when walking in these areas and do not feed them. Biting and stinging insects, including mosquitoes, are a nuisance between April and November, particularly in areas close to fresh water and swamp land. If you plan to visit parks and reserves, wear a good insect repellent.

TRAVEL AND HEALTH INSURANCE

Travel insurance is highly recommended. It can help in the event of loss or theft of personal goods, or if travel arrangements fall through.

Foreign visitors should also obtain insurance for emergency medical and dental care, which can be expensive in the US. It is useful to carry a medical ID card containing information on your blood type, allergies, medications, and an emergency contact number.

DIRECTORY

IN AN EMERGENCY

Emergencies
Tel 911.

Medical Center of Louisiana
2021 Perdido St. **Map** 2 B5.
Tel (800) 256-2311.

New Orleans Dental Association
Tel (504) 834-6449.

Police (Non-Emergency)
Tel (504) 821-2222.

Touro Infirmary
1401 Foucher St. **Map** 7 E4.
Tel (504) 897-7011.

LOST AND STOLEN PROPERTY

Airport Operations
Upper Level, West Lobby,
New Orleans International Airport.
Tel (504) 464-2672.

HOSPITALS AND PHARMACIES

RiteAid
2669 Canal Street.
Map 2 B4.
Tel (504) 827-1400.
www.riteaid.com

Walgreens
1801 St. Charles Avenue.
Map 8 A2.
Tel (504) 561-8458 (24 hours).
900 Canal St. **Map** 4 B3.
Tel (504) 568-1271.
www.walgreens.com

Banking and Currency

MasterCard logo

Throughout New Orleans there are various places to access and exchange your money. Banks are open during the week, and there are also numerous ATMs. Foreign currency can be exchanged for a fee in many banks and major hotels, but exchange rates tend to be high. For the best rates, withdraw US currency directly from your account using an ATM. Prepaid debit cards are available in lieu of traveler's checks; however, there may be high fees. The best option is to carry debit and credit cards to make purchases and withdraw cash.

ATMs outside a branch of Hancock Bank, New Orleans

BANKS AND BUREAUX DE CHANGE

Banks are generally open from 9am to 4pm Monday to Friday. There are some, however, that open as early as 8:30am and stay open until 5pm.

Traveler's checks issued in US dollars can be cashed at most banks and exchange bureaus, as long as you have some form of photographic ID, such as a passport or a driver's license. The front desk of your hotel might also be able to exchange traveler's checks into cash. Always ask about commission fees before any transaction, as these can vary greatly.

A currency exchange counter is usually available at the main branches of large banks. Banks open to the general public include Capital One and Whitney. Numerous branches of these can be found in the French Quarter, the Central Business District, and along St. Charles Avenue. There is a bureau de change at the airport, but exchange rates tend to be better at banks.

When changing money, be sure to request US currency in bills no larger than $20 or $50, since many business are unable to accept $100 bills.

ATMS

Most banks in New Orleans have automated teller machines (ATMs) in their lobbies or in an external wall. ATMs can also be found in various restaurants and bars around town, mainly in the French Quarter. These machines enable you to withdraw US bank notes, usually $20 bills, directly from your bank or credit card account at home. Be aware, however, that a fee might be levied on your withdrawal, depending on the bank; it is advisable to check the bank's policy before going ahead with your transaction.

Before leaving home, ask your credit card company or bank which American ATM systems or banks will accept your card, and check the cost of each transaction. Make sure, too, that you can remember your PIN (Personal Identification Number). The largest ATM systems are Plus and Cirrus, which accept VISA, American Express, and MasterCard, as well as a number of US bank cards.

ATMs give you 24-hour access to your cash; however, do take care when using them in deserted areas, especially after dark, and always be vigilant of people around you.

CREDIT AND DEBIT CARDS

Credit and debit cards are part of everyday life in New Orleans, just as they are in other parts of the country. The most widely accepted credit cards in the US are **VISA, MasterCard, American Express**, and Discover Card.

Besides being a more convenient and much safer alternative to carrying a lot of cash, credit cards also offer some useful additional benefits, such as insurance on your purchases. They are also essential if you want to reserve a hotel room or book a rental car, and can be useful in emergencies, when cash may not be readily available.

Prepaid debit cards, such as VISA's TravelMoney Card, are increasingly being used

American Express charge cards

to replace traveler's checks; they are available at many grocery and convenience stores throughout the city. Note that these cards may carry high fees. A similar service is offered by **Thomas Cook**'s Travel Moneycard. Thomas Cook can also issue foreign currency as cash or traveler's checks.

MONEY TRANSFERS

In an emergency, it is possible to have money wired to you from almost anywhere in the world via **Western Union** or **MoneyGram**.

Coins

American coins come in 1-, 5-, 10- and 25-cent, as well as $1, denominations. Each coin has a popular name: 1-cent coins are known as pennies, 5-cent coins as nickels, 10-cent coins as dimes, 25-cent coins as quarters, and 1-dollar coins (and bills) as bucks.

25-cent coin (a quarter)

10-cent coin (a dime)

5-cent coin (a nickel)

1-cent coin (a penny)

Bank Notes

The units of currency in the United States are dollars and cents. There are 100 cents to a dollar. Bank notes, or "bills," come in $1, $2, $5, $10, $20, $50, and $100. The $2 bills are rarely seen. Each bank note features a different US President. Security features include subtle color hues and improved color-shifting ink in the lower right hand corner of the face of each note.

1-dollar bill ($1)

5-dollar bill ($5)

10-dollar bill ($10)

20-dollar bill ($20)

50-dollar bill ($50)

100-dollar bill ($100)

DIRECTORY

CREDIT AND DEBIT CARDS

American Express
*Tel (800) 221-7282
(check replacement).*
*Tel (800) 528-4800
(stolen credit cards).*
www.americanexpress.com

Thomas Cook/ MasterCard
*Tel (800) 223-9920
(check replacement and stolen credit cards).*
www.thomascook.com

VISA
*Tel (800) 227-6811
(check replacement).*
*Tel (800) 336-8472
(stolen credit cards).*
www.visa.com

MONEY TRANSFERS

Moneygram
Tel (800) 666-3947 (US).
Tel 0800 833 833 (UK).
www.moneygram.com

Western Union
Tel (800) 325-6000 (US).
Tel 0800 8971 8971 (UK).
www.westernunion.com

Communications and Media

US postal service logo

A full range of telephone and Internet services is available in New Orleans. Public telephones have become a rare sight, and the few that remain are frequently out of service. Prepaid cell phones are widely available in most pharmacies and convenience stores, and VoIP computer programs are inexpensive options for local and international calls. Stamps can be purchased not only at post offices, but also at many drugstores and hotels; additional postal services are available from private courier firms. Local newspapers, magazines, and websites are useful for information on events around town, and national and foreign newspapers are also easily found.

INTERNATIONAL AND LOCAL TELEPHONE CALLS

Toll-free numbers (prefixed by 800, 866, 877, or 888) are common in the United States and well worth taking advantage of, though some hotels may impose an access charge for these calls. It is also possible to dial these numbers from abroad, but

USEFUL DIALING CODES AND NUMBERS

• Direct-dial call outside the local area code, but within the United States and Canada: dial 1.
• International direct-dial call: dial 011, followed by the country code (UK: 44; Australia: 61; New Zealand: 64), then the city or area code (omitting the first 0), and the local number.
• International call via the operator: dial 01, then the country code, the city code (minus the first 0), and the local number.
• International directory inquiries: dial 00.
• International operator assistance: dial 01.
• An 800, 866, 877, or 888 prefix indicates a toll-free number.
• All directory assistance: dial 411.
• Useful area codes: New Orleans metro area: 504; Cajun Country: 337; Baton Rouge: 225; southeast Louisiana (except New Orleans): 985.

note that they will not be toll-free from outside the US.

When making a local call from a public telephone, 50 cents will buy you 3 minutes' time. For long-distance domestic calls, the cheapest rate runs from 11pm to 8am on weekdays and at weekends. It is also possible to make direct calls from your hotel room, but be aware that they usually carry hefty surcharges. Unless you are using your own international telephone card, it is better to use a payphone.

Directory assistance is free of charge by dialing 411 (local) or 00 (international). Operator assistance is available by dialing 0 (local) or 01 (international). All operator-assisted calls carry a surcharge. For emergency services only (fire, police, or ambulance), call 911 free of charge.

International rates vary depending on which country you are contacting.

Public telephone sign

CELL PHONES

Most foreign cell phones will work in the US, but expect to pay high fees. The only US network operators supporting GSM phones (world phones) are AT&T Mobility and T-Mobile. Be sure to check fees, roaming rates, and availability with your mobile phone provider before you leave home. Prepaid cell phones are widely available from many stores and may be a more affordable option if you are planning to use a cell phone frequently.

PUBLIC TELEPHONES

Although public telephones can be found in the city, they are increasingly rare and frequently out of service. Rates start at 50 cents for the first 3 minutes for local calls and go up to $8 for international calls. Some phones accept credit cards. Dial (800) CALLATT (225-5288), then, at the prompt, key in your credit card number and wait to be connected. You will be charged at normal rates.

INTERNET AND EMAIL

There are free Wi-Fi hotspots for Internet access throughout the city. These are available to patrons in hotels, cafés, bars, and some restaurants. You may also try the **French Quarter Postal Emporium** or **FedEx Kinko's** shops, which also offer fax, printing, and shipping services. Many hotels have fully-equipped

An Internet café in New Orleans

Coin-operated newspaper boxes in the French Quarter

business centers where guests can use a computer; if not, they will have Wi-Fi access, or dataports where you can connect your laptop.

Any high-speed connection will support the use of Skype or other VoIP programs, enabling you to place local or international voice and video calls for pennies a minute from your laptop, smart phone, or Wi-Fi-enabled device. Computer-to-computer calls are free.

POSTAL SERVICES

Post offices are usually open from 9am to 5pm Monday to Friday, with some branches also open on Saturday mornings. Drugstores and hotels sell stamps, and there are also vending machines at some department stores and transportation terminals. Stamps bought from vending machines are often a little more expensive.

Surface mail sent overseas from the US takes several weeks, so it is better to use airmail, which takes five to ten working days.

All domestic mail goes first class and takes one to five days (longer if you do not include the zip code). You can pay extra for Priority Mail for a delivery of two to three days, or for Express Mail, which offers next-day deliveries in the US, and within two to three days to many foreign countries.

Standard US mailbox

Be sure to use the right mailbox for the required service. Mailboxes are painted blue, while Express and Priority boxes are silver and blue.

Private courier services such as **UPS**, **DHL**, and **FedEx** offer next-day deliveries to most destinations both domestic and international.

NEWSPAPERS, MAGAZINES, AND WEBSITES

The only local daily newspaper in New Orleans is *The Times-Picayune*, found in hotel lobbies and street dispensers throughout the city. *Gambit*, a free weekly paper distributed in cafés, shops, and hotels, is a good source of in-depth entertainment and lifestyle news. Several local monthly magazines, like *Where Y'at Magazine*, *Offbeat*, and *New Orleans Magazine*, offer local news, restaurant and nightlife information, event listings, and festival information. For comprehensive national and international news, look to the *New York Times* or *USA Today*, both of which are available from coin-operated boxes all over the French Quarter and CBD. Foreign newspapers are available at major bookstores and some of the larger hotels.

There are many useful websites for local news, entertainment, restaurant listings, and events. Among the best ones are www.nola.com, www.bestofneworleans. com, www.frenchquarter. com, and www.neworleans online.com.

TELEVISION AND RADIO

In addition to the national TV networks (ABC, CBS, NBC, and FOX), most hotels have cable or satellite hook-up, offering many more channels. Some cable channels focus on one specific area – for example, ESPN is devoted to sports and CNN to the news.

Most radio stations broadcast pop music, but if you hunt around (especially on the FM band) you can often pick up entertaining local stations. WWL (870 AM and 105.3 FM) broadcasts local news; National Public Radio WWNO (89.9 FM) focuses on national news and classical music; the Jazz & Heritage Foundation station WWOZ (90.7 FM) plays R&B, jazz, Latin, Cajun, and zydeco; and Tulane University's WTUL (91.5) offers local and indie music, as well as music listings and community events.

TRAVEL INFORMATION

Many airlines have direct flights to New Orleans, and charter and domestic services are numerous. Growing competition between airlines has resulted in reduced prices in low season, making flying an even more attractive alternative to bus or train travel. Amtrak trains run from major US cities to New Orleans, and long-distance luxury bus services offer a less frantic and often

Passenger jet arriving in the city

less expensive way to travel for those arriving from other North American cities. For visitors arriving by car or bus, there can be little to beat the spectacular views of the city when driving into New Orleans by way of the River Road. If you are planning to stay in the city center, it is not necessary to rent a car; most of the sights are within easy walking distance of one another.

Passenger jet at Louis Armstrong International Airport

ARRIVING BY AIR

All the major US airlines, including **American Airlines**, **Southwest Airlines**, **United Airlines**, and **Delta Air Lines**, have scheduled services to New Orleans. Most of them also offer flights from abroad, but these will usually entail a stop at another US airport en route. **Air Canada** offers scheduled flights direct from Toronto to New Orleans, while American Airlines, Delta, and United all operate from the United Kingdom.

LOUIS ARMSTRONG INTERNATIONAL AIRPORT

New Orleans' Louis Armstrong International is the ninth-largest airport in the United States. Customs, sightseeing information, baggage claim, car-rental desks, and ground transport-ation into the city are located on the lower level of the airport. The top level contains services for travelers departing from New Orleans, including foreign-exchange offices,

ticket and insurance counters, restaurants, bars, baggage handlers, and shops. The Tax-Free Counter refund offices *(see p206)* can also be found on this level.

There are nine Telephone Display Devices (TDD) throughout the airport. Whitney National Bank, situated in the ticket lobby, is the only banking facility in the airport; however, automated teller machines (ATMs) can be found in several places: in the East Lobby near Concourse B; in the ticket lobby next to the bank; in the West Terminal; and on the Lower Level, near the Southwest Airlines Baggage Claim and the Charter Baggage Claim.

There is a baggage storage-check service, called VIP Baggage Check, on the ground floor of the airport. For security reasons, lockers are no longer available. There is also a Traveler's Aid booth located in the East Baggage Claim. Traveler's Aid provides assistance to travelers in distress, as well as offering tourist information. The

hours that this counter is open may vary, as it is run by volunteers.

TICKETS AND FARES

The cheapest round-trip fares to New Orleans are generally economy or APEX tickets on scheduled flights; these must be booked in advance. The competition between travel agencies and the numerous airlines serving New Orleans makes it well worth shopping around. Keep an eye out for promotional fares and package tours, which offer good deals on charter flights.

Off-season fares are cheap, and you will often get a better deal if you fly in the middle of the week. During holiday periods like Christmas and special events such as Mardi Gras *(see pp28–9)*, seats are always in high demand, and air fares can rocket to more than double their usual price.

Travelers at a check-in desk, Louis Armstrong International Airport

Amtrak train arriving in New Orleans

ON ARRIVAL

Upon arrival, foreign visitors from countries participating in the Visa Waiver Program *(see p206)* must show a valid passport and complete a customs declaration form and an I-94 form provided by the airline. Visitors from other countries must present a visa issued by a US consular official. Join the line for non-US citizens, and show your passport and forms to the immigration officer. Expect to be asked questions, be photographed, and to have your fingerprints taken.

If you need to catch a connecting flight, clear customs and immigration, then retrieve your luggage, go through the security screening, re-check your luggage, and follow the signs to your connecting flight.

GETTING TO AND FROM THE AIRPORT

Louis Armstrong International Airport is located about 12 miles (19 km) from the city center. Bus and taxi stands are located outside the terminal on the first level.

There are two **Airport Shuttle** services linking the airport to the Central Business District, which costs $20 per trip. To travel to the airport, call at least 2 hours in advance. The E-2 Airport Downtown Express, run by **Jefferson Transit**, is the only public bus route to and from the airport. The 45-minute trip costs $2. The bus stops at the intersection of Loyola and Tulane Avenues until 6:50pm on weekdays. After this time and at weekends, it stops at the intersection of Tulane and Carrollton Avenues, where you must transfer to the number 39 Tulane **RTA** bus to reach downtown. This bus operates seven days a week, from 5:30am until midnight.

Taxicabs are plentiful, and the standard rate is $33 from the airport to the city center.

ARRIVING BY TRAIN

Visitors traveling to New Orleans by train or bus arrive at Amtrak's Union Passenger Terminal *(see p221)*, on Loyola Avenue, at the edge of the Central Business District, near the Superdome.

Noted for their comfort and luxury, all long-distance **Amtrak** trains have a full complement of refreshment facilities and sleeping accommodations.

At peak times, passengers are advised to reserve seats in advance on many services. Amtrak offers a range of special deals and packages, including 5-, 15-, and 30-day passes that allow unlimited travel. Note that these are available only for international travelers.

From Amtrak's terminal in the CBD, there are plenty of taxis that will take you to the main hotel areas.

Greyhound bus logo

ARRIVING BY BUS

Long-distance coach services are operated by **Greyhound Bus Lines** and arrive at Union Passenger Terminal *(see p221)*. This terminal, which is shared with Amtrak, provides full baggage, ticketing, and package express services throughout the day and into the early hours of the morning. Greyhound buses are modern, clean, and safe. Some services are express, with few stops between major destinations, while others serve a greater number of cities. If you are planning to break your journey several times along the way, or you wish to tour the country, there are various packages designed to suit your requirements. Overseas visitors should also note that passes may be less expensive if you buy them from a Greyhound agent outside the US.

DIRECTORY

ARRIVING BY AIR

Air Canada
Tel (888) 247-2262.
www.aircanada.com

American Airlines
Tel (800) 433-7300.
www.aa.com

Delta Air Lines
Tel (800) 221-1212.
www.delta.com

Southwest Airlines
Tel (800) 435-9792.
www.southwest.com

United Airlines
Tel (800) 864-8331.
www.united.com

GETTING TO AND FROM THE AIRPORT

Airport Shuttle
Tel (504) 522-3500.

Jefferson Transit
Tel (504) 818-1077.
www.jeffersontransit.org

RTA
Tel (504) 248-3900.
www.norta.com

ARRIVING BY TRAIN

Amtrak
Tel (800) 872-7245.
www.amtrak.com

ARRIVING BY BUS

Greyhound Bus Lines
Tel (800) 231-2222.
www.greyhound.com

Getting Around New Orleans

Yellow New Orleans taxicab

Although most of the city's popular tourist sights in and near the French Quarter are easily accessible on foot, New Orleans also has a useful public transportation system, with bus routes covering the city. No visitor should miss the opportunity to travel on the oldest streetcar in the nation. A Jazzy Pass allows unlimited travel on RTA buses and streetcars for one, three, five, or 31 days. Riverboats also provide a pleasant way to see the sights along the basin of the Mississippi River. Taxis are affordable, convenient, and highly recommended for trips after dark to areas outside the French Quarter. Bicycle and scooter rentals offer a fun and convenient transportation alternative.

GREEN TRAVEL

From the airport, there are two green options to reach downtown: the Airport Shuttle *(see p215)*, which uses propane hybrid vehicles, and public bus services.

Public transportation is an affordable, safe, and eco-friendly way to see New Orleans. The Regional Transit Authority (RTA) buses *(see p215)* run on biodiesel, and the electric streetcar gives off no emissions. The Jazzy Pass is a good deal if you plan on using public transport often.

Walking is the greenest option in the downtown areas. You can easily explore the French Quarter, Central Business District, Marigny/Bywater, and Riverfront on foot; in addition, a variety of guided and unguided walking tours *(see p218)* are offered in the Garden District and French Quarter.

Renting a bicycle is another fun way to experience the city at a leisurely, intimate pace; some rental companies offer guided bike tours. Scooter rental is also available, providing easy parking and quick access to the entire city.

Note that trips to sites outside New Orleans will require traditional transport – either a car or tour bus.

BUSES

Bus stops are indicated by white and yellow signs displaying the RTA logo. The route numbers of the buses stopping there are usually listed at the bottom of the sign. All New Orleans buses are equipped for disabled access and have bike racks mounted on the front.

Buses stop only at designated bus stops, which are located every two or three blocks, depending on the area of the city. On boarding the bus, put the exact change or number of tokens in the fare box, or show your Jazzy Pass to the driver. This pass can be bought through the RTA offices, at tourist information kiosks, Walgreens, and in a small number of hotels. Always ask for a transfer when you pay, since this will enable you to change to another bus should your itinerary require it.

To indicate that you want to get off, pull the cord that runs along the window, or tell the driver. The "Stop requested" sign above the front window will light up. Instructions for opening the doors are posted near the exit. Make sure you look carefully for oncoming traffic when alighting from the bus. If you are unsure where to get off, ask the driver.

Smoking, drinking, eating, and playing music are all prohibited on buses. Guide dogs for the blind are the only animals allowed on RTA vehicles. Front seats are reserved for senior citizens and disabled passengers.

St. Charles Avenue streetcar on Canal Street

STREETCARS

The Riverfront streetcar line travels a distance of 2 miles (3 km) along the Mississippi Riverfront, from Esplanade Avenue, at the far side of the French Quarter, to the New Orleans Convention Center in the Central Business District. The streetcar runs approximately every 20 minutes from 7:10am–10:30pm during the week, and from 8:40am–10:30pm on weekends. Pay the driver or swipe your Jazzy Pass when you board; you can exit from either the front of the car or the back,

A biodiesel RTA bus, a green way to travel around New Orleans

depending on how crowded the streetcar is. Remember to pull the cord to indicate that you want to disembark.

The first stop for the St. Charles streetcar is at the corner of Canal and Carondelet streets. The streetcar turns onto Canal Street, then back around on St. Charles Avenue for the trip uptown. It travels the length of St. Charles Avenue, turning on to Carrollton Avenue at the Riverbend, and terminating at Claiborne Avenue. The return trip is the reverse of the outbound trip until Lee Circle, where it turns onto Carondelet Street to get to Canal Street. This line operates 24 hours a day and runs every 7 minutes, but is less frequent off peak.

The Canal streetcar route starts at the Riverfront, at the foot of Canal Street, and runs to City Park Avenue. There is also a spur line along North Carrollton Avenue, linking Canal Street to the New Orleans Museum of Art and City Park at Beauregard Circle. It runs approximately every 30 minutes from 7am–2am.

TAXIS

Taxis, better known as cabs, are easily found at airports, bus and train stations, major hotels, and regular taxi stands. If you need to get somewhere on time, it is best to call a taxi company *(see p219)* and arrange a pickup at a definite time and place. Most hotels have lines of taxis waiting outside. In general, drivers are knowledgeable and friendly, and all fares should be metered according to the distance traveled. All taxis have a light on their windshield to indicate when they are available.

WALKING

Because the city is made up of distinct neighborhoods, it is often simplest to take public transportation to a particular area and then to explore on foot. The French Quarter is compact, and you can stroll around it. Only outside the Quarter do you need to watch for traffic; "Walk" and "Don't walk" signs appear on major streets

Pedestrians in Jackson Square

to prevent jaywalking. Wear comfortable shoes: some sidewalks and streets in New Orleans are very old and hard to navigate. Parts of Mid-City, Uptown, and the Central Business District are best avoided at night, but it is wise to be cautious at all times in all areas of New Orleans.

RIVERBOATS AND FERRIES

Steamboats began plying the Mississippi River at the start of the 19th century, bringing new settlers to New Orleans from the north. Today, the riverboats offer tours stopping at popular destinations. The **Creole Queen** *(see p88)* runs two cruises: a day trip to the Chalmette Battlefield, where the Battle of New Orleans *(see p17)* took place, and a night cruise that includes dinner accompanied by live jazz. The steamboat **Natchez** *(see pp64–5)* offers a 2-hour tour in the morning and a

Traditional paddlewheeler cruising the Mississippi River

night cruise with an excellent buffet and live jazz.

The Canal Street ferry *(see p88 and p221)* crosses the river daily, carrying pedestrians and vehicles from the CBD to Algiers Point, on the West Bank.

CYCLING

Bicycling in New Orleans is easy and convenient thanks to the city's sunny weather, flat landscape, and bike-friendly initiatives. It's a pleasant, leisurely way to see the city and experience the charm of its historic neighborhoods. **Bicycle Michael's** and **The American Bicycle Rental Company** offer rental services, as well as guided tours. All city buses are equipped with bike racks, allowing you to combine modes of transport. Be sure to lock your bike securely when you park it, as bicycle thefts are common.

DIRECTORY

RIVERBOATS & FERRIES

Creole Queen
Canal St at Riverwalk. **Map** 5 D2.
Tel (504) 529-4567.

Natchez
Canal St at Riverwalk. **Map** 5 D2.
Tel (504) 569-1401.

CYCLING

The American Bicycle Rental Company
317 Burgundy Street. **Map** 4 C2.
Tel (866) 293-4037.

Bicycle Michael's
622 Frenchmen Street. **Map** 3 E4.
Tel (504) 945-9505.

GUIDED TOURS

Whether you go by bus, bicycle, swamp boat, or on foot, guided tours in and around New Orleans are led by knowledgeable licensed guides who can show you much more than if you were exploring on your own.

Walking tours in the French Quarter, Uptown, and Mid-City neighborhoods cover themes such as history, jazz, architecture, cemeteries, and more. Bicycle tours will take you through the Faubourg Marigny, Treme, Mid-City, and Garden District, covering distances of up to 20 miles (32 km). Narrated bus tours service all areas outside the French Quarter and include trips beyond the city to some beautifully preserved 18th- and 19th-century plantation homes. The close proximity of bayous and wetlands makes a swamp-boat tour an exciting afternoon excursion where you can experience the local wildlife. Transportation from the city to the boat launch is provided.

Reservations are required for all but the walking tours.

DRIVING

A good public transportation network *(see pp216–17)* and short distances between sights make driving in New Orleans unnecessary. However, a car is convenient if you wish to visit the surrounding countryside. Driving in the city takes patience, good skills, good humor, and the ability to read the road and the street signs quickly. Be prepared for heavy traffic and a severe shortage of parking facilities.

Streetcar and heavy traffic on Canal Street

RENTING A CAR

To rent a car in New Orleans you must be at least 21 years of age, with a valid driver's license. Rates may be higher for anyone under 25. All agencies require a major credit card or a large cash deposit, a reservation voucher, and insurance. In the event of a breakdown, call the rental firm first. If you are a member of the AAA *(see p221)*, you can also contact them for emergency assistance.

All rental cars are automatic, with power brakes and steering, and air-conditioning. Refill the car with gas before returning it, or you will have to pay a service charge and inflated gas prices.

ROAD SIGNS

Colorful signs point the way to the main tourist areas, such as the French Quarter. Street-name signs are affixed to light posts and telephone poles, as are directional signs; however, many are damaged or missing, so it is wise to carry a map. Large red hexagonal stop signs are posted at intersections without traffic lights.

TRAFFIC REGULATIONS

Traffic travels on the right side of the road, and seatbelts are compulsory for both drivers and passengers; children under five must travel in a child seat.

You can turn right on a red light unless there are signs to the contrary, but you must come to a stop first. If you see a flashing amber light at an intersection, slow down, check for oncoming traffic, then proceed with caution. Passing (overtaking) is allowed on both sides on multi-lane roads, including Interstate highways, but it is illegal to change lanes across a solid double yellow or double white line. If a school bus stops on a divided highway, the traffic traveling in the same direction as the bus must stop until the bus moves on; on a two-way road, traffic in both directions must stop.

Citywide speed limits are 35 mph (56 km/h) on divided streets and 25 mph (40 km/h) on non-divided streets, unless otherwise posted. Speeds in school zones are limited to 20 mph (32 km/h) during the hours posted on the signs.

Streetcars cannot stop very quickly, so it is important to

ONE WAY
Traffic flows in a single direction

SPEED LIMIT 35
Maximum speed in mph

RIGHT TURN ONLY
Right turn restriction

Slippery road

Left turn allowed

STOP
Stop at intersection

TRAFFIC SIGNS

A range of different signs offer information and instructions for drivers. Speed limits may vary every few miles, depending on the conditions of the road and the amount of traffic. In more remote areas, drivers must watch out for wildlife that may stray onto the roads, especially alligators and armadillos.

ensure you look carefully when crossing streetcar tracks.

Driving under the influence (DUI) of alcohol or drugs is illegal and punishable by a heavy fine, loss of your license, or even a jail sentence.

PARKING

Parking in the city is difficult and expensive. Parking areas and garages often post prices at the entrance. Many downtown businesses have designated parking lots and offer discounted or free parking for patrons. In addition to being often closed to traffic, the streets in the French Quarter are very narrow; street parking here can result in your car being damaged by passing vehicles or exuberant revelers. There are parking meters all over the city, some of which accept notes and credit cards. Be sure to make a note of the time limits, especially in the French Quarter, where your car may be towed if you are even only one minute over the time limit.

The tow-away crew in New Orleans is very active. Never disregard parking prohibitions, such as near a fire hydrant or a crosswalk, at bus stops, in disabled, reserved, or parade route areas, and during street cleaning. Parking on any major city street or thoroughfare is forbidden during Mardi Gras *(see pp28–9)*.

No Parking and No Stopping signs

The airport has a large long- and short-term parking area if you wish to leave your car there and take a taxi into the city. Rush hours in the city are from 7–9am and from 4–6pm Monday to Friday.

FUEL

US gas (petrol) prices are low compared to those in Europe. Gas stations are sparse in the downtown area. All pumps accept credit cards, but if using cash, you must pay before you pump. Many stations have a convenience store where you can pay for gas and buy refreshments. Always fill up before driving into remote areas.

PENALTIES

If you have been issued a ticket and wish to contest the charges, you may request a hearing at **Traffic Court**.

If you parked on the street and cannot find your car, it may have been towed away. Call the **Claiborne Auto Pound** and give the following information about your car: license plate number, make and color, and where you parked it. To retrieve it, you will have to pay the fine, and present your driver's license and registration or rental voucher.

If your car is not at the pound, it might have been stolen. In this case, call the police department *(see p209)* to find out how to proceed.

ROAD CONDITIONS AND HAZARDS

New Orleans is notorious for large potholes, some of which can damage a car or cause loss of control. Drive carefully and check to make sure there is paved road ahead. Heavy downpours can cause street flooding. Drive slowly through standing water or choose another route.

Royal Street during Mardi Gras, when parking is not allowed

Traveling Outside New Orleans

Public transportation outside the city is scarce, so the best way to experience the areas around New Orleans is by renting a vehicle or joining an organized bus tour. Take a day or two for a trip down to Avery Island or into Cajun Country; drive the Great River Road along the Mississippi and visit the plantations; or go exploring in the bayous. If hunting, fishing, or boating interests you, Louisiana is truly a "Sportsman's Paradise."

Oak Alley Plantation, between New Orleans and Baton Rouge

TRAVELING BY TRAIN

The only long-distance passenger train line in the US is Amtrak. Long-distance trains have dining and sleeping cars; in general, reservations are recommended. All trains arrive and depart from New Orleans' **Union Passenger Terminal**, in the Central Business District. There are always taxis outside the terminal, which is just a short ride away from the French Quarter, the Garden District, and the major downtown hotels.

The *Crescent* train travels every day to New Orleans from New York by way of Atlanta and intermediate points. The *City of New Orleans* train departs daily and goes to Chicago and points between. The *Sunset Limited* travels to and from the West Coast (Los Angeles) and also to and from Florida three times a week, with stops at intermediate points. The schedules for all of these trains may vary from season to season. Amtrak offers discounts for seniors, travelers with disabilities, students, and children. There are also a number of good-value tour packages, group rates, and promotional discounts.

LONG-DISTANCE BUSES

Whether you are going to other parts of the United States or traveling around Louisiana, **Greyhound Bus Lines** offers the cheapest way to get around. The buses are comfortable, clean, and modern; there are generally on-board toilets, a water cooler, and TV screens.

Buses to the larger cities and popular tourist destinations in Louisiana run fairly frequently. Travel to the smaller towns in Cajun Country or to off-the-beaten-path areas is not as well defined. Your best bet is to book a tour or rent a car.

Greyhound's Discovery Pass offers up to 60 consecutive days of unlimited travel anywhere in the US and Canada. Tickets may be less expensive if you buy them in advance, but walk-up or unrestricted fares are also readily available. Ask about any discounts when you purchase your ticket. Reductions are offered to children, seniors, members of the military, students, and travelers with disabilities.

Greyhound will provide assistance to disabled travelers, including priority seating. In some cases, a personal-care assistant may travel for free. For further details, call the ADA Assist Line (800-752-4841).

SPEED LIMITS

Speed limits in the US are set by the individual states. There are heavy fines for going well above the limits, which in Louisiana are as follows:
• 55–70 mph (89–113 km/h) on highways and Interstates;
• 20–35 mph (32–56 km/h) in residential areas;
• 20 mph (32 km/h) in school zones.

Speed limits vary every few miles, so keep a close eye out for the signs. On an Interstate highway it is best to drive at or slightly above the speed limit; if you wish to drive more slowly, stay in the right-hand lane. The left lanes are for passing only (overtaking).

DAY TRIPS AND TOURS

A number of companies – among them **Gray Line**, **Kayak-Iti-Yat**, **New Orleans Tours**, **Pearl River Eco Tours**, and **Tours by Isabelle** – offer

A swamp-boat tour of the wetlands

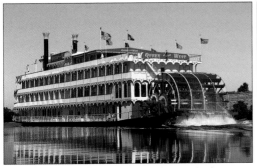

Queen of the West, a paddle steamer run by American Cruise Lines

trips and tours outside the metropolitan New Orleans area. Each trip will take at least one full day. If you set aside two or more days, you will have just enough time to savor the great diversity of Louisiana, including the bayous, spicy food, and lively music in Lafayette, Breaux Bridge, and other Cajun Country towns. The rice and sugar plantations along the Mississippi River can also be discovered, as can the spectacular wilderness of the Atchafalaya Basin. Swamps and bayous are all around the city, and many popular boat tours allow you to explore the wetlands.

RULES OF THE ROAD

Traffic accidents are high in this region so use caution at all times and be aware of other drivers and hazards such as debris in the road, unstable road surfaces, and standing water.

Drivers and passengers are required by law to wear seatbelts at all times. Also note that littering is not permitted anywhere along any road, highway, or Interstate.

The **AAA (Automobile Association of America)** offers maps, emergency roadside services, and discounts at hotels, restaurants, and various tourist spots. The AAA has a reciprocity agreement with many automobile clubs abroad, so it is worth finding out if that is the case with your home club. If not, rental agencies often offer roadside service for an extra fee.

Many roads out in Cajun Country may be under water at certain times of the year, so be aware. Watch for pedestrians, cane trucks, oil tankers, and loose cattle when driving.

MISSISSIPPI RIVER FERRIES AND CRUISES

The **Canal Street Ferry** ride across the Mississippi River to Algiers Point *(see p88)* is an experience in itself, offering excellent views between the Mississippi and New Orleans. The passenger boarding gate is located on the upper floor of the ferry terminal at the foot of Canal Street. Passengers with cars and bicycles board on the street level of the ferry terminal. The trip takes about 15 minutes. The first ferry leaves at 6am; the last departs at midnight. You may not smoke, drink alcohol, or eat food aboard the ferry. The ride across the river at dawn or sunset is one of the best bargains in New Orleans (it's free), and the view of the skyline and riverfront from the other side is an experience to remember.

Blount Small Ship Adventures and **American Cruise Lines** offer tours on the Mississippi, from New Orleans up to Baton Rouge, Memphis, and other cities north along the river. Cruises last from one to two weeks, focusing on historic sites

American Cruise Lines logo

such as plantations and old towns. There are also some cruises that travel out of the Mississippi River and into the Gulf of Mexico to destinations in the Caribbean and Mexico.

DIRECTORY

TRAVELING BY TRAIN

Union Passenger Terminal
1001 Loyola Avenue.
Map 4 A4.
Tel (800) 872-7245.
www.amtrak.com

LONG-DISTANCE BUSES

Greyhound Bus Lines
Tel (800) 231-2222.
www.greyhound.com

DAY TRIPS AND TOURS

Gray Line
Tel (504) 587-1401.
www.graylineneworleans.com

Kayak-Iti-Yat
Tel (985) 778-5034.
www.kayakitiyat.com

New Orleans Tours
Tel (504) 212-5925.
www.bigeasytours.com

Pearl River Eco Tours
Tel (866) 597-9267.
www.pearlriverecotours.com

Tours by Isabelle
Tel (877) 665-8687.
www.toursbyisabelle.com

RULES OF THE ROAD

AAA (Automobile Association of America)
Tel (800) 852-7216.
www.aaa.com

MISSISSIPPI RIVER FERRIES AND CRUISES

American Cruise Lines
Tel (800) 460-4518.
www.americancruiselines.com

Blount Small Ship Adventures
Tel (800) 556-7450.
www.blountsmallship adventures.com

Canal Street Ferry
Foot of Canal St. **Map** 5 D4.
Tel (504) 376-8100.
www.dodt.state.la.us

STREET FINDER

The map references given with all sights and venues described in this book refer to the maps in this section. A complete index of street names and all the places of interest marked on the Street Finder can be found on the pages following the maps. The key, set out below, indicates the scales of the maps and shows what other features are marked on them, including transport terminals, hospitals, post offices, emergency services, churches, and information centers. The maps include not only the sight-seeing areas (which are color-coded), but the whole of central New Orleans and all the districts important for hotels *(see pp160–69)*, restaurants *(see pp170–85)*, shopping *(see pp186–93)*, and entertainment *(see pp194–203)*. The map on the back inside cover shows the city's public transportation routes.

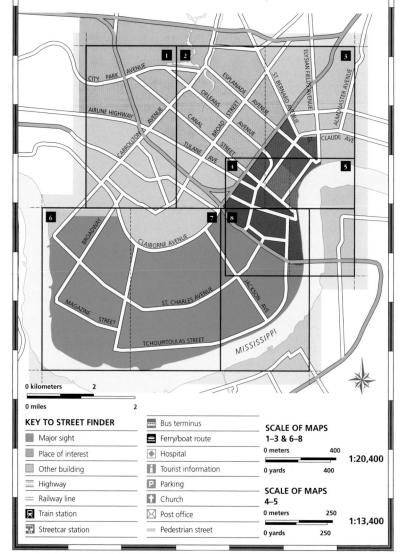

0 kilometers   2

0 miles   2

KEY TO STREET FINDER

- Major sight
- Place of interest
- Other building
- Highway
- Railway line
- Train station
- Streetcar station

- Bus terminus
- Ferry/boat route
- Hospital
- Tourist information
- Parking
- Church
- Post office
- Pedestrian street

**SCALE OF MAPS
1–3 & 6–8**

0 meters   400

0 yards   400

1:20,400

**SCALE OF MAPS
4–5**

0 meters   250

0 yards   250

1:13,400

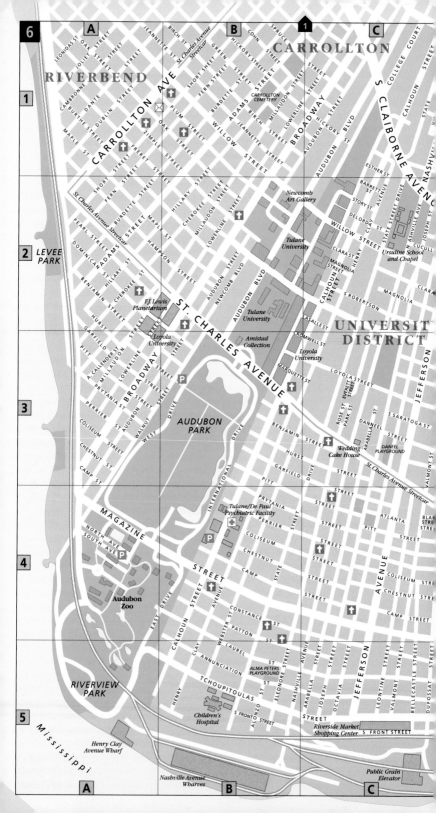

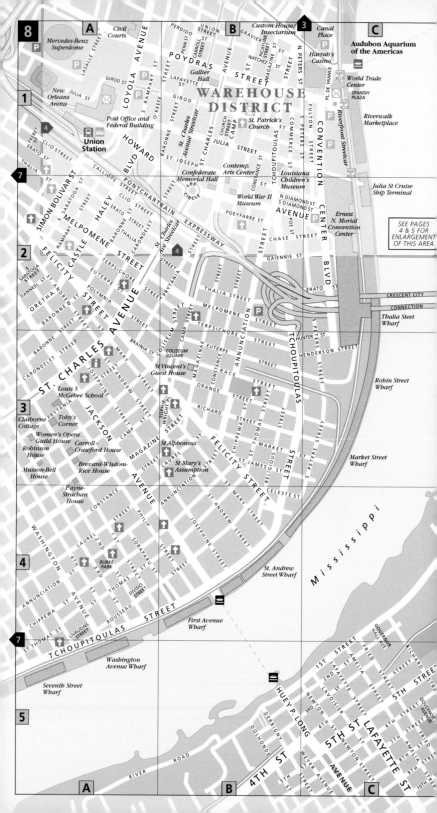

Street Finder Index

T

Taft Place	**2 B2**
Tchoupitoulas Street	**4 C4,**
	6 B5, 7 D5, 8 A4
Teche Street	**5 F4**
Tensas Street	**2 B1**
Terpsichore Street	**7 F2, 8 B2**
Thalia Street	**1 C5,**
	2 A5, 4 A5, 7 F1, 8 A1
Toledano Street	**7 E1**
Toulouse Street	**1 C2,**
	2 A2, 3 D5, 4 C2, 5 D2
Touro Street	**3 E1**
Trafalgar Street	**2 C1**
Treasure Street	**3 D1**
Treme Street	**3 D4, 4 C1**
Tulane Avenue	**1 C3, 2 A4**
Tunica Street	**2 C1**

U

Ulloa Street	**1 C3**
Union Street	**4 B3, 8 B1**
Upperline Street	**7 D1**

Urquart Street	**3 E3**
Ursulines Street	**2 B2,**
	3 E4, 5 D1, 7 C1

V

Valence Street	**7 D2**
Vallette Street	**3 F5, 5 F3**
Valmont Street	**6 C3**
Vendome Place	**1 C5**
Verna Street	**2 B2**
Verrett Street	**3 F5, 5 F3**
Versailles Street	**1 C5**
Vicksburg Street	**1 C1**
Victory Avenue	**2 A1**
Vincennes Place	**1 C5, 6 C1**
Violet Street	**1 A1**
Virginia Court	**1 C1**
Virginia Street	**1 C1**
Vision Street	**1 C1**

W

Walmsley Street	**1 B5**
Walnut Street	**6 A3**

Washington Avenue	**1 C4,**
	7 E1, 8 A4
Webster Street	**6 B4**
Weiblen Street	**1 C1**
West Drive	**6 A3**
West End Boulevard	**1 B1**
W. Stadium	**8 A1**
Weyer Avenue	**8 C5**
Willow Street	**2 C5,**
	4 A2, 6 B1, 7 F2
Wilshire Street	**2 C1**
Wilson Street	**2 B2**
Winthrall Place	**2 C1**
Wisner Boulevard	**2 B1**
Wood Avenue	**1 A1**
Woodland Place	**1 B1**

Y

York Street	**7 D1**
Yupon Street	**2 B1**

Z

Zimple Street	**6 A1**

General Index

Acknowledgments

Dorling Kindersley would like to thank the many people whose help and assistance contributed to the preparation of this book.

Main Contributor
Marilyn Wood is an American travel writer who has written guidebooks to a number of cities, including New York, Toronto, Boston and London.

Additional Contributors
Ian McNulty, Sarah O'Kelley, Peter Reichard, Harriet Swift.

Additional Photography
Cheryl Gerber, Ian McNulty, Ian O'Leary, Rough Guides/Greg Ward.

Additional Picture Research
Rhiannon Furbear, Rosie Meyer, Ellen Root.

Revisions Designer
Mariana Evmolpidou.

Revisions Editor
Anna Freiberger.

Design and Editorial Assistance
Brigitte Arora, Claire Baranowski, Jyl Benson, Uma Bhattacharya, Chapel Design & Marketing Ltd., Louise Cleghorn, Hannah Dolan, Gadi Farfour, Fay Franklin, Jo Gardner, Lydia Halliday, Vinod Harish, Mohammad Hassan, Jacky Jackson, Jasneet Kaur, Juliet Kenny, Vincent Kurien, Esther Labi, Maite Lantaron, Carly Madden, Alison McGill, Ian McNulty, Sonal Modha, Mary Ormandy, Christina Park, Sangita Patel, Mani Ramaswamy, Sands Publishing Solutions, Azeem Siddiqui, Wendy Toole, Conrad Van Dyk, Dora Whitaker.

Dorling Kindersley would like to thank the following for their permission to photograph at their establishments and for their assistance with photography: New Orleans Museum of Art; St. Louis Cathedral, Cabildo, Presbytere and all other churches, museums, restaurants, hotels, shops, and other sights too numerous to thank individually.

Picture Credits
Key:
a-above; b-below;/bottom; c-centre; f-far; l-left; r-right; t-top.

Works of art have been reproduced with permission of the following copyright holders: Portrait of a Young Girl 1935, © ADAGP, Paris and DACS, London 2011 – 122b.

The Publisher would like to thank the following individuals, companies and picture libraries for their kind permission to reproduce their photographs:

ALAMY IMAGES: F1online digitale Bildagentur GmbH/Udo Frank 208cla; EditorialFotos 173tl; SCPhotos/Dinodia 213tl; Stephen Saks Photo 173c; Visions of America, LLC/ Joseph Sohm 69bc, 70cl; AMERICAN CRUISE LINES: 221tl, 221cb; AMTRAK: Mick Nussbaum 215tl; AUDUBON AQUARIUM OF THE AMERICAS: David Bull/Audubon Nature Institute, New Orleans 31cr; 90tr/cra/bl/br; 91tl/cra/bl; AUDUBON ZOO: 113crb.

BIG EASY PHOTOS: Brent Daniel 47tl, 160cl, 219t; BUSH ANTIQUES: 187br.

CONTEMPORARY ARTS CENTER: 10cra; CORBIS: 137 (insert); Bettmann 36cla, 37tr/tl/crb; Richard Cummins 85t; DK Images 211cb; Philip Gould 36bl, 134cla; John Hicks, 135br; Robert Holmes 47tl, 136–7, 135tr; 201bl; Francis G. Mayer 37bl; National Geographic Society/Krista Rossow 219bl; Underwood & Underwood 36br; COREL STOCK PHOTO LIBRARY: 22tl, 23tr/b, 209b, 212cr, 212clb, 214t/c/b.

JOHN DEMAJO: 132tr; DICKINSON COLLEGE, Carlisle, Pennsylvannia: 48cl.; DREAMSTIME. COM: Anne Power 220 cla.

FLICKR.COM: www.flickr.com/photos/ infrogmation/3345144615/ 200tr; FRENCH ART NETWORK: 48br; FRENCH MARKET: 207bl.

GETTY IMAGES: Foodpix/Melanie Acevedo 172cla; GREYHOUND LINES, INC.: 215cb.

PAUL AND LULU HILLIARD UNIVERSITY ART MUSEUM: Timothy Hursley 155t; HISTORIC NEW ORLEANS COLLECTION: Jan Brantley 15bl, 16t, 17tr/bl, 18tr/c, 19tr/clb, 32cla, 60–61 (except 61cl); HOUMAS HOUSE PLANTATION: 145br; HOTEL MONTELEONE: 196bl.

IMAX THEATRE: 91br.

LEONARDO MEDIA LTD.: 171cr; LOUSIANA OFFICE OF TOURISM: 133tl, 133br, 200tl; LOUISIANA PHILHARMONIC ORCHESTRA: 197cl; LOUISIANA

Phrase Book

South Louisiana has a rich heritage of blending its disparate cultures, and New Orleans is no exception. French, Spanish, Cajun French, Creole French, English, German, and even some Native American words have all been mixed together into a New Orleans patois. The following is a list of the most frequently used words and phrases, plus a guide to correct pronunciation.

Words and Phrases

armoire	(arm-wah) **cupboard or wardrobe**
arpent	**measure of 180 ft (55 m)**
au dit	(oh-dee) **ditto or "the same"**
aw-right	**accepted greeting or acclamation on meeting friends or acquaintances**
banquette	(ban-ket) **sidewalk**
baptiser	(bap-tee-zay) **to give a name to something**
bateau	**boat**
bayou	(bay-you or bye'o) **a waterway or creek**
boeuf	(berf) **cow, meat, steak**
Boureé	**Cajun card game**
bousillage	(boor-sill-arge) **mixture of Spanish moss and mud, used to insulate walls**
brulé	(bru-lay) **burned, toasted (as in *café brulé*)**
cabinette	**outhouse**
cocodrie	**alligator**
Cajun	**descendants of the Acadians who settled in South Louisiana in the 18th century**
charivari	(shi-va-ree) **noisy mock serenade to a newly married older couple**
chaudron	**a cauldron or large kettle**
cher	(share) **widespread term of endearment in Cajun French**
cold drink	**soda with ice**
coulée	(cool-ay) **ravine or gully**
Creole	**descendant of original French or Spanish settlers**
Creole of color	**descendant of French or Spanish settlers with African blood**
doubloons	**aluminum coins thrown to Mardi Gras crowds**
dressin' room	**polite term for the bathroom**

fais-do-do	(fay-doh-doh) **literally "go to sleep"; Cajun term for a community dance where parents bring their children, who often fall asleep to the music**
fourche	**the fork of a creek (as in Bayou Lafourche)**
gallery	**balcony or porch**
gris-gris	(gree-gree) **voodoo charm**
Guignolée	**New Year's Eve celebration**
jour de l'An	**New Year's Day**
krewe	**private club that sponsors a parade and a ball during Mardi Gras**
lagniappe	(lan-yap) **"something extra" at no cost**
levee	**embankment for flood control or riverside landing**
neutral ground	**the median of a large avenue or street (the St. Charles Avenue streetcar runs on the neutral ground)**
nonc	**uncle**
nutria	**South American rodent imported to Louisiana in the late 18th century. The nutria is an important part of the fur industry**
ouaouaron	(wah-wah-rohn) **bullfrog**
parish	**civil and political division in Louisiana (like a county)**
patois	(pat-wah) **dialect: different Cajun communities speak their own patois**
pirogue	(pee-row) **long, shallow canoe**
praline	(praw-LEEN) **candy made with sugar, cream, and pecans, very popular in New Orleans**
rat de bois	(rat-de-bwah) **opossum**
shotgun house	**long, narrow house**
T or Ti	**petite, junior, a nickname (T-frere = baby brother)**

Vieux Carré	(voo-cah-RAY) **literally "Old Square", the French Quarter**
ward	**political division of New Orleans**
where y'at?	**how are you?**

Street and Town Names

Atchafalaya	(chaf-fly) **large (800,000 acres) swampy wilderness area in South Louisiana**
Tchoupitoulas St	(chop-a-TOOL-us)
Burgundy St.	(bur-GUN-dy)
Chartres St.	(CHART-ers)
Euterpe St.	(YOU-terp)
Melpomene Ave.	(MEL-pom-meen)
Metairie	(MET'ry) **suburb of New Orleans**
Terpsichore St.	(TERP-si-core)
Opelousas Ave.	(opp-a-LOO-sas)
Lafayette	(laugh-e-YET) **unofficial capital of Cajun Country**
Plaquemine	(PLACK-a-meen) **town and parish south of Baton Rouge**
Baton Rouge	(bat'n ROOZH) **capital of Louisiana**
Thibodeaux	(TIBB-a-doh) **common surname, also a town in Cajun Country**
Natchitoches	(NACK-uh-dish) **oldest town in the Louisiana Purchase area**
Ponchatoula	(ponch-a TOOL-ah) **town on the north shore of Lake Pontchartrain**

Cajun & Creole Cooking

andouille	**pork and garlic sausage**
beignet	**square, deep-fried doughnut, dusted with powdered sugar**
boudin	**spicy pork, rice, and onion sausage**
bread pudding	**French bread soaked in milk and egg, baked, and served with whiskey sauce**
bouillabaisse	**French seafood stew**
café au lait	**dark roast coffee served with steamed milk**
chicory	**coffee additive, made of roasted, ground roots**
crawfish	(cray-fish) **often called "mudbugs," a delicious, small, lobster-like crustacean found in the creeks and bayous in Louisiana**

dirty rice	**rice mixed with chicken gizzards and livers, green pepper, onions, and spices**
etouffée	**method of cooking crawfish or shrimp, simmered with vegetables**
filé	**ground sassafras leaves, used to thicken gumbo**
grillades	**meat smothered with thick tomato gravy, always served with grits**
grits	**ground, hulled corn, cooked and served with butter, salt, and pepper**
gumbo	**spicy soup with okra, tomatoes, seafood, served over rice**
jambalaya	**thick stew of rice, sausage, seafood, vegetables, and spices**
muffuletta	**huge sandwich of cold cuts, cheese, and olive salad, served on Italian bread**
okra	**pod vegetable, usually served in gumbo**
oysters Rockefeller	**oysters on the half shell, covered with a creamy spinach sauce, and baked on a bed of salt**
po'boy	**sandwich of fried seafood, roast beef, ham, or a mixture, served on French bread**
remoulade	**spicy mayonnaise-based seafood sauce**
roux	**mixture of butter and flour, mixed with water and seasonings; used as a base for many soups, gravies, and sauces**
shrimp Creole	**shrimp cooked with tomato sauce and seasoned with onions, green pepper, celery, and garlic**
Tabasco™	**hot, red pepper sauce made only at Avery Island; often used for any brand of pepper sauce, of which there are hundreds of brands available**
tasso	**local highly seasoned smoked ham**

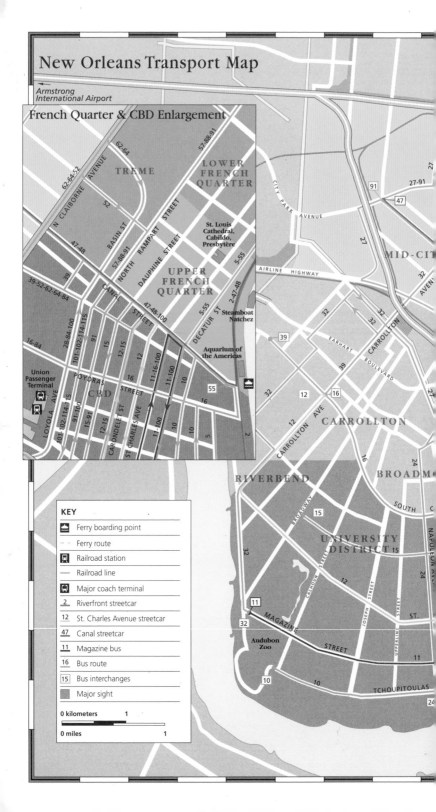

New Orleans Transport Map

Armstrong
International Airport

French Quarter & CBD Enlargement

TREME

LOWER
FRENCH
QUARTER

N CLAIBORNE AVENUE

62-64-52

62-64

57-88-91

52

BASIN ST

NORTH RAMPART STREET

DAUPHINE STREET

47-48

57-88-91

UPPER
FRENCH
QUARTER

St. Louis
Cathedral,
Cabildo,
Presbytère

39-52-62-64-84

CANAL STREET

39

47-48-100

5-55

5-55

2-47-48

DECATUR ST

Steamboat
Natchez

16-84

28-84-100

101-102-114-115

91

15

12-15

12

11-16-100

11-100

Aquarium of
the Americas

Union
Passenger
Terminal

POYDRAS STREET

CBD

101-102-114 15

91-100

15-91

12-15

CARONDELET ST

16

ST CHARLES AVE

11-100

10

10

10

55

16

2

AIRLINE HIGHWAY

CITY PARK AVENUE

91

47

27

27-91

MID-CIT

27

32

AVEN

EARHART

39

CARROLLTON

BOULEVARD

39

32

12

16

32

CARROLLTON AVE

CARROLLTON

16

24

RIVERBEND

BROADM

SOUTH

BROADWAY

15

UNIVERSITY
DISTRICT 15

32

CALHOUN STREET

12

JOSEPH STREET

15

NAPOLEON AVE

24

ST.

11

MAGAZINE

32

11

Audubon
Zoo

STREET

10

10

TCHOUPITOULAS

24

KEY

⛴	Ferry boarding point
- -	Ferry route
🚉	Railroad station
—	Railroad line
🚌	Major coach terminal
2	Riverfront streetcar
12	St. Charles Avenue streetcar
47	Canal streetcar
11	Magazine bus
16	Bus route
15	Bus interchanges
	Major sight

0 kilometers   1

0 miles   1